HENRY 'ORATOR' HUNT
AND THE ILCHESTER BASTILLE

The Tree of LIBERTY — with, the Devil tempting John Bull.

Henry 'Orator' Hunt
and the
Ilchester Bastille

Mick Davis

HOBNOB PRESS

First published in the United Kingdom in 2024
by The Hobnob Press
8 Lock Warehouse,
Severn Road, Gloucester
GL1 2GA

www.hobnobpress.co.uk

© Mick Davis 2024

Mick Davis hereby asserts his moral rights to be identified as the author of the Work.

All rights reserved. No part of this publication may be reproduced, stored in a retrieval system, or transmitted in any form or by any means, electronic, mechanical, photocopying, recording or otherwise, without the prior permission of the publisher and copyright holder.

British Library Cataloguing in Publication Data
A catalogue record for this book is available from the British Library

ISBN 978-1-914407-71-0

Typeset in Adobe Garamond Pro 11/14 pt.
Typesetting and origination by John Chandler

Front cover image: Henry Hunt by Adam Buck, circa *1810.* © *National Portrait Gallery, London*
Back cover image: W Bridle gaoler of Ilchester, by George Cruikshank, 1821

CONTENTS

Introduction	ix
1. Manchester 16 August 1819. 1.15pm	1
St Peter's Field 1819	3
The Arrests	5
2. The Gathering Storm	13
The Old Enemy	13
The British Volunteer Corps	14
The Price of Victory	16
The Technological Revolution	18
The Fight for Reform	20
The Spencean Philanthropists	22
The Despard Plot of 1802	23
King Ludd 1811-1817	24
Major Cartwright & the Campden Clubs 1812	26
Spa Fields 1816	27
The Crown & Anchor	29
The Blanketeer's March 1817	32
The Pentrich Rising June 1817	33
The Aftermath of Peterloo	34
The Cato Street Conspiracy 1820	36
3. The Making of an Orator	39
The Wiltshire Yeomanry	42
Marriage & Family	44
The King's Bench	47
Mrs Vince	52
4. Two Peas in a Pod	57
William Cobbett	57
Enter Henry Hunt	61

Bristol 1807	63
The King's Bench, Newgate & The Tower	65
The Candidate for Bristol 1812	67
The Corn & Property Bills 1815	69
The Westminster Election of 1818	72
Peterloo and Bail 1819	74

5. The Trial of Henry Hunt — 75

Trial, Transcript & Sentence	75
The Defence Case	86
Prosecution Closing Speech	92
Mr Justice Bayley Sums Up	94
The Verdict	96

6. Hulk Educated Monster? William Bridle 1779-1851 — 100

Birth & Family	100
Somerset Fencible Cavalry	101
The Prison Hulks	105
John Commins	107
The *Retribution*	110
Debtor Relief	114

7. The Ilchester Bastille — 116

Early History	116
Joseph & Edward Scadding 1757-1808	117
Execution of Mary Norwood 1765	118
Attempted escape by Ward, Maggs and others. 1786	119
The 19th Century, Dr Lettsom	121
1808 William Bridle Takes Charge	123
Sir Francis & The Loaf 1812	124
Bridle Expands the Jail	126
Daniel Lake Taskmaster 1815	127
The Typhus Outbreak of 1817-18	134
The General Election of 1818	135

8. A Perfect Paradise — 138

Hunt's First Impressions	138
The General Election of 1820	147
Jail Matters	149

The Campaign Begins.	153
Mr & Mrs Hobbs	154
Hunt 'Peeps' at the Jail	156
Petition of Charles Hill	159
Petition of James Hillier	160

9. Hunt v Bridle — 163
The Magistrates Inquiry 19 April 1821	163
The Commons Commission	165
Bridle's Defence June 1821	182
Aftermath	202
The Commission's Report: 4 December 1821	206

10. Pastures New — 210
Visits & Petitions	210
Hunt's Breakfast Powder	217
Dr John Robertson	220
Business as Usual?	221
Cobbett Returns November 1819	222
William Cobbett c1831	227

11. Trial & Sentence — 230
The Trial of William Bridle 15 August 1822	233
The Sentence 22 November 1822	238

12. Sydney Gardens Bath 1824 — 243

13. Destitution & Despair — 251
London & The End of the Road	255

Appendix I Shelley: The Mask of Anarchy — 266

Appendix II Clarke & Madden — 274

Bibliography — 280
Index of Persons and Places — 282

INTRODUCTION

THE FAMOUS RADICAL speaker, Henry 'Orator' Hunt was imprisoned in Ilchester jail, Somerset for his part in the 'Peterloo Massacre' of 1819, an event which both horrified and stimulated reformers and reactionaries alike. Hunt was a colleague of the more famous political campaigner William Cobbett whose life, activities and fractured relationship with Hunt are examined here in some depth. Whilst imprisoned in Ilchester jail Hunt wrote his memoirs and a flurry of political pamphlets. Arrogant, passionate and from a wealthy farming background, he was infuriated at being treated like a common criminal and denied what he considered to be his rights. Ilchester was his second taste of jail, the first occurred in 1800 when he served six weeks in London's King's Bench prison which was more like a gentleman's club.

His jailor for over two years at Ilchester was William Bridle and the two men grew to hate each other with a passion; they could not have been more different in background and attitude. Bridle was from a struggling Somerset family who left home at 15 to join the Somerset Fencible Cavalry, a local force to counter any invasion from France and put down any thought of revolt at home. When that movement disbanded in around 1802 he moved on to become first mate on the prison hulk *Retribution* moored at Woolwich before accepting the governorship of Ilchester jail.

Hunt's constant campaigning and published polemics about his prison situation as well as much behind-the-scenes political intrigue resulted in Bridle being dismissed from his position at the jail, after which he a published book of his own denying the allegations which had included assault, rape, corruption, embezzlement and just about anything else that Hunt could think of to throw at him. There is a brief account of the history of Ilchester jail during and before this period which has been little recorded along with notes on some of its more famous inmates.

Hunt's life and political career was tied for better or worse to that of William Cobbett, and their fraught relationship is examined, as are the lives and families of both parties against the backdrop of the French wars, prison conditions and the radical social themes of the times.

In many ways Bridle is the more interesting of the three and certainly the least known. He became governor of Ilchester in 1808 until his altercation with Hunt in 1821, after which he ran Sydney Pleasure Gardens in Bath until his financial ruin in 1832. Much research has gone into his activities after that time throwing light on the career of a fascinating character. He had much support and sympathy amongst people who did not believe Hunt's allegations but was unable to re-establish his reputation and died in the utmost poverty in a London workhouse in 1851, a broken man mentally and physically.

Mick Davis
1 April 2024

Mick Davis has had twelve books published, ranging from biography, criminology, prehistory and local history. He lives and works full time as a historian and author in Frome, Somerset.

1
MANCHESTER
16 AUGUST 1819. 1.15 pm

Monday 16 August 1819 was a beautiful summer's morning, warm, sunny and with a gentle breeze blowing across St Peter's Field in Manchester. Monday was the traditional day off for handloom weavers and others of the artisan class and the entire area was packed with people creating a harmonious atmosphere, men women and children in their best clothes singing and dancing, but this was no summer fair. The estimated 60,000 people – it may have been over twice that number depending upon the viewpoint of the estimator – had gathered to hear demands for the reform of parliamentary representation. They had come, the curious, the hecklers, the political zealot and honest working people seeking the reform of a corrupt electoral system, to listen to the words of one man. Henry Hunt whose words, despite a commanding voice earning him the nickname 'Orator' Hunt, could only be heard by a tiny minority of the crowd, so great was their distance from the two wagons lashed together which formed the hustings.

The meeting was originally arranged for 9 August with mock elections but notices had been posted around town by the magistrates warning people off and declaring the meeting to be illegal. But, to the great amusement of those who could read, it contained a grammatical error cautioning *all persons to abstain at their peril*. Fearing trouble from the authorities that meeting was abandoned. Hunt was furious at the delay but could do nothing but wait cooped up in the cottage of Joseph Johnson, a former brush maker and now part owner of the *Manchester Observer* with whom he had little sympathy. He agreed to chair the meeting provided that, 'the largest assemblage maybe procured that ever was seen in this country'. With time on his hands he went to the magistrates to see if there was any arrest warrant out for him and was assured that there was none. There is no indication that Hunt's intentions for the great day were other than entirely peaceful, quite the reverse in fact; he resisted all calls for his supporters to carry cudgels as it would give the authorities 'every opportunity to excite a riot that they may have a pretence for spilling our blood'.

In the past similar gatherings had been mocked in the press as ragtag gatherings of drunks and layabouts. In order to be treated seriously it was thought that some order should be brought to the proceedings, and retired infantry soldiers and local militia men were asked to organise spinners, weavers, bricklayers, colliers and other tradesmen into disciplined bands, marching, halting, about-face countermarching to shouted commands with bugles and drums to avoid their activities being dismissed out of hand. This was also done to keep the various geographical groups together under their own banners so they could re-assemble at the end of the meeting and find their way home. News of the military-style operations must have increased the fears of the magistrates and led to the banning of the meeting planned for the 9th which was smartly sidestepped by rescheduling it for the 16th, but without the mock elections.

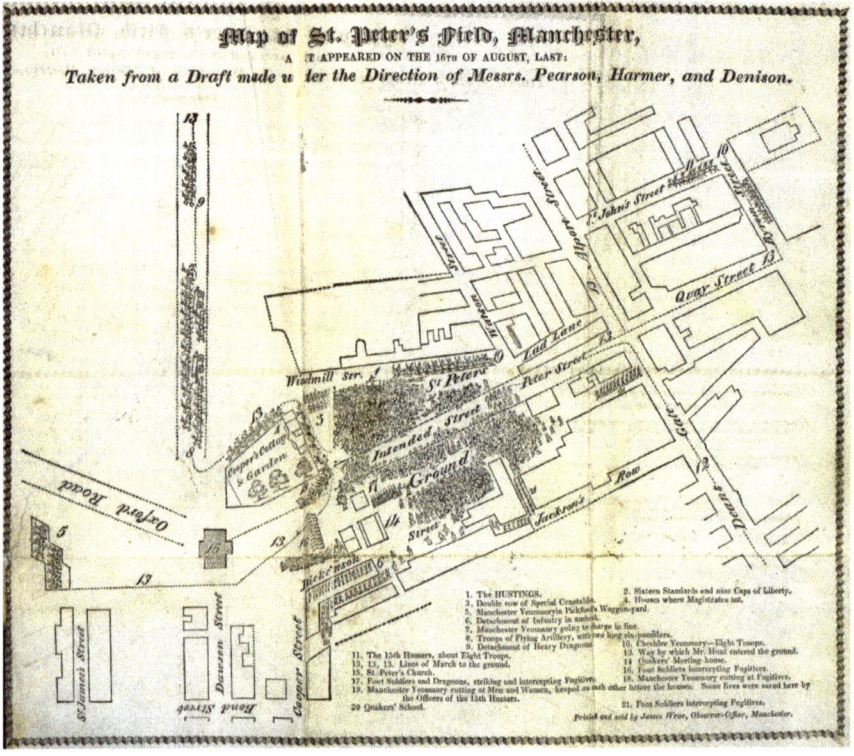

St Peter's Field 1819

St Peter's Field 1819

Hunt's makeshift platform stood near the Windmill public house, decked out with blue and white bunting. He was an imposing figure in his trademark white hat, symbolising the purity of his intentions. With him on stage were John Knight, a cotton manufacturer and reformer, Joseph Johnson, the organiser of the meeting, John Saxton, managing editor of the *Manchester Observer*, the radical publisher Richard Carlile, and George Swift, reformer and shoemaker. There were also a number of reporters, including John Tyas of *The Times* sharing the platform with members of the recently formed Manchester Committee of Female Reformers, led by their president Mary Fildes; in fact a particular feature of the meeting was the number of women present. Female reform societies had been formed in North West England during June and July 1819, the first in Britain. Many of the women were dressed distinctively in white, and some formed all-female contingents, carrying their own flags. Very quickly St Peter's Field, an area of 14,000 square yards, was packed with tens of thousands of men, women and children. The field was overlooked from the house of a Mr Buxton at 6 Mount Street 100 yards away and occupied by the magistrates, who had a bird's eye view of proceedings. Between them and the stage a passage had been formed lined with constables. This was soon blocked by Hunt's supporters, fearing that it was a path for the authorities to effect an arrest once the appropriate warrants had been sworn – which it was. This defensive action, however, was later used by the magistrates to justify their use of the military as the only means of effecting an arrest. The magistrates were apprehensive and viewed some of the banners with alarm, fearing violence – or so they claimed. Seemingly innocuous today they were felt provocative at the time.

> *Annual Parliaments and Universal Suffrage.*
> *Let us Die like Men and not to be Sold like Slaves.*
> *Death or Liberty!*

Slogans like these and the adoption of the 'cap of liberty' used by the French revolutionaries must have caused alarm amongst those charged with keeping order. The Phrygian Cap, as it was otherwise known, either worn or carried aloft on poles, consisted of a soft conical cap with the apex bent over. Thought to have originated in ancient Turkey, it became a symbol of freedom from slavery in Republican Rome and was adopted as a symbol of the revolution by both the American and French revolutionaries.

In Byrom Street and in overall charge of military operations on the day was Lieutenant Colonel Guy L'Estrange, who ordered his troops to stand by, and as Hunt took his place the atmosphere became electric. The multitude were

The Cap of Liberty

now roaring their approval and increasing in number minute by minute. We do not know when the tipping point was reached but the huge crowd had greeted Hunt's appearance with a deafening roar of approval. As he began to speak, William Hulton, a young and rather timid man, who was unfortunately chairman of the select committee of magistrates, was urged on by his fellow magistrates and the growing concern of local businessmen, to 'do something'. There seems to have been no detailed plan of action on behalf of the authorities other than for the military to come to the aid of the special constables under Joseph Nadin if they felt unable to cope with the situation. Hulton prepared warrants for the arrest of Hunt and others as soon as proceedings were underway, and asked Nadin if he could affect the arrest, 'No', replied Nadin, 'not with these, nor with any number of constables, I refuse to execute it without military assistance.'

Hulton ordered the Manchester & Salford Yeomanry Cavalry to advance and assist with the arrests. Resplendent in their sky blue jackets with white facings topped with black shako hats and truncated cones, they must have formed impressive figures in this peacock dress, each man's arrogance augmented by the power of his horse and sabre, during a period

William Hulton, Chief Magistrate

when a soldier was to be distinguished by his ability to stand out rather than camouflage. The officers had little in common apart from their class background but all rejoiced in dressing up, showing off their horses, mares or geldings, and playing soldiers with no fear of having to face a real war.

They moved at speed towards the hustings, thereby claiming their first victim, two-year-old William Fildes knocked from his mother's arms and trampled to death under the horses' hooves. Seeing their arrival Hunt tried a tactic that had worked before – of giving the troops three cheers, with many in his audience believing the gesture to be sincere and that the cavalry was there to protect them. This time the ruse failed and may have been interpreted as a gesture of defiance. The horsemen regrouped near the magistrates and now was the time to read the Riot Act, which would have allowed local officials to order illegally assembled groups of more than twelve people to disperse within one hour. Refusal was a felony offence which carried the death penalty. Opinions differ as to whether it was read at all or simply drowned out by the uproar around it. There was certainly much less than an hour between this and military intervention.

The Lord Lieutenant of Lancashire had ordered that the yeomanry's sabres be sharpened, and 63 had been sent to the cutler for that to be done. The yeomanry drew their newly sharpened sabres and advanced furiously into the mass of people. Some seemed to have gone berserk; panic broke out and people ran for their lives. The men on the horses and the horses themselves had no experience of crowd control or operating at a tightly packed event and were becoming increasingly disorganised, striking left and right indiscriminately with their sabres, unable to control their mounts and panicking amid the crush of bodies.

The Arrests

AS THEY APPROACHED the platform to seize their prey some of the special constables were seen to raise their truncheons in a form of salute – a grave error. Mistaking these for protesters bearing cudgels they struck several down with the flat of their swords and onto the ground with the unarmed reformers. At last the cavalry reached the hustings and Captain Hugh Birley in command said to Hunt, 'I have a warrant against you and arrest you as my prisoner' to which Hunt replied, 'I will willingly surrender myself to any civil officer who will show me his warrant.'

Deputy Constable of Manchester Joseph Nadin stepped forward, once memorably described as having a 'Neanderthal forehead under a black hat and immense brown coat which made him the most recognisable figure in early 19th century Manchester; a coarse man with a hatred of the working class; a corrupt and brutal thug who ran his own network of spies'. As he approached Hunt the yeomanry moved forward and began to hack and stab at everything in sight, cutting down the banners and flags in particular. Many of these standards or banners had been lovingly created in the homes of the various reform groups that had travelled many miles to attend the rally and were fiercely defended as though in time of war. Such trophies were hungrily sought after by the attacking horsemen. It is as well at this stage to record Hunt's own version of the event as he sat writing his memoirs in Ilchester jail many months later,

> The moment that I entered the field, ten or twelve bands struck up the same tune, *See the Conquering Hero Comes;* eighteen or twenty flags, most of them surmounted by a Cap of Liberty, were unfurled, and from the multitude burst forth such a shout of welcome as never before hailed the ears of an individual, possessed of no other power, no other influence over the minds of the people, except that which he had gained by an honest, straight-forward discharge of public duty. With some difficulty, and by slow degrees, the carriage was drawn up within a few yards of the Hustings, where the crowd was so dense as to forbid the approach of the carriage any nearer.
>
> We alighted, and, an avenue being made for us, we ascended the Hustings. The ladies composing the Committee of Female Reformers had followed close to the carriage up to this point, and therefore it was absolutely necessary to dispose of them in some place of safety, to prevent their being trampled under foot. Some part of them were placed in the carriage, which we had left, and the remainder were assisted upon the Hustings. Another shout now filled the air, as a compliment to me, and I took off my hat, to endeavour to address this immense multitude, with a full conviction that the very orderly conduct of the people would deprive their enemies of all pretence whatever to interrupt the proceedings.
>
> I had scarcely uttered two sentences, urging them to persevere in the same line of conduct, when the Manchester Troop of Yeomanry came galloping into the field, and formed in front of a house occupied by a Mr Buxton, where it was said the Magistrates had assembled for the purpose of keeping the peace. As soon as the military appeared, the people, (as is always the case under such circumstance) began to disperse and fly from the outskirts. To prevent the confusion likely to arise from such a circumstance, I caused three cheers to be given, which had the desired effect of restoring the confidence of the people, who did not, indeed, suspect it to be possible that the devil himself would have

authorised the Yeomanry to commit any violence upon them, as there was not the slightest symptom amongst them that could have created any real fear in the mind of the most timid.

Before, however, the cheering was sufficiently ended to enable me to raise my voice again, the word was given, and from the left flank of the troop, the trumpeter leading the way, they charged amongst the people, sabring right and left, in all directions, sparing neither age, sex, nor rank. In this manner they cut their way up to the Hustings, riding over and sabring all that could not get out of their way.

In this magnanimous exploit several fell dead, and hundreds were wounded; and this was done in cold blood, with the most savage ferocity, without the slightest provocation having been given by the people, and without one act of resistance, without ONE STONE, ONE STICK, or ONE FINGER having been raised even to resist, much less to provoke, such a bloodthirsty, such a cowardly, wanton, cruel, and murderous act.

At length it turned out that these diabolical deeds were committed in order, as it was pretended, to execute a warrant, to apprehend myself and others who were upon the Hustings with me. Now I most solemnly declare, that this warrant could have been executed with the greatest possible ease, by any single constable, without the aid of the military, or any breach of the peace whatever; and I have not the slightest doubt in my own mind, that the magistrates were fully sensible of this fact at the time when they ordered the ferocious yeomanry to charge and cut down the people. The object was to strike terror into the minds of the assembled multitude, and to pull down reform by the sword, regardless of the blood that would be spilt in the enterprise.

Their mission to execute the arrest warrant having been achieved, the yeomanry set about destroying the stage, seizing banners and flags from the stand as souvenirs. According to Tyas, the yeomanry then attempted to reach flags in the crowd, 'cutting most indiscriminately to the right and to the left to get at them' – only then, he claimed, were brickbats thrown at the military: 'From this point the Manchester and Salford Yeomanry lost all command of temper'.

As the stones began to fly sticks and cudgels were raised and Hulton called upon the 15th Hussars led by Guy L'Estrange to clear the area. This troop had arrived late to the party, uncertain of their role and without much of a clue as to what had gone on, but the order to, 'disperse the crowd' was all too clear and within five minutes all three large bodies of cavalry had forced their way into the multitude from different directions cutting and slashing indiscriminately seemingly beyond all control. To describe it as a 'charge' would be inaccurate, there was simply insufficient room for such a manoeuvre – a fast trot would probably be more accurate. Many witnesses amongst the protesters testified that the Hussars used the flats of their swords while it was the yeomanry that had precipitated the disaster and behaved viciously, even to the extent of injuring the constables and their own men. It was they who had caused most of the injuries, trampling on the people as they struggled to get away. Contemporary accounts estimate there being about 1,000 troops and 400-500 constables.

The Cavalry Advance

There are many eyewitness reports claiming that some of the yeomanry were drunk, 'because they rolled about on their horses', claimed one man while another stated that, 'he could hardly sit on his horse, he was so drunk, he sat like a monkey'. There seems to be no direct evidence of this but perhaps it was the only explanation people could come up with to explain their incredible behaviour. There were also reports that the yeomanry had long been insulted and laughed at with taunts of cowardice by the local population, so perhaps this was their revenge. Some witnesses even told of people being rescued from the yeomanry by the hussars. Nobody was spared, not women nor the very old. It was as though some form of tribal instinct had taken hold: relatives, friends and acquaintances were no longer recognised in the frenzy of brotherly bloodlust and comradeship. Of course, the yeomanry cavalry was local and several victims recognised their assailants. Once the protesters had fled, their attackers contented themselves with collecting banners, caps of liberty and other abandoned souvenirs. The cavalry too had their casualties, hit by bricks or stabbed at by iron railings and lengths of wood. By 2 o'clock, a mere 20 minutes since the yeomanry had arrived at Buxton's house, it was all over. Samuel Bamford a hand loom weaver described the scene in his memoirs,

> The sun looked down through a sultry and motionless air… over the whole field were strewn caps bonnets hats shawls and shoes and other parts of male and female dress trampled torn and bloody. Yeomanry had dismounted some easing their horse's girths some wiping their sabres. Several mounds of human beings are still remained where they had fallen, crashed down and smothered. Some of these still groaning – others with staring eyes, were gasping for breath and others would never breathe more. All was silent save those low sounds and the occasional snorting and pawing of steeds.

Now in custody, Hunt was taken first to Buxton's house with Johnson, Saxton, Elizabeth Gaunt who was covered in blood, and others before being placed in the charge of L'Estrange. The constables tried and failed to knock off Hunt's white hat. While he was being hissed at and pulled by the coat and collar Tyas saw him being beaten on the head with sticks. Hunt asked Nadin if they could see the arrest warrant but this was refused, as was conveyance by carriage, and they were paraded through the Manchester streets by a detachment of hussars to the New Bailey prison, during which exercise he was again struck several times but without serious injury. Within ten minutes the crowd had been dispersed, at the loss of possibly 18 lives and more than 600 injured. Only the wounded, their helpers, and the dead were left behind. For some time afterwards there was rioting in the streets, most seriously at New Cross, where troops fired on a crowd attacking a shop belonging to someone rumoured to have taken one of the women reformers' flags as a souvenir. Peace was not restored in the town until the next morning, and in Stockport and Macclesfield rioting continued into the 17th. There was also a major riot in Oldham that day, during which one person was shot and wounded.

Not all agreed with Hunt's version of events. Initial reports two days later on the 18th in the *Globe* newspaper reported that,

> An hour having expired after the reading of the Riot Act the warrants of the magistrates were carried into effect. The Yeomanry cavalry in support of the

police officers armed with warrants from the magistrates dashed through the crowd surrounded the hustings and arrested Henry Hunt and others who are carried off the field and sent immediately under escort to New Bailey prison whilst the caps of liberty and the banners of rebellion were destroyed and trampled in the dirt. While the seizure was made by the Yeomanry the 15th Hussars and the 31st and 88th Regiments of foot, a brigade of artillery and the Cheshire Yeomanry made their appearance on the ground. At the moment of surrounding the hustings a shower of brickbats and paving stones were hurled at the Yeomanry several of whom were struck, one so severely, that he dropped the reins and his horse fell by which he was pitched off and his skull was fractured. He was carried to the infirmary and at 4 o'clock all hope of his recovery was fled. Besides this gentleman six other persons were killed one of them was Mr Ashworth of the market place who is on duty as a special constable.

On 19 August the *Morning Post* received an eyewitness account,

At about 11 o'clock thousands upon thousands, men and women paraded down Mosley Street three and five abreast mostly with large sticks which they stamped triumphantly against the flagged causeways as they passed any respectable houses or buildings.

The flags were extremely numerous of various colours some too of silk; most of them bearing the usual mottos on these occasions. Several of them surrounded with coloured caps of liberty or else the red cap was carried on a pole surrounded with Laurel between two of their emblems indeed, the numerous concourses at 12 o'clock exceeds my bounds of calculation; but at one the hour when *Hunt* arrived in an open carriage, (a woman too supposed to be Mrs *Johnson* on the box) a great addition poured in with banners flying and bands of music playing. The whole area of the ground was now literally crammed full, from well-informed persons at least it is said to be 100,000.

Hunt and the lady mounted the platform… they were immediately enveloped with caps of liberty and other revolutionary emblems. The meeting was addressed by several orators showing much menacing attitude and the shouts seem to rend the very air and shake the very foundation of the ground, the constables were tauntingly insulted wherever they were observed to stand, sticks and hats always waving on every acclamation. About half past one the magistrates deemed it expedient to read the riot act and immediatly after the platform was surrounded in a masterly manner and the whole posse above with all their emblems taken into custody.

The whole of this grand manoeuvre would have taken place without bloodshed had not the mob assailed the military and civil authorities with every resistance in their power and particularly with missiles. Consequently, cavalry charged in their own defence, not without first being witness to a pistol shot from the multitude against one of the Gentleman of our yeomanry who now lies in imminent danger. Also, Ashworth one of our special constables was killed on the spot. And I regret to state that several other loyal special constables have been hurt in the conflict. Soldiers forbear with great humanity from firing but several of those infatuated persons have felt the Sabres as many have been taken into the infirmary wounded. Great difficulty afterwards remained in clearing the streets and avenues from the lingering mob.

At 6 o'clock the streets were more free from intruders than this immense crowd could have justified us to expect possible. The military from Cheshire are billeted in the town. The rest in barracks with the exception of our own Yeomanry who are still on duty. Great praise is due to them for that unexampled manly contact on this occasion.

The exact number of those killed and injured has not been established with certainty, as there was no official count or inquiry, and many injured people fled to safety without reporting their injuries or seeking treatment, but hiding their wounds for fear of retribution from the authorities. The Manchester Relief Committee, a body set up to provide help for the victims, gave the number of injured as 420, while radical sources listed 500. Three of William Marsh's six children worked in the factory belonging to Captain Hugh Birley of the Manchester Yeomanry, and lost their jobs because their father had attended the meeting. James Lees was admitted to Manchester Infirmary with two severe sabre wounds to the head, but was refused treatment and sent home after refusing to agree with the surgeon's insistence that, 'he had had enough of Manchester meetings.'

An in-depth study by Michael Bush, *The Casualties of Peterloo* produced a list of 654 casualties, of which at least 168 were women, four of whom died either at St Peter's Field or later as a result of their wounds. It has been estimated that fewer than 12 % of the crowd was made up of women, suggesting that they were at significantly greater risk of injury than men by a factor of almost 3:1. Richard Carlile claimed that the women were especially targeted, a view apparently supported by the large number who suffered from wounds caused by weapons. Eleven of the fatalities listed occurred on St Peter's Field. Others, such as John Lees of Oldham, died later of their wounds, and some like Joshua Whitworth were killed in the rioting that followed the crowd's dispersal from the field. Bush puts the fatalities at eighteen. The event was first labelled the 'Peterloo Massacre', by the radical *Manchester Observer* newspaper in a bitterly ironic reference to the Battle of Waterloo which had taken place just four years earlier. Historian Robert Poole has called it, 'the bloodiest political event of the nineteenth century on English soil', and 'a political earthquake in the northern powerhouse of the industrial revolution'.

But how did it get to this?

2
THE GATHERING STORM

THE PERIOD BETWEEN the loss of the American colonies in 1775 and the Great Reform Act of 1832 must count amongst one of the most fascinating periods of British history. The American revolution sent shockwaves through the establishment and stimulated radical thought and reaction amongst all sections of the population. The suppression of Tom Paine's *Rights of Man* in 1791, with its belief that men have inherent, natural rights such as freedom of expression, religion, and freedom from persecution, made it one of the most widely read books of its time. The turn of the 18th and 19th centuries saw one of the greatest upheavals in the country's history, with the land going through a period of great political and economic transformation. By the last decade of the 18th century Enlightenment thinking had encompassed most of the intellectual thought of the time, with its central doctrines of reason, individual liberty and humanism in opposition to an absolute monarchy and the domination of the church. Despite their territorial rivalry, England and France had many cultural and intellectual exchanges during this period, marked by the growth of ideas and the spread of knowledge and education. Many of the leading thinkers and writers of the time, including Voltaire and Rousseau, had close ties to both England and France. The industrial revolution stimulated a growing class consciousness in the face of lives of unrelenting toil and drudgery. Stimulated by events abroad, protest and repression developed their own momentum and it is worthwhile examining some of the major events and pockets of opposition which existed during that time.

The Old Enemy

FROM 1795 UNTIL 1815 England had been almost continually at war with France, the situation driven by a mix of political, economic, and colonial conditions, including competition for control of global trade and territory. The conflicts took place on a number of fronts not only in Europe, but also in North America, the Caribbean and India. Its origins can be traced back to the medieval period, when the two nations were bitter enemies in the Hundred Years' War, but it was during the 18th century that their rivalry reached its peak, as both nations competed for dominance in Europe and around the world. Both had extensive colonial empires, and their respective governments sought to expand their influence and control over key territories and resources. France was a major continental power, its ambitions a threat to England's security and interests. One of the most significant events was the Seven Years' War, which lasted from 1756 to 1763. Fought primarily in Europe and North America, it was the largest and most costly war in European history, with significant territorial gains for England, including the acquisition of Canada and several French colonies in the Caribbean.

The wars left England as the dominant naval and colonial power in the world, while France was left weakened and embittered, never to recover. The war also contributed to a growing sense of nationalism and identity in both nations as they sought to assert their cultural and political influence on the world stage. It has been estimated that the conflict amounted to a colossal £800m before it was finally brought to an end by Wellington's victory over Napoleon at Waterloo on 18 June 1815.

The conflict led to many challenges to trade. The cloth industry in particular was left facing a number of problems. International trade and shipping was disrupted, making it difficult to import many raw materials from other countries. This led to a shortage at home which in turn drove up prices and made it difficult for manufacturers to trade at a competitive rate. In addition, the wars had a major impact on the export market for English cloth. England had been a major supplier to continental Europe, and now many of the traditional export markets were closed. This led to a decline in demand for English cloth, which in turn affected the profitability of cloth manufacturing, with its obvious effect on wages and employment. The wars had accelerated the pace of technological change, as manufacturers sought to improve efficiency and reduce costs. Since the end of the war the wages for spun yarn had fallen from 3d to 2d a pound, reducing workers income to about 15/- for a six day working week. Despite these challenges the industry was able to adapt to changing circumstances. Many manufacturers focused on producing for the domestic and military market as well as developing new contacts outside Europe. helping exports to grow and thrive.

The British Volunteer Corps

IN MARCH 1794, in response to the perceived threat of invasion by revolutionary France, the government issued a circular to the Lord

Lieutenants and High Sheriffs of the counties suggesting that, 'Gentlemen of Weight or Property' should assist in forming volunteer infantry and yeomanry cavalry corps. A yeoman was a person of respectable standing, nominally a small farmer working his own land and one social rank below a gentleman, and the yeomanry was initially a rural, county-based force. By late 1797 51,000 men had joined, climbing to 116,000 in 1798 and 146,000 in 1801, of which almost a quarter were cavalrymen. At its height in 1804, there were 380,258 enrolled; it was the largest voluntary movement of the 18th century.

British Volunteer Force 1798

The Yeomanry Cavalry was the mounted section of the British Volunteer Corps, a military auxiliary established for civil defence. Members were required to provide their own horses and were recruited mainly from landholders and tenant farmers, with the middle class featuring prominently in the rank and file. Officers were largely recruited from among the nobility and landed gentry, and although they were funded in part by public subscription, raised in each county, a commission could involve significant personal expense. Understandably the scheme was particularly important to those counties facing the English Channel. Cavalry forces were preferred to infantry partly because they would be better suited for suppressing internal disorder, and partly because those socially advanced enough to pay for their own horses and equipment were likely to favour the establishment side in any conflict.

A typical troop consisted of between 50 and 80 men pledged to serve within their own or adjacent counties in the event of invasion by the French. Gamekeepers, park keepers, and hunters, who were clothed by their masters, were encouraged to join due to their knowledge of the country and ownership of rifles. The Pitt government was much perturbed not only by events in France but by those radicals at home thought of as sympathetic to events there, like Tom Paine the author of the *Rights of Man* in 1791. So much so that Pitt's administration suspended the Habeas Corpus act in March 1794; the full title of the bill was, '*An Act to Empower His Majesty to secure and detain such persons as His Majesty shall suspect are conspiring against his person and Government*'. Habeas Corpus was one of the most important safeguards against the abuse of government power, requiring anyone in detention to be produced in court within a specified time with reasons given for their imprisonment. Its suspension gave the authorities the power of detention without charge whenever they chose and was not lifted until June of the following year.

Another, less publicised, role of the cavalry was the maintenance of internal order, although some in the government thought that a considerable risk was being taken with what amounted to arming sections of the general population, and many had strong reservations in what were extremely uncertain and volatile times. Others opposed the plan as an attempt to establish self-supporting private paramilitary armies.

Many corps made it clear that they were not to be called up for normal military service, subjected to military discipline, or marched beyond their predetermined geographical limits. Volunteers were wary of the government's intentions, concerned that they might be forced to act under regular military command, and specified that they were not to be transferred to any other corps nor to serve under other officers without the consent of all members. Volunteers were not subject to long periods of training and were not required to leave home except in an emergency. The effects of a huge voluntary force could have been profoundly disruptive to social relationships and the distribution of power on national and local levels. Large bodies of armed men were given considerable financial and organizational autonomy and allowed to nominate their own officers and terms of service.

The Price of Victory

AFTER VICTORY AT Waterloo England was on a high. Church bells rang out, bonfires were lit, grand dinners held and the common soldier was awarded the Waterloo medal, the first time such an honour had been bestowed upon such lowly subjects. Yet the euphoria of victory soon gave way to reality and despair. England was still an agricultural country mostly living off the land, a slave to the elements and the whims of the landowners. The war years had seen degrees of growth and stability, an economy boosted by the insatiable demands of the war machine for clothing, munitions, tents, sails, food and everything required to keep the wheels turning. Victory brought this to a standstill. The winter of 1815 saw the return of about 350,000 discharged soldiers and sailors, now without jobs, and joined by an estimated 15,000 convicts, felons who had been coaxed into the army and navy from various jails and prisons hulks. Churchwardens and local constables were asked to pay particular attention as, 'the greatest exertions will be necessary to restrain depredations and murder.' The recruitment of those convicts willing to serve had worked well in the short term, but there was no plan for the resettlement of a battle-hardened army of desperate men looking for employment and somewhere to live. Many soldiers had not received their pay and there was an acute economic slump, accompanied by chronic unemployment and harvest failure.

1816 was known as the Year Without a Summer because of severe climate abnormalities causing average temperatures to decrease drastically. Summer temperatures in Europe between the years 1766 and 2000 were the coldest of any on record. In all probability this was a 'volcanic winter' and due to the colossal eruption of Mount Tambora in the Dutch East Indies during April 1815. The resulting agricultural disaster led to major food shortages and destitution for many, with several factors combining to make things worse. The enclosure act of 1801 removed the right to the old common land, a source of firewood, rabbits, fruits and berries, replacing it with a criss-cross of fences, hedges and dry stone walls. Movement to the towns was piecemeal and the labourer was left with little choice but to put up with his lot or starve. In the towns landowners built back-to-back tenements – slum dwellings, rat infested hovels where cholera and typhoid would soon be rife – but close to factories. People were crammed in together, and to pay the rent were sometimes sleeping eight to a bed in a room containing up to 20 people, with the owners under no obligation to repair and maintain the properties; toilets were just an open sewer.

In 1799 prime minister Pitt had introduced a graduated tax on incomes to help pay for the war. The better-off paid tax on anything over £60 per year – the working man was lucky to earn £8 and so was largely unaffected. After the war the tax was dropped, but money had to come from somewhere and so indirect taxation on goods, had to be increased, and this included everyone – especially the poor. As though the situation wasn't bad enough, on 10 March

1815 the House of Commons passed the Corn Law Bill which blocked the import of cheap corn, by forbidding importation below a set price, and later by imposing steep import duties, making it too expensive to bring it in from abroad, even when food supplies were short. The law increased the profits and political power of the landlords, raised food prices and the cost of living for working people, hampering the growth of other sectors, such as manufacturing, by reducing disposable income. Over the period 1811 to 1820 family earnings fell by about 25% for factory workers and 38% for domestic outworkers.

The Technological Revolution

THE INDUSTRIAL REVOLUTION and the rise of the machines brought significant changes to the country's economy, creating new wealth. But it also led to the further decline in the workers' living standards, particularly in the textile mills of northern England. At the beginning of the 19th century the wealth of the country had depended largely upon the cloth produced from the wool of home-grown sheep, woven by hand on the looms of country cottages in southern England. A series of technological breakthroughs swept all this away. Kay's flying shuttle of around 1733 was one early example. James Hargreaves's spinning jenny of 1764 speeded the process of production tremendously – one machine able to take the place of 80 individual weavers. Increasingly the independent spinners and weavers were going to the wall and the source of the country's wealth begin to shift from the southern counties to the north centred upon Manchester.

Workers were required to work long hours in cramped and poorly ventilated conditions. Many suffered from injuries and illnesses as a result of the dangerous machinery they operated. Wages were very low, which often forced them to live in squalor and poverty. Innovation leading to increased production and a greater variety and quality of goods might have meant an increase in the quality of life for all, but instead led to an increase in the population so that any increased wealth had to be shared amongst more people – maintaining previous levels of poverty.

The mass production of goods also allowed for cheaper prices and a greater availability of products, leading to increasing demand and the beginnings of consumerism. This concentrated vast amounts of money in the hands of the few, as factory owners and managers became increasingly wealthy.

The determination of one man in particular, Richard Arkwright (1732 –1792), inventor and entrepreneur, is credited as the driving force behind the development of the spinning frame. He took out his first patent in 1769 and was the first to develop factories as we know them, housing both mechanised

Richard Arkwright

carding and spinning operations, combining power, machinery, semi-skilled labour and the new raw material of cotton to create mass-produced yarn. The massively increased output was estimated as a fifty-fold increase in production per man-hour; and with the appropriate supervision production could take place 24 hours a day. Steam power was soon added, meaning that factories no longer needed to be sited near rivers, and workers were brought from their cottages into one specialised workplace. He was the first to use James Watt's engine to power textile machinery, and as the factory system took off the government removed the costly import tariff on raw cotton. This was great progress in output and technology, but who gained most benefit?

As there were not enough local people to supply the labour required he built a large number of cottages nearby, preferring weavers with large families so that women and children could be employed. Arkwright's machines made skilled workers jobless and in 1779 arsonists destroyed his new Chorley Mill, which employed only cheap unskilled labour, often children, and apart from an engineer to repair the machines should they break down, everyone else was expendable. The machine-destroying Luddites were yet to emerge, but their grievances were first aired around Arkwright. In 1780 Ralph Mather published a book, *An Impartial Representation of the Case of the Poor Cotton Spinners in Lancashire, &c.* detailing the new factory system:

> Arkwright's machines require so few hands, and those only children, with the assistance of an over looker. A child can produce as much as would, and did upon an average, employ ten grown up persons. Jennies for spinning with one hundred or two hundred spindles, or more, going all at once, and requiring but one person to manage them. Within the space of ten years, from being a poor man worth £5, Richard Arkwright has purchased an estate of £20,000; while thousands of women, when they can get work, must make a long day to card, spin, and reel 5,040 yards of cotton, and for this they have four-pence or five-pence and no more.

One of the most significant effects of the factory system was the creation of a new class of worker. Prior to the Industrial Revolution most people worked in agriculture or in small-scale crafts. The new system meant that people were driven from the land and into the factories. The rise of the working class called for new forms of social organization, and workers began to combine into protective groups in order to fight for better wages and working conditions.

The Fight for Reform

THE DRAMAS OF American independence and the French Revolution did not just inspire intellectual debate in educated circles. Influenced by Paine's notion of universal rights, and beginning to make connections between their economic struggles and political corruption, working people began to organise into political groups for the first time, calling for reforms that would enable them to take a more active part in deciding how the country was governed.

The London Corresponding Society (LCS) was established in 1792, in the words of its founder Thomas Hardy 'as a means of informing the people of the violence that had been committed on their rights, and of uniting them in an endeavour to recover those rights'. Soon the society was in communication with other reform groups in northern towns, including Manchester and Sheffield. The breeches-maker and LCS member Francis Place credited the Society with improving the morals and education of its humbly-born members, but the government regarded radical societies – especially those with a large membership and nationwide association, as dangerous – at its peak it probably had 10,000 members. Their fears were greatly increased by the violent turn taken by the revolution, and once war with France broke out in 1793 the authorities sought to restrict the activities of reform societies, under the guise of national security. British reformers, they argued, were far too similar to French Jacobins, the most powerful and extreme revolutionary faction. Government-sponsored journalists propagated this message in the press, while spies on the ground penetrated radical meetings and provided exaggerated reports of treasonous plots.

One of the immediate impacts of the French Revolution was a sense of fear and uncertainty among the ruling class. The events in France were seen as a warning of what could happen if the most desperate needs of the common people were not met, and this fear led to a crackdown on dissent and a strengthening of the existing political order. The Reign of Terror which followed the revolution with its massacres and executions suggested that any reform would be accompanied by violence, which Pitt's government set out to pre-empt by increasingly punitive measures.

At the same time, the events inspired many in England to demand greater political rights and freedoms. The ideas of liberty, equality, and fraternity were widely discussed and many saw them as a model for their own fight for political reform. The *Rights of Man* was widely read, with those who could not read having it read to them in groups. It sold as many as a million copies and was eagerly studied by reformers, Protestant dissenters, democrats, London craftsmen, and the skilled factory-hands of the new industrial north.

People were being driven to drastic measures by hunger and poverty. Those in power feared their money and position, and in 1816 a number of factors combined to drive the country into a severe depression. Increased industrialisation combined with the demobilisation of the forces led to mass unemployment which, coupled with the loss of production of war materials, affected engineering companies, and the production of coal fell by a third. The hosiery trade which had been in decline for several years was deeply affected.

Since the previous century there had been calls for parliamentary reform, and an end to 'rotten boroughs' in particular. They were a parliamentary constituency with an electorate so small that voters were susceptible to control in a variety of ways, mainly by financial reward or threats of eviction. The word *rotten* conveyed the idea of corruption as well as long-term decline. Due to the lack of secret ballots and their dependency on the landlord in these areas most or all of the few electors could not vote as they pleased, and rarely were the views or personal character of a candidate taken into consideration. In the Commons a majority of the members was elected by only 154 voters; the best part of one million people of Lancashire were being represented by only two county MPs with two members for Liverpool.

There were numerous radical organisations, demonstrations, idealists and fantasists that led to the tragedy of Peterloo – a period of free thought and debate perhaps not seen since the civil war. Riots were countrywide and many sought a new life abroad, even to America which required no documents for entry. Reformer and essayist William Cobbett believed that the government was using informers and *agents provocateurs* to stir matters up and introduce even more repressive laws. At that time only 11% of adult males had the vote, very few of them in the industrial north, which also suffered the worst poverty. Reformers sought parliamentary reform and the vote for all men as the solution, and organised mass campaigns to petition parliament for change. When a second slump occurred in early 1819, radical reformers mobilised huge crowds in attempts to force a change in government.

One of the problems was that, in its paranoid state, government confused attempts at peaceful reform with armed revolution, and the persecution of peaceful reformers forced many underground and towards violent means. Many of the revolutionary plots were of the government's own making, either intentionally or otherwise, some instigated or at least encouraged by government agents. Repressive acts of 1793-1800 might be seen as justified as a reaction of a wartime administration intent upon tightening political control at home, to avoid dissent and seen as diminishing the war effort. Pitt's government may well have been seizing the opportunity to make political capital out of conspiracy scares to intimidate the extra-Parliamentary opposition by muddying the waters.

A big shake up in attitude had occurred with the declaration of war in 1793. Many liberals, previously eager to show their radical ideals, shrank away for fear of exposing themselves as traitors by sympathising with the revolution, but there were many organisations who held fast to their beliefs, planning and plotting with endless utopian discussions at inns and coffee houses. Some brief outlines of the main societies and protests from the wilder shores of the movement might be useful.

The Spencean Philanthropists,

ONE THE MOST influential groups of Utopian thinkers were the Spencean Philanthropists, a group taking their name from the radical speaker Thomas Spence (1750–1814) who advocated violent revolutionary action, and were involved in unrest and propaganda with the aim of overthrowing the government. Spence ran a bookstall in High Holborn and in 1794, with other members of the LCS, he agitated and campaigned tirelessly for radical change to Parliament. In contrast to other reform associations of the period, it drew largely upon working men (artisans, tradesmen, and shopkeepers) and was itself organised on a formal democratic basis, although much infiltrated by spies on the government payroll. In May 1794 William Pitt suspended Habeas Corpus in an attack upon the societies and their attendees, and Spence's activities caused him to spend seven months in Newgate jail on a charge of high treason, followed in 1801 by a sentence of twelve months' imprisonment for seditious libel – publishing material advocating insurrection against the established order. Spence was an advocate of the common ownership of land and equality of the sexes. Born in poverty, he died the same way in 1814 after further long periods of imprisonment. His plan was for the establishment of self-contained parochial communities, in which rent was paid to the parish, who would own the land which would be the only form of tax.

His demands were,

1 The end of aristocracy and landlords;
2 All land should be publicly owned by 'democratic parishes', which should be largely self-governing;
3 Rents of land in parishes to be shared equally amongst parishioners, as a form of social dividend;
4 Universal suffrage (including females) at both parish level and through a system of deputies elected by parishes to a national senate;
5 A social guarantee extended to provide income for those unable to work;
6 The right of infants to be free from abuse and poverty.

He first published his ideas in a penny pamphlet, *Property in Land Every One's Right* in 1775 and further explored his political and social concepts in a series of books about the fictional Utopian state of Spensonia.

The Despard Plot of 1802

THE DESPARD PLOT was a failed conspiracy by led by Colonel Edward Despard, a former army officer and colonial official. Evidence suggested that he planned to assassinate George III and seize key strong points in London such as the Bank of England, the Tower of London and the Royal Arsenal, as a prelude to a wider uprising by the population of the city. Having secured these and other strongpoints they would march on Parliament. The plan of action made sense militarily, and had the army and navy gone over to their side may have made some progress. But they miscalculated the mood of the people, overestimating the scale of their support as well as making impossible promises such as giving all military personnel who took part one guinea per week and ten acres of land to cultivate. The government was aware of the plot five months before the proposed date of attack but held back, gathering evidence until the week before. Despard and his co-conspirators were arrested and charged with high

Colonel Despard at his trial

treason and convicted of plotting an uprising. Not even an appearance by Horatio Nelson the country's greatest hero on his behalf could save him, and his execution on 21 February 1803 was attended by a crowd of around 20,000.

Hunt, who had visited Despard in prison wrote in his memoirs,

> ... my opinion is, that Colonel Despard fell a sacrifice to the intrigues and the spy plots of the ministers of that day, and their detestable agents, that the verdict was obtained against him by perjury, and that he was in no degree guilty of the charges that were preferred against him.

William Cobbett commented 'If you abhor treason, you are told Despard was a madman; if you are discontented with public affairs, you are told he was a hero.'

King Ludd 1811-1817

BY FAR AND away the most famous opposition to the new industrial order was the Luddite movement. Whereas the debating societies and coffee houses allowed the literate and informed to debate and ponder, those without education or idealistic aspirations and at the cutting edge of poverty were compelled to take matters into their own hands. Named after the mythical figure, Ned Ludd, who supposedly led the movement, the Luddites sought to protect traditional craftsmanship and livelihoods from the encroachment of new machinery and factory-based production. They were convinced that direct action was the only way to protect their way of life from being entirely destroyed by the industrial revolution. By 1811 the movement had gained momentum in the textile-producing regions, particularly in Nottinghamshire and Yorkshire. The Luddites met at night on the moors surrounding industrial towns to practice military-like drills and manoeuvres. Driven by desperation and hunger, attacks were organised on factories, aiming to wreck the specific types of machinery that posed a threat to their livelihoods in each region. In the Midlands these were the 'wide' knitting frames used to make cheap and inferior lace articles. In the North West, weavers sought to eliminate the steam-powered looms threatening wages in the cotton trade. In Yorkshire, workers opposed the use of shearing frames and gig mills to finish woollen cloth.

In 1812 the government introduced the Frame Breaking Act, making the destruction of machines a capital offence. Hundreds of Luddites were arrested, and some executed, further inflaming the situation. As the destruction of machinery spread and the movement gained supporters, factory owners responded with a firm and often ruthless stance to suppress the rebellion. The

Ned Ludd in 1812

government saw the movement not only as an assault on private property, but also on the sanctity of contracts and the social order itself, and in consequence sought to strengthen laws protecting property rights and suppress any form of labour agitation. In addition to the raids, Luddites coordinated public demonstrations and the mailing of letters to local industrialists and government officials explaining their reasons for destroying the machinery and threatening further action if the use of 'obnoxious' machines continued. There were clashes with government troops at Burton's Mill in Middleton and at Westhoughton Mill, both in Lancashire. The Luddites sent death threats to magistrates and food merchants and were probably responsible for some attacks on them. What is interesting is that the movement seems have had no political ambition other than direct action in its own specific interests. There seems to have been no attempt to link up with wider political protest movements or demands for revolutionary reform.

The movement acted as a catalyst for policy changes during the period from 1811 to 1817 and achieved far more than the coffee-house dreamers. While the government remained firmly committed to safeguarding their economic interests, they also began to acknowledge the necessity of social reforms to avert further unrest. The Factory Act of 1819 was the first step towards regulating factory employment and limited working hours for children. Then in 1824 the Combination Act of 1800 which had prohibited workers from forming trade unions or engaging in collective bargaining was repealed, granting workers the right to form unions and advocate for better conditions. The Luddite movement was pivotal in the struggle between the working people and the ruling class during the early stages of industrialisation.

Major Cartwright & the Campden Clubs 1812

MAJOR JOHN CARTWRIGHT (1740–1824) was born into a well-off Nottinghamshire family with strong connections to the landowning gentry. His political career was shaped by his experiences as a soldier and landowner and he became committed to the movement for democratic reform. Originally a naval officer with estates in Lincolnshire his title was derived from his post in the county militia. He had served as an officer in the army during the American Revolutionary War, which exposed him to ideas of liberty, equality, and democratic principles. After returning from military service, he became increasingly involved in political and social activity, focusing on the extension of voting rights and parliamentary change. He became a leading figure in the early parliamentary reform movement, advocating universal suffrage and annual parliaments. He believed that widespread participation in the political process was essential for the well-being of the nation and the preservation of freedom; 'the true cause of suffering is misgovernment and its proper correction parliamentary reform'. Cartwright was instrumental in the foundation of the Campden Clubs, named after the parliamentary leader John Campden during the civil war. They began in London during 1812 as political campaigning and debating societies dedicated to parliamentary reform. The intention was to bring together middle-class moderates and lower-class radicals in the reform cause. There were at least 25 clubs throughout the country but they were forced underground, and eventually disbanded in the face of legislation and pressure from the authorities. A capacity to organise and control was more alarming to the government than the rampages of undisciplined rioters. Cartwright was a prolific writer and speaker, publishing several works on political reform, including *Take Your Choice! Representation or Taxation* (1776) and *England's Alarm* (1803). He had founded the Society for Constitutional Information in 1780, a group aimed at promoting democratic ideals and constitutional reform. In later years Cartwright remained committed to his radical principles, and continued to be an influential figure within the reform movement, inspiring and supporting other activists in their pursuits of democratic change.

Spa Fields 1816

SPA FIELDS was situated in Clerkenwell, London, the centre of which was a large pub called Merlin's Cave. It was the venue for what was to be the first of three meetings featuring Hunt as the speaker on 15 November 1816 against a background of increasing discontent over taxes and prices. The invitation came from Arthur Thistlewood, a farmer's son from Lincolnshire, who had trained as a land surveyor but gave it up upon obtaining a commission in the army at the age of 21. He made an unsuccessful attempt at farming before moving to London in 1811. Travels in France and the United States inspired Thistlewood with revolutionary ideas, and soon after his return to London he joined the Spencean Philanthropists. By 1816 Thistlewood was well known as a dangerous character and followed closely by the police. Cobbett was suspicious and warned Hunt against any involvement with him. Although wary of the violent intentions of the organisers, Hunt, who could never resist an audience, met them before the meeting and persuaded them to moderate some of their more extreme demands. The meeting was peaceful, Hunt waxed lyrical about the evils of high prices and over-taxation, the greed of the borough-mongers and sinecurists and the necessity for parliamentary change. He made no appeal for violence but advised his hearers to sign a petition 'before physical force was applied'. The petition embodied the full radical programme of the day:

- universal (male) suffrage
- annual general elections
- secret ballots

Hunt was by now a very popular speaker and this first meeting was attended by around 10,000 people. It ended peacefully, with Hunt and Sir Francis Burdett being elected and asked to deliver a petition to the Prince Regent, requesting electoral reform and relief from hardship and distress. Burdett declined to take part, causing accusations of cowardice, and despite two attempts to present the petition Hunt was refused admittance.

The second meeting had been organised for 2 December so that a report on the reception of the petition could be delivered along with more speeches. Secretly, the Spenceans planned to use the occasion to encourage rioting all across the country and then seize control of the government by taking the Tower of London and the Bank of England. They hoped to let Hunt entertain the crowds and engage the troops while they got on with the real work of revolution. On the day Thistlewood and his followers led an excited section of the gathering away towards Newgate, presumably aiming to free the prisoners in a romantic re-enactment of the storming of the Bastille. They slipped off before Hunt arrived, knowing that he would disapprove of their violent intentions. On his way to the meeting Hunt met John Castle, part of Thistlewood's group, who told him that the Tower of London had been taken and that he should head there instead, but Hunt had long been suspicious of the man and continued to the agreed venue.

Aiming to seize the Tower, the rioters raided a gunsmith's shop at Snow Hill on the way during which one of their number was accidentally shot. They exchanged gunfire with troops at the Royal Exchange and other outbreaks of violence took place, notably at the Minories, but after the soldiers refused to hand over the Tower as Thistlewood had anticipated, the rioters dispersed. The police had known of their plan through a spy and Thistlewood's attempt at revolution ended in an embarrassing non-event. It is claimed that he attempted to flee to North America but, along with three other leading Spenceans, John Hooper, Thomas Preston, and James Watson, he was arrested and charged with high treason. Watson was tried first and the chief prosecution witness was John Castle, who it emerged was a government spy who had infiltrated the Spenceans. Castle's evidence was discredited by defence counsel when it emerged that he had a criminal record and that his testimony was unreliable. The jury concluded that Castle was an *agent provocateur* and Watson was acquitted, at which point the prosecution presented no evidence against the other defendants and all four were released. Cobbett, writing after the Cato Street events, summed up the situation,

> This is…the game that was played by Edwards and Castles; these two scoundrels were the most violent, and urged on their unfortunate victims to deeds of

desperation, yet they escaped not only punishment but even indictment. What a lesson for all Reformers, to avoid the snares of the most violent men, who are generally the agents of Government! All these worthies contrived to get into my company, Castles ONCE, Edwards ONCE, and this said person who played such an active part in Colonel Despard's affair ONCE, and here only once each; once was quite enough for me.

The establishment and its press of course attempted to blame everything on Hunt the, 'arch revolutionary'. In a brilliant piece of prose Cobbett gave some fatherly advice to his great friend,

Guard against excess in future. Take in a little sail and add a little to your ballast. Exchange a little of the courage of the lion for a little of the wisdom of the serpent. Give up a little, and only a little, of the stubbornness of the oak, for a little and only a very little of the pliancy of the reed. Do this and trust to the folly and knavery of these stupid and malignant wretches to make you a great man.

Despite Thistlewood's naïve adventurism Spa Fields was a triumph for Hunt and his policies of democratic reform, and helped to shift the main reform movement away from conspiratorial gatherings of incendiaries towards mass meetings and open debate; at least for the time being.

The Crown & Anchor

SOME WEEKS LATER, on 22 January 1817, the provincial radicals held a meeting at the Crown and Anchor pub in the Strand attended by 70 delegates. Missing from the meeting was Sir Francis Burdett, aged 47 in 1817, a veteran campaigner for reform who had served a number of jail terms for his activities despite being a wealthy baronet. He was seen as the leader of the radical faction in the Commons and campaigner against the slave trade, but had come to despise Hunt and Cobbett as vulgar upstarts, and they disliked him in equal measure. Major Cartwright, now approaching 80, Cobbett, and Hunt debated the issue of whether reform should be by household or universal suffrage. Hunt, favouring the latter, won the debate. On 28 January 1817 the delegates sent their representative off to Parliament. He was Lord Cochrane, a naval officer and long-standing campaigner for parliamentary reform, MP for Honiton in Devon 1806-07 and later for Westminster. His reformist views had made him many enemies, particularly when he attacked corruption in the navy. Hunt had the honour of bearing the petition signed by half a million

The Tree of Liberty

people to Parliament through excited crowds which was then, 'unrolled … many yards in length and was carried on the heads of the crowd perfectly unharmed'. Lord Cochrane ' took charge of our petitions …we… bore him on our shoulders across Palace Yard to the door of Westminster Hall, the old rafters of which rang with the shouts of the vast multitude outside'.

The Prince Regent had been given a boisterous reception earlier in the day when, as he was returning to Carlton House from the Lords to open the new session of Parliament, his carriage was mobbed and either a stone or a bullet (it was never identified – Hunt claimed a potato) broke the glass of his coach window. Debate in the Commons was interrupted and Parliament adjourned. The government took the view that such events demanded countermeasures, which were manifested in the Seditious Meetings Act passed by Lord Liverpool's government on 31 March and continued in force until 24 July 1818. It was designed to ensure that all reforming, 'Societies and Clubs ... should be utterly suppressed and prohibited as unlawful combinations and confederacies'. No meeting of more than fifty persons could be held without the prior consent of the magistrates. The measures were a re-enactment of Pitt's repressive legislation of the 1790s and became known as the 'Gag Acts', which included a provision making it high treason to assassinate the Prince Regent, which was not unreasonable, under the circumstances.

The Crown & Anchor after Peterloo 1819

At the same time Home Secretary Viscount Sidmouth issued a Home Office circular informing magistrates of their powers to arrest persons suspected of disseminating seditious libel. He announced that, 'an organised system has been established in every quarter under the semblance of demanding Parliamentary reform but many of them I am convinced have… revolution and rebellion in their hearts.' For good measure Sidmouth ordered the apprehension of all 'printers of seditious and blasphemous materials, all writers of the same, and demagogues'.

At the end of March, 1817 William Cobbett left for the United States, telling no one until after his arrival, when he announced that he would no longer be able to express himself freely if he remained: 'The laws, which have just been passed, especially if we take into view the real objects of those laws, forbid us to entertain the idea, that it would be possible to write on political subjects according to the dictates of truth and reason, without drawing down upon our heads certain and swift destruction.' Another motivation, and the effect upon friends and colleagues, is discussed in a later chapter.

The Blanketeer's March 1817

BY 1817 MOST of England's soldiers were stationed in either India or France, leaving around 16,000 in the country which was not thought to be enough to 'police the nation'. Sidmouth as Home Secretary was very keen to build up the volunteer yeomanry cavalry regiments, with the government paying for arms and ammunition while the volunteers paid for their outlandish uniforms, horses and other expenses. The officers were the minor aristocracy, factory and landowners, with lower ranks consisting of tradesmen and the self-employed. The working population, largely excluded, was under no illusion as to the purpose of these private armies, particularly in the towns where they were treated with fear and contempt.

A demonstration was organised by John Bagguley, an 18-year-old tool maker who had been travelling around Manchester advocating parliamentary reform for the previous two years. The event was to be held in Manchester on 10 March 1817. The intention was for the participants, about 40,000, who were mainly Lancashire weavers, to embark upon a nine-days march to London carrying blankets, so that they could sleep on the floors and in the barns of various sympathisers on the way. Many had notes pinned to their sleeves to petition the Prince Regent over the desperate state of the textile industry in Lancashire, and to protest against the suspension of the Habeas Corpus Act during the previous month. William Cobbett responded to the suspension thus: 'When our children's children shall read of this event, they will be all anxiety to know ... what was the cause of putting, for several months at the least, the *Personal Safety of every man,* however innocent he may be, within the *absolute power* of a Secretary of State, or of Six Privy Councillors.'

Before the march had begun magistrates read the riot act and the King's Dragoon Guards broke up the meeting arresting 27 people including Bagguley, throwing the meeting into disarray. Nevertheless, several hundred men set off in the drizzling rain pursued by the cavalry, who attacked them before they had got much further than Macclesfield and many no further than the River Mersey at Stockport. Many marchers scattered, dropped out or were taken into custody by the constables and yeomanry; the majority were turned back or arrested under vagrancy laws before they reached Derbyshire. In Stockport, over two hundred were arrested but with the jails full the authorities had nowhere for them and simply sent them home. During the scuffles an incident left several marchers with sabre wounds and one bystander was killed, although reports differ as to whether he was shot or sabred across the head by a mounted soldier, succumbing to his injuries several days later. Unconfirmed reports claim that one sole marcher, named as Abel Couldwell, reached London after eight days and delivered the petition to the Home Office. Bagguley was released from solitary confinement after seven months without charge and unshaken in his resolve. The Blanketeer's action had formed part of a series of protests and calls for reform that were to culminate in the events at Peterloo and the repressive Six Acts. Some of those arrested were held without trial for months before their eventual release and the event was used to support the government's case for continued emergency measures. Parliament renewed the suspension of Habeas Corpus again in June and it was not reinstated until the following March, at which time legislation indemnifying officials for any unlawful actions during the period of suspension was also passed.

The Pentrich Rising June 1817

STIMULATED BY THE suspension of Habaes Corpus, this group saw the only way forward as armed rebellion, and on the night of 9–10 June 1817 a band of around 300 men, mainly stocking knitters, quarrymen and iron workers, led by Jeremiah Brandreth an unemployed stockinger, set out from South Wingfield to march to Nottingham, about 20 miles distant, where they were told that a provisional People's Government was being set up. Never more than a few hundred, they were lightly armed with pikes, scythes, lumps of wood and a few guns. They spent around four hours searching around the area for food, arms and recruits before eventually setting out. By early morning they had reached Eastwood, some eight miles from Nottingham. There, two magistrates accompanied by twenty fully armed men and 15th Light Dragoons, met them. One of the magistrates described the confrontation: 'we came in sight of the mob who though at three quarters of a mile's distance from us no sooner saw the troops, then they fled in all directions...throwing away their arms'. Not a single shot was fired and within a very short space of time,

48 men were captured in the initial round-up. One, William Oliver, was yet another government spy, and this rather pathetic attempt at an uprising was quashed almost before it began.

Eighty-five of the marchers were incarcerated in Nottingham and Derby jails, before being brought to trial at Derby, charged in the main with, 'maliciously and traitorously [endeavouring]...by force of arms, to subvert and destroy the Government and the Constitution'. Twenty-three were sentenced, three to transportation for fourteen years and eleven for life. As for the ringleaders, despite the totally inept organisation, the government was determined to make an example of them, hoping that, 'they could silence the demand for reform by executions for high treason'. On Friday, 7 November, 1817 Brandreth, and two others were hanged and beheaded at Friar Green Gate, Derby jail. Although the customary quartering was remitted by the Prince Regent the executioner cut

Jeremiah Brandreth in Irons 1817

off their heads with an axe and held Brandreth's up to the crowd exclaiming, 'Behold the head of the traitor, Jeremiah Brandreth.' This was the last use of the axe for decapitation in Britain, and apparently the execution block can be seen by request in Derby Museum. Many liberal thinkers of the time were disgusted by the verdicts and executions. Lord Sidmouth was much criticised for his use of Oliver as *agent provocateur* who was not called as a witness by either side, – possibly the entire affair took the form it did at his encouragement.

The Aftermath of Peterloo

PETERLOO WAS A shock to ordinary people; a turning point in British history, with a significant impact on the development of democracy. The authorities had used extreme force to suppress a peaceful meeting, and the deaths of innocent people had outraged many, sparking a wave of protests and demonstrations across the country, increasing public awareness and stimulating demand for political reform. The government responded by cracking down even harder on the reform movement. Its leaders were arrested and imprisoned so that before the end of 1820 every leading working-class radical of importance was in jail and support for change slipped rapidly into decline, while the working classes of England returned docilely to their factories.

The Six Acts

In December 1819 legislation known as the 'Six Acts' was introduced by home secretary, Viscount Sidmouth, designed to curb demonstrations and to check the growth of radical propaganda and organizations, they were drawn up in a certain amount of panic over the events at Peterloo and were in force by December.

The six acts were:

- The *Training Prevention Act,* now known as the Unlawful Drilling Act 1819 (60 Geo. 3 & 1 Geo. 4 c. 1), made any person attending a meeting for the purpose of receiving training or drill in weapons liable to arrest and transportation. More simply stated, military training of any sort was to be

conducted only by municipal bodies and above.
- *The Seizure of Arms Act* (60 Geo. 3 & 1 Geo. 4 c. 2) gave local magistrates the powers, within the disturbed counties, to search any private property for weapons and seize them and arrest the owners.
- *The Misdemeanours Act* (60 Geo. 3 & 1 Geo. 4 c. 4) attempted to increase the speed of the administration of justice by reducing the opportunities for bail and allowing for speedier court processing.
- *The Seditious Meetings Act* (60 Geo. 3 & 1 Geo. 4 c. 6) required the permission of a sheriff or magistrate in order to convene any public meeting of more than 50 people if the subject of that meeting was concerned with church or state matters. Additional people could not attend such meetings unless they were inhabitants of the parish.
- *The Blasphemous and Seditious Libels Act* (or Criminal Libel Act) (60 Geo. 3 & 1 Geo. 4 c. 8), toughened the existing laws to provide for more punitive sentences for the authors of such writings. The maximum sentence was increased to fourteen years' transportation.
- *The Newspaper and Stamp Duties Act* (60 Geo. 3 & 1 Geo. 4 c. 9) extended and increased taxes to cover those publications which had escaped duty by publishing opinion and not news. Publishers were also required to post a bond for their behaviour.

Despite their sweeping powers the measures were rarely implemented. It was the last of the six, which greatly increased taxes on printed matter, newspapers, periodicals and pamphlets, that had perhaps the greatest effect. Publishers and printers had to provide securities for their good behaviour, and any publication appearing at least once a month costing less than 6d. was subject to a tax of 4d. The act also restricted the freedom of the established press and radical publications simply went 'underground', which may have increased their appeal.

The Cato Street Conspiracy 1820

FOLLOWING ON FROM Peterloo various radicals again thought mass meetings to be futile and favoured more direct action. A plan was hatched to assassinate all the British cabinet ministers and the Prime Minister, Lord Liverpool, while they were together at a dinner at the Earl of Harrowby's house in Grosvenor Square. The conspirators would then seize key buildings, overthrow the government and establish a 'Committee of Public Safety' to oversee a violent revolution. The plot was named after their meeting place near Edgware Road in London. How widespread the conspiracy was is uncertain but it was a time of

Arthur Thistlewood at the time of his trial

great unrest; rumours abounded including one that the London-Irish community and a number of trade societies, notably shoemakers, were prepared to lend support, while unrest and awareness of a planned rising were widespread in the industrial north and on Clydeside.

The leader once more was Arthur Thistlewood, having seemingly learnt nothing from his previous attempts at insurrection in 1816 nor the fate of his predecessor Guy Fawkes many years before. With continuing disregard for his own safety, he had challenged the Home Secretary, Lord Sidmouth, to a duel early in 1818 and was imprisoned in Horsham jail for twelve months. Unfortunately for him, he was again the subject of government spies; his second-in-command was George Edwards a government agent. Lord Harrowby had been tipped off days before and the dinner cancelled, assuming that it was organised in the first place and not just a ruse, so that the plotters fell into a carefully laid trap. Indeed it is possible that the whole scheme was instigated by Edwards. He was never called as a witness and was not to be found before the trial was held, the prosecution possibly fearing acquittals, as had happened in the Spa Fields trial. Thirteen were arrested after a vicious melée at Cato Street on 23 February, during which a constable, Richard Smithers, was run through and killed by Thistlewood's sword. A number of others managed to escape during the confusion including Thistlewood himself who was captured the following day. Five of the conspirators were tried and convicted of high treason. Lord Chief Justice Abbott proceeded to sentence,

> That you, and each of you, be taken from hence to the gaol from whence you came, and from thence that you be drawn upon a hurdle to a place of execution, and be there hanged by the neck until you be dead; and that afterwards your heads shall be severed from your bodies, and your bodies be divided into four quarters, to be disposed of as his majesty shall think fit.

Work began on the construction of the gallows outside the gates of Newgate Prison, with additional barricades erected to keep back the expected large crowds of spectators and an extra platform added behind the usual structure. Additional security was deployed in the form of troops of soldiers. The new stage was covered in sawdust to absorb the blood and the men's coffins lined up in readiness. Construction work continued throughout the weekend and on 1 May 1820 Arthur Thistlewood, William Davidson, cabinet maker, John Thomas Brunt, bootmaker, Richard Tidd, bootmaker and James Ings, butcher, prepared to meet their fate. The Sheriff for the City of London, Mr Rothwell, was in charge of the actual arrangements for carrying out the sentence and decided to do away with the usual humiliating drawing to the place of execution on a hurdle. The condemned men remained unapologetic to the last and the dreadful sentence was respited to mere hanging and decapitation rather than the full quartering of the bodies. After final gestures of defiance as the ropes were put around their necks their lives were terminated; but that was not the final act, and investigations have led to a fascinating tale which is told in full in Appendix 1.

After 1820 the so-called 'Enlightened Tories' like Peel, who first entered the cabinet in 1822 as Home Secretary, were watering down the repressive approach of the immediate post-war years repealing the Combination laws, giving rights to Roman Catholics and mitigating the savagery of the penal system. Revolutionary conspiracy was largely off the agenda and reform on the cards, as the establishment realised that change had to take place and began to listen. Peel introduced a number of important reforms to British criminal law. He reduced the number of crimes punishable by death, simplified the law by repealing a large number of criminal statutes and consolidated their provisions into what were known as Peel's Acts.

3
THE MAKING OF AN ORATOR

Henry Hunt was the son of an ancient and respectable farming family, born on 6 November 1773 at Widdington Farm, Upavon to parents Thomas and Elizabeth (Powell) The family had owned large amounts of land in Wiltshire and Somerset since coming over with William the Conqueror, which was confiscated when they backed the wrong side in the Civil War. Despite their loyalty, to the extent of joining the future king in exile, their property was not returned at the Restoration, and the resilient family had to begin the long haul back to solvency and respectability through hard work and judicious investment in farming, coupled with what was probably the more traditional route of Thomas making a sound marriage to a wealthy farmer's daughter in 1772.

At the age of five Henry spent a year at a boarding school at Tilshead on Salisbury Plain where he learnt to read, basic maths and iron discipline. He and his fellows were 'better fed than taught' as he remarked later, but nonetheless he had fond memories of his time there with the master describing him as a good scholar if a little 'volatile' at times. His education continued at Hursley in Hampshire, until the age of ten and upon the death of his grandfather the family went to live at Littlecot Farm in the parish of Enford in Wiltshire. According to his memoirs it was here that he became aware of poverty and developed a sympathy for the poor. His next education was at the grammar school in Andover, which was very different from his previous experiences and during which time he and his fellows were regularly beaten with the birch.

His mother Elizabeth died in 1788 at the age of 36 when he was 16 and his father suggested that he consider going to Oxford and then into the church, explaining what he perceived to be the undoubted advantages of the calling,

> ...if you should be a clergyman, I have now an opportunity of purchasing the next presentation to a good living, and you will then have secured to you

for life £1,000 or perhaps £1,200 a year and you will have nothing else to do for six days out of the seven but hunt shoot and fish by day and play cards and win money off the farmer's wives and children by night. This is the life of modern clergymen; and they might do very well, and get on very smoothly, in this way, if they did not screw up their tythes too high, and get drunk too often, so as to cause a serious complaint to be made to the bishop by some of the parishioners; which you may rest assured they never will do by you, let your conduct be ever so immoral or ever so irreligious, provided that you let the farmers have their tythes at an easy rate. Do that, and no complaint will ever be made against you to the bishop.

Thomas continued that the only way to achieve exulted rank in their profession was through 'the most prostituted sycophancy and a total dereliction of every manly noble feeling of independence.' Evidently father was not a big fan of the clergy, despite being a churchwarden, and must have been delighted at his son's rejection of the suggestion. Young Henry was determined to become a farmer and set about learning the trade, beginning work as a ploughboy on his father's farm. According to his own account he became more proficient and productive at working the land, tilling the soil, building hayricks and thatching than anyone before him, a remarkable arrogance and self-belief that was to carry him through life. His introduction to politics was at the hands of his local vicar, Rev. Carrington, whom he described as 'an excellent scholar and a very sensible, liberal minded worthy man.' Writing his memoirs in 1821, in one of his many flights of invective he described the good clergyman's opponents,

> He was at that time denominated by the vulgar, illiterate, grovelling, low-bred slaves of the day, a Jacobin; and this excellent, enlightened being, who possessed more real love of country than a legion of the reptiles with which he was surrounded, was constantly exposed to the petty insults of some of his big-bellied, big-headed, empty-pated neighbours, who termed themselves loyal and constitutional subjects, and who took upon themselves to point him out as an enemy to his country, because he did not choose to shut his eyes and join in the war-whoop, the savage, stupid, idiotic cry against the patriotic efforts that were then making by the friends of liberty in France, to rescue their fellow countrymen from the accursed yoke, the double bondage of superstition and tyranny.

Henry was at this time very patriotic, a 'loyalist' as they were known, but at the same time receptive to what were explained to him as the exciting events in America and France. He had a great respect and admiration for his father, although they often clashed over his stubbornness and sometimes wilful disobedience to the extent of open defiance. In June 1794 he made his own way to Portsmouth to witness the launch of the *Prince of Wales* man of war before King George, who was honouring Lord Howe's victory over the French. His father had forbidden him to attend and taken his horse, and so he took his father's horse in return and rode the 50 or so miles to see the ceremony. Upon arrival the gates were closed and he was denied permission to board. He ran up a ladder to gain access to the ship and attempts were made to manhandle him back to the shore in front of huge crowds, but eventually his pursuers relented and he was allowed to remain. The event seems to have affected him profoundly and perhaps he spent much of his career trying to recapture that first feeling,

> I was permitted remain on board and to be launched in the *Prince of Wales;* having got on board more than an hour after all other communication had been cut off from her and I obtained this gratification in the presence of thousands who held the success of my daring perseverance by giving me three cheers. This was the first act of my life that gained me the cheers of a large multitude and I was not a little proud of the compliment.

The Launching of the Prince of Wales 1794

The Wiltshire Yeomanry

HUNT DESPISED THE Jacobins of revolutionary France and was a firm patriot with all the unshakeable certainties of youth. He explains his feelings at the time in the first volume of his memoirs,

> There was about this time great talk of an invasion by the French. The ministers, having granted large subsidies, and having imposed new taxes, found it necessary to frighten John Bull with the idea of being invaded. Great alarm was therefore excited throughout the country; volunteer corps and troops of yeomanry were raising all over the island. Provisions had by this time increased in price, every article of common consumption was nearly doubled, and great dissatisfaction was evinced amongst the labouring poor; there were riots in many parts of the country, and much mischief was done by burning wheat-ricks, and pulling down mills, in consequence of the high price of bread. But the dread of invasion was in every one's mouth, and nothing else was talked of. I, therefore, was one who anticipated nothing less than an immediate attempt, and I applied to my father, and requested that he would purchase me a proper charger, and let me enter into a troop of the yeomanry cavalry.

In Wiltshire the idea was taken up with enthusiasm, and the first troop of Wiltshire Yeomanry consisted of 60 men formed in Devizes, under the command of Mr James Sutton with the motto *Primus in Armis,* signifying that they were the first local body of cavalry, chiefly drawn from the class of yeomanry, to be formed into a regiment. It was resolved to raise nine more troops in the county, and the circulars inviting recruits to join announced that hunters, coursers, and other bold riders would be particularly acceptable. The first official notice concerning the Wiltshire Yeomanry appeared in the *London Gazette* of 8 July 1794, and the final arrangements of the officers in the issue of 22 August, by which time the county possessed its full complement of ten troops, namely, Devizes, Salisbury, Warminster, Bradford, Chippenham and Calne, Malmesbury, Swindon, Marlborough, Everly, and Hindon. The uniform of each consisted of blue coatee, white leather breeches, long black gaiters, and a black leather helmet, with black plume over the ridge, and a small red feather plume at the side; while the Devizes troop was allowed to have Number 1 inscribed on its buttons, to denote the fact that it was the first to be raised in the kingdom. In the year 1796 the Salisbury troop was inspected by George III, who broke his journey on the way to the fashionable watering-place of Weymouth for the purpose. In the following year the ten troops were formed into the regiment of Wiltshire Yeomanry Cavalry, Lord Bruce being appointed colonel with a medal being struck to commemorate the banding together of the troops. In June 1798, all the ten troops paraded together at Devizes for the first time for three days and marched to Beckhampton Down, where Lady Bruce presented five standards. The regiment on this occasion consisted of 28 officers and 595 non-commissioned officers and men.

At the peace of Amiens in 1803 the Wiltshire Regiment was not disbanded, like some others, and upon the renewal of hostilities in 1804 its strength increased to 804 of all ranks. In the following year the great power and efficiency of the regiment caused it to be called out for permanent duty, when it was also inspected and praised by the Duke of Cumberland. Hunt was determined to join despite some wise words from his father, who was well aware of the character of the commanding officer,

> Look for instance at our neighbours; there is Mr Astley of Everly, [Otherwise Everleigh 20 miles north of Salisbury] who is surrounded by every comfort; he has at his command not only horses, servants, and carriages, but he has a numerous body of tenantry, who submit to be his mere vassals, and will do any act, however dirty or mean, at his nod. He is your commander of the troop of Yeomanry; he keeps hounds; and has many manors well stocked with game; and he is a magistrate of the county, and ignorant as he is, yet he dispenses the laws, or rather issues his arbitrary mandates to the whole surrounding neighbourhood. In fact, he possesses great power, and all his power is derived from his wealth alone.

As usual Hunt followed his own inclination and joined the regiment despite his father's wise words. He continues,

> I enrolled my name as a member of the Everly, Troop of Yeomanry, under the command of the *gallant* Captain Dugdale Astley. I knew the Captain to be a poor creature, and as little cut out for a warrior as any man I had ever met with; he was built like Ajax, but as for skill or valour I believed him to possess neither.

After drill and training came the troops' first opportunity for action. Among their number was William Dyke, one of the largest farmers in the area, who occupied the position of cornet, the lowest rank of commissioned officer. He had been attacked and abused in Salisbury market place for selling his corn at a legal but much reduced measure. The locals threatened even greater retaliation on the following week and the gallant band were stirred into action, determined to turn out in force to quell any riot. When the time came to march on Salisbury Captain Astley was, 'away on business', and Lieutenant Poore had been called to London leaving Cornet Dyke as the senior officer and the cause of the whole affair, but unfortunately he was, 'seized with a violent pain in his bowels', and likewise unable to attend. Now leaderless, apart from a sergeant-major, they managed to ride on as far as a public house in Amesbury where they got hopelessly drunk before receiving the news that all was quiet in Salisbury and returning home – to the absolute disgust of young Henry who was denied his chance of glory.

In 1797, as the threat of invasion grew, the various yeomanry corps, received letters or circulars from the Lord Lieutenants of their respective counties to enquire if, in case of the enemy landing, they would volunteer their services to the full extent of their various military districts. Hunt's district was Wilts, Hants, and Dorset, and a day was appointed for the Everly troop to assemble, and to give their answer to this application. Many were having reservations about the whole enterprise, fearing that its role was to maintain discipline at home on behalf of the authorities rather than hold back French when they invaded. The officers commanding the troop encouraged the men to remain within their county protecting their farms and livestock, and not engage in adventures outside of their area. At a stormy meeting in 1798 Hunt gave an impassioned speech before resigning in disgust at their cowardice, thus making an enemy of his neighbour and commanding officer Captain Astley, who was outraged when Hunt criticised him publicly for refusing to serve outside the county. Grave repercussions were to follow.

Marriage & Family

ON 19 JANUARY 1796 Henry Hunt, aged 22 of Enford, married Ann (Nancy) Halcomb (born 20 May 1775) by licence in Devizes; her parents ran the Bear Inn in Devizes market place. Hunt's father, who was a very close friend of her father, had often praised the daughter highly but disapproved of the match, thinking that his son could do much better as she had no fortune. However, her father managed to hand over a £1,000 dowry which Hunt immediately lent to relatives. They moved two miles from Widdington Farm to Chisenbury House, a large old-fashioned but handsome mansion with 52 windows liable to the window tax – some of which Hunt proceeded to block. Initially they seemed very happy at their new home but it was, nonetheless, a very expensive residence at which he and his wife entertained frequently. His hard work and success at farming enabled him to maintain it all, claiming that, 'I had at all times plenty of money, and I had every comfort and luxury about me but in the midst of all this apparent extravagance I never forgot the poor, all my servants were well paid and well fed…' Once settled he paid close attention to his farming activities, paying frequent visits to social events at Devizes. They had a daughter, Ann, born 28 March 1798 at Enford, followed by Henry II born 23 August 1800 and Thomas who was born 27 May 1802.

Father Thomas Hunt died in 1798 and, despite Henry's frequent disobedience and pig-headedness, the pair had maintained a deep respect for each other and Henry would have felt his loss keenly. As the eldest of six children he became the owner by either freehold or lease of 3,000 acres in Wiltshire and a large estate in Somerset. As heir to his father's estates Henry fully expected to take over the role of principal overseer of the poor in his parish of Enford with responsibility for doling out money to the needy. The position was subject to the sanction of the local magistrates and, despite his name being at the top of the list, he was passed over at the instigation of Astley and in favour of those wanting to reduce the amount given out. The reality was that this brash and boastful young man's face simply did not fit. His large income, easy relationship with his farm workers and labourers, with his undoubted arrogance and delight in displaying it antagonised the local landowning aristocracy. His position as that of a small landowner, but substantial tenant farmer, produced an income equal to many of the local establishment and yet he did not fit into the category of yeoman or gentry, and he had upset his neighbours of both categories.

Despite his fallout with Astley, Hunt's courage and attitude to military discipline was noticed and appreciated by Colonel Charles Brudenell Bruce, leader of the Marlborough Troop of the Wiltshire Yeomanry, with whom he claimed to have been on excellent terms, and he was invited to join. The 14-mile distance between Chisenbury and Savernake prevented Hunt from attending the troop drills as regularly as was required. When he did attend his remarkable fondness for talking and treating the troop to animated orations on loyalty, military discipline, and kindred subjects, as well as entering into constant arguments with the sergeants on points connected with drill, was a great irritation to Lord Bruce, who was looking for a convenient opportunity to get rid of him. This occurred in November 1798 when Hunt refused to attend a meeting at Savernake on the 19th. Hunt was amazed some days later to receive a letter informing him that his services were no longer required in the Marlborough Troop. He did turn up to a meeting sometime later, only to find that his name was not on the list and that he had been dismissed. In a fury Hunt said to Bruce, 'Then you are no longer my colonel nor I your subject and I shall expect satisfaction,' a direct challenge to a duel which was illegal, and Bruce took Hunt to court. The case was heard on 28 January 1799 at the King's Bench in Westminster Hall and could have been settled with an apology – the judges pressed for that very thing, but Hunt in his arrogance refused. He claimed that the real reason behind the prosecution was due to his performance at a game shoot where, professing himself to be a most excellent shot, he proved it by bringing down bird after bird, amounting to ten brace of pheasants – following which he was accused of shooting on his lordship's land without permission. It was at the instigation of Bruce's father,

Charles, Lord Bruce, Head of the Wiltshire Yeomanry

outraged at this supposed trespass, that his dismissal from the troop had been finally achieved. The court was having none of it, Hunt was convicted, sentenced to six weeks' imprisonment in the King's Bench prison and fined £100.

As an interesting aside and indication of the role of the yeomanry, on 7 June 1810 a mutiny broke out among the 2nd Wilts Local Militia stationed in Devizes, caused apparently by an unnecessary strictness of discipline. A sergeant was committed to the guardroom at the barracks in Back Street, and after evening parade, a party of the regiment, feeling this to be greatly unfair, forced the door and released the prisoner. The mayor summoned to his aid the Yeomanry Cavalry, who arrived the following morning with Colonel Lord Bruce at the head of as many troops of the yeomanry as could be mustered at so short a notice. The mutinous corps was disarmed and a ringleader, named Marmion was flogged on the Green. Although the Volunteer Corps had been disbanded following the defeat of Napoleon in 1815, the yeomanry was retained as a politically reliable force which could be deployed in support of the civil authorities. They often served as mounted police until the middle of the 19th century.

The King's Bench

Originally, the Court of the King's Bench was mobile and travelled around the country with the monarch hearing cases in various locations. However, in the thirteenth century, it began to operate from a fixed location in Westminster Hall, where it remained until replaced by the High Court of Justice in 1875. In Hunt's time the court was presided over by the Chief Justice of the King's Bench, appointed by the monarch and responsible for overseeing its proceedings, assisted by a staff of judges, lawyers, and clerks. One of its most significant features was its jurisdiction over common law cases based on the accumulated rulings of judges rather than on statutes – an important part of the legal system. In addition to its role in resolving disputes, the court also played an important part in the development of English constitutional law. Many important legal precedents were established there, including the principle of Habeas Corpus, which established the right of individuals to challenge their detention and seek release from custody. Despite its importance, the court was not without its flaws, being often criticised for its slow and cumbersome procedures, and claims that its decisions were sometimes influenced by political considerations rather than a strict adherence to the law. However, the legacy of the court lives on, with many of its important legal precedents continuing to influence the development of the country's legal system.

The Court of the King's Bench

The jail itself was in Belvedere Place, Southwark, South London, initially used as a detention centre for debtors. Over time it became a place of confinement for a wider range of offenders, including political prisoners, those convicted of serious crimes such as murder and theft, and those who had been accused of sedition or treason. The prison was much like any other of the time, overcrowded and dirty, but privately run so that inmates had to provide their own food and bedding. Often five or six hundred people were squeezed into two hundred and twenty-four tiny cells, most less than nine feet long. Those without funds lived by begging or on the charity of their fellows. with no access to fresh air or natural light. Food and medical care were often inadequate, with outbreaks of typhus quite common, and inmates were frequently subjected to physical abuse by the prison guards. Despite these appalling conditions, the prison was a highly profitable enterprise, generating significant revenues for the crown through fees and charges levied on prisoners and their families. Prisoners also had to pay a release fee at the end of their sentence, and if they could not afford it they had to remain in prison. The prison was burnt down by the Gordon Rioters in 1780 but was quickly rebuilt.

That poor state of affairs was of course for those prisoners with no money – perhaps two-thirds of the total were confined within the prison walls. For the better off the jail operated a system of liberties, or Rules, as they were called, that allowed detainees to live in lodgings within an area about three miles in circumference around the main prison block. It is estimated that one-third of prisoners lived in 'the Rules', and by the early 19th century the keeper was receiving £3,590 per year: £872 from the sale of beer and £2,823 derived from various fees and liberties. The apparent laxness of the prison led to it being described as 'the most desirable place of incarceration for debtors in England.'

Those able to do so could pay for one of the eight 'state rooms', and within the wider prison area there were facilities that make it sound like a pretty soft sentence. The yard had a coffee house, two pubs, butchers' stands, chandlers' shops and a surgery. On some occasions there was an open-air market where hawkers of all kinds plied their wares along with racket grounds and fives courts. All this was of course dependent upon how much money you or your supporters could provide, and as most of those confined were under its control until they could pay their debts or finish their sentence, there would not have been many who could live in such 'luxury'. Those sentenced were not supposed to stray beyond the boundaries of the Rules, but enforcement was loosely applied and when Lord Chief Justice Ellenborough was applied to for an extension of the permitted area he replied gravely that he really could see no grounds for it since to his certain knowledge they already extended as far as the East Indies.

Beginning at the end of December 1800 and into the following January, Hunt served his time under these pleasant conditions. He rented a spacious private room and was given the, 'run of the key' upon lodging a bond of £5,000 to be paid if he 'escaped'. For this he was allowed to come and go as he pleased providing that he returned at night. He found his situation with a parlour maid and an open fire far more comfortable than any inn. During his time there he became an avid reader of *Cobbett's Register* and longed to meet Cobbett in person. During his court case, Hunt had met Henry Clifford, a radical lawyer who was involved in the campaign for adult suffrage. Clifford introduced Hunt to several of his political friends, including Francis Place, Thomas Hardy and Horne Tooke. The one with whom Hunt felt most at home was Samuel Waddington, with whom he shared two spacious apartments and discussed politics. Hunt was now becoming more attracted to radical ideas, increasing his distance even further from local landowners, as he describes in his memoirs:

It was while he was undergoing his sentence, that, I became acquainted with him [Samuel Waddington], and I passed my six weeks as pleasantly as I ever passed any six weeks of my life. To be sure it put me to a great expense, and a considerable loss, in taking me from my family, home, and business; but I gained more real information, more knowledge of the world, and of men and manners; more insight into mercantile, political, and theological affairs than I should have gained in so many years, if I had continued in the country, employing my time in farming, shooting, fox hunting, and attending to the exercise of the yeomanry cavalry. It is more than probable that I should never have taken the lead, (such a lead!) in the political affairs of my country, if I had not thus early been placed in such a situation, and in such company, by the sentence of the Court of King's Bench. Before that period, I had, it is true, a natural and an inherent abhorrence of tyranny and oppression, and my excellent parent had instilled into my breast a pure love of justice…

When I was in the King's Bench my time passed very pleasantly, and as a great portion of it passed in the best of society, amongst some of the most intelligent men of the age, my time was not thrown away. I was induced to think for myself, and to form my own opinion of public men and public measures, without placing, as I had hitherto done, an implicit reliance upon the opinions of others whom I supposed to have had more experience, and better means of judging of such matters, than I had. I began not only to think but to act, for myself.

Hunt returned home from London in a very discontented frame of mind, believing himself to have been treated with the grossest injustice; he began getting into disputes with his neighbours, prosecuting several for trespassing on his land when hunting. With the steadying hand of his father now removed, a very successful farming business, plenty of money and still in his 20s, Hunt began to enjoy life – or so it seemed to him at the time,

I kept an excellent table, had a good cellar of wine, and there was never any lack of visitors to partake of it. The old adage, 'that fools make feasts and wise men partake of them,' I cannot refrain from acknowledging to have been pretty much realized at Chisenbury House. When I look back, and recollect the train of hangers-on that constantly surrounded my table, amongst the number of whom was always a parson or two, I am induced to exclaim, in the language of Solomon, "it was all vanity and vexation of spirit!" My life was a scene of uninterrupted gaiety and dissipation—one continued round of pleasure.

I had barely time to attend to my own personal concerns; for no sooner was one party of pleasure ended than another was made. The hounds met at this cover to-day, at that tomorrow, and so on through the week. Dinners, balls, plays, hunting, shooting, fishing, and driving, in addition to my large farming concerns, which required my attendance at markets and fairs, and which business I never neglected.

Despite the foregoing he made the unlikely claim that,

I took my bottle as freely as any of them; but, thanks to a good constitution, never to excess, or rather never so *as to become inebriated*.

Despite all his carousing, political activity was never far from his mind. As he saw it, Pitt's government was spreading fear of invasion throughout the country in order to justify heavy taxation and political submission amongst working people but despite his reservations and with his customary bravado he offered his services,

Our Lord Lieutenant of Wiltshire, Lord Pembroke, had caused circular letters to be written to the clergymen, churchwardens and overseers of every parish, to return an account of all the moveable property, live and dead stock and at the end of it to state what he would voluntarily place at the disposal of the government, in case of an actual invasion; he was also to declare whether he was employed in any volunteer corps, and if not, whether he would place himself under the Lord Lieutenant and act as pioneer, driver, &c. In the parish of Enford, a public meeting was called, which was held at the inn. I, having lately been dismissed from the Wiltshire yeomanry by Lord Bruce, the colonel, and having no confidence either in the courage or skill of the colonel or any of the officers belonging to that regiment, but having, by considerable pains and perseverance, obtained a pretty correct knowledge of military tactics, I hereby engage to enter myself and three servants, completely equipped, and mounted upon valuable hunters, as volunteers into the regiment of horse that shall make the first charge upon the enemy; unless the Lord Lieutenant should think that an active and zealous friend to his country, well mounted, and ready to perform any service, however desperate, accompanied by three servants, also well mounted, can serve the cause of his country better by placing himself at the disposal of the Lord Lieutenant of the county.

Hunt made a complete list of everything he owned and offered it to the cause, and it was then that he first spoke in public at his local pub in Enford in support of Lord Pembroke's appeal.

> My neighbours stared, and I believe some of them thought me mad with enthusiasm. And as well as I can recollect, so far were they from following my example, that they all contented themselves with offering some a waggon and four horses, some a cart and two horses, some a few quarters of corn; but no one went further than offering a waggon and four horses and a few quarters of oats. In fact, when the returns came to be examined, the offer that I had made exceeded that of all the farmers of the whole district, for many miles round.

Hunt assumed that he would be in full command of this troop, which did not go down at all well with Pembroke and the county authorities. Despite instructions that all offers were to be accepted, he informed Hunt that his services would not be required. One more snub from the establishment which had the effect of removing what remained of his traditional loyalism.

Mrs Vince

MILITARY AMBITIONS ASIDE, his personal life was about to take a very different turn. He fell in love with the wife of one of his best friends, Henry Chivers Vince III (1765-1831). Hunt had known Mrs Catherine Vince since before 1800 and they had been involved in what was, according to him, a passionate but platonic relationship, but one almost beyond the obsessive, as he admits in his memoirs. Catherine Vince was the illegitimate daughter of Colonel Harry Bisshopp, a son of the sixth baronet of Parham, West Sussex, whose seat was the Elizabethan mansion in that place. She had been born in Ireland while her father was serving there, before moving to Storrington in Sussex, a highly educated and beautiful woman with a keen interest in politics. The couple stayed together until Hunt's death in 1835 and it is most unfortunate that we know so little about her. Not a single word or opinion has been attributed to her in any of Hunt's voluminous writings, and there would seem to be no portrait.

By mid July 1802 they could stand being apart no longer and having arrived separately at the Brighton racecourse they hired a carriage and made for London together. The deed was done and there was no turning back, Hunt left his wife with an allowance of £250 a year and a fully furnished house in Marlborough. Daughter Ann was to live with the mother at their new home while the boys, Tom and Henry, were to live with their father; either party was to have unlimited access to the children. Thomas stayed with Nancy until the age of five after which he joined his brother before moving to London. Hunt describes the situation in his memoirs,

> The reader will perceive that I have of late very seldom mentioned the name of Mrs Hunt. The fact is, that I did not at this period enjoy that domestic felicity, of which I had heretofore partaken. I was, as I have more than once stated, gay, thoughtless, and dissipated. I seldom ever spent a retired, quiet evening at home, enjoying the rational amusements of my own domestic fireside. We had always company at home, or I was one of a party abroad; myself and Mrs Hunt were living a true fashionable life, and we entered into all its levities and follies. This course had drawn us into more fashionable, more accomplished society; and I own that to me polished manners were a great attraction, and that those who possessed them, possessed superior powers to fascinate. Amongst this number I frequently met a lady, who had been bred up and educated in the highest and most fashionable circles; she was tall, fair, and graceful, and, as far as my judgment went, every charm and accomplishment, both corporeal and mental, that could adorn an elegant and beautiful female, appeared to be centred in her. I never concealed in the smallest degree the pleasure which I felt in her society. Though for upwards of twelve months, which was ever since we had become first acquainted, my attentions had been very marked, yet they had not attracted any particular notice I thought. Alas!...my wife had watched the progress of this attachment with anxiety and pain; she mentioned her fears, and expostulated in becoming terms against the imprudence of my conduct, which might give occasion to the world for ill-natured remarks; and she represented to me that, although my attentions were open and undisguised, they were very pointed and visible to everyone.
>
> It will be asked, what said the husband of the lady? for she was a married woman. It would ill-become me to say more than is absolutely necessary upon that subject; but, unfortunately, he was careless and inattentive, and knew not how to prize the treasure that he possessed; and besides, as he never entertained, nor ever had any reason to entertain, a shadow of doubt respecting his wife, we were constantly left together. This intimacy had now continued nearly two years, and as the lady was going to stay with her family in a distant county, I was invited to pay her a visit while she was there. Instead of staying a week or ten days, I remained a month. During the whole of the time, my attention was incessant; I could not join in any scheme of pleasure or amusement, unless she was one of the party.

There were many who, finding it in their interest to besmirch his character, accused him of turning his wife out of doors to starve, and various other accusations of immoral behaviour which he was at great pains to deny with his usual injured passion,

> If any one of those who have been railing against me, will come forward; if any person, male or female, will come forward and establish one act of seduction against me, even from the earliest period of my life, up to this hour; if they will produce one illegitimate offspring of mine, or prove that there ever has been such, even by common report; I hereby solemnly promise not to write, or have published, one more line as long as I remain in this prison. And further; if anyone will come forward and prove, that I have ever been the inmate of a brothel, or been ever seen within the walls of a house of ill-fame, since the day I was married, twenty-five years ago; or that I ever, in the whole course of my life, seduced, and afterwards deserted, a female; I do hereby solemnly declare, that upon such proof being established, I will, within one month from the time I leave this gaol, voluntarily banish myself from this country; and so far from ever appearing again in public, I will never again set foot upon British ground.
>
> After this great change in my domestic affairs, I made full as great a change in my course of life. I immediately abolished all the accustomed carousals and feasts that I had been in the habit of giving at Chisenbury-House. I continued the society of a few select friends, but I cast off the busy, fluttering, flattering throng—the fawning, cringing crew—that had been used to crowd my table. I took a house in Bath, and spent the following winter in comparative retirement, in which I was blessed with the society of two or three rational and intelligent friends.

After his separation from Nancy he did not renew the lease on Chisenbury House when it ended in October 1802, and spent much time in Bath and Bristol trying to rescue his investment in a Bristol brewery which he had built under his own supervision near a spring called Jacob's Well in Clifton. He had been cheated over a period of time by a young man whom he had trusted totally. Lodging in Clifton he tried to improve the situation by direct supervision, but this early attempt at 'organic beer' using only malt and hops without additives failed, and he managed to extract himself by 1809, having lost in the region of £8,000 while his partner vanished to America. A brewery of that name was still listed as a going concern in 1880.

Gradually, Hunt became more involved in radical thought and activity, with its opportunity to appear on stage in front of an adoring audience; it

HUNT's *Genuine* BEER.

HUNT's first appearance in public life was as a *public Brewer*. In January, 1807, we find him advertising in the Bristol Gazette, that he had established a Brewery at Clifton.---" The Families of Clifton and Bristol," says he, " are respectfully informed, that they may now be supplied with *genuine* Table Beer, produced from the best malt and hops, and wholly exempt from *any other ingredient whatever*." He afterwards offered to make, and we believe did make, a voluntary Affidavit to the same effect. On consulting the Records of the Court of Exchequer, however, we find, that a very few months after the date of the above Advertisement, seventy gallons of *other ingredients* were seized from HENRY HUNT, of " the Clifton *Genuine* Brewery ;" and were *condemned* in Michaelmas Term, 1807. This awkward little accident, it seems, gave the Bristol men a sort of distaste for Hunt's *genuine* Beer, and no great relish for his Affidavits; and the consequence was, that he shut up his Brewery, and turned *genuine* Patriot.---(*New Times.*)

I never heard such a tale!!! Sure this never can be our Orator, Henry Hunt. He, good man!! is honestly labouring day and night to keep our Constitution pure and unadulterated. The Brewer was day and night infusing poison into the Constitution of all his fellow-subjects.

1807 Hunt's Genuine Beer

has been said that he would 'go to the opening of an envelope' a crack shot, a very handsome man powerfully built, an excellent boxer and a fine horseman, he attracted attention wherever he went and wore a white wide-awake hat – broad-brimmed felt with a low crown emphasising his pure intentions, and of course to make sure that he would stand out in any crowd. Hunt became greatly impressed by the ideas and achievements of Sir Francis Burdett, who stood as an independent in the Middlesex by-election of 1804 against the Pitt government's repressive system and was defeated by five votes.

In 1805 he was able to try out his speaking skills before a wider audience. Henry Dundas, otherwise Lord Melville, one of William Pitt's closest friends, was treasurer of the navy when Alexander Trotter, the navy's paymaster, admitted that he had transferred £8 millions of public money from the Bank of England to his own private account at Coutts, loaning the funds at interest, from which he benefited. These transactions caused no loss of public money, but rather the loss of interest on that money. Meetings of protest were held nationwide, including one in Devizes not far from Hunt, who turned up and gave a speech denouncing Melville's behaviour and corruption in general. This he counts as his first entry into public life. On 8 April the Commons voted to censure Melville. The debate on whether to progress to impeachment proceedings climaxed dramatically – 216 votes for, 216 against. In vividly described scenes, the speaker, 'white as a sheet', sat silently for ten full minutes before casting his vote in favour of impeachment. This single vote resulted in the first significant parliamentary defeat for a Pittite government in over twenty years. Melville's trial reached the House of Lords, but ended in his acquittal.

4
TWO PEAS IN A POD

William Cobbett

TEN YEARS BEFORE the birth of Hunt and some 60 miles distant at a pub called the Jolly Farmer, in Farnham, Surrey William Cobbett was born on 9 March 1763 the third son of George Cobbett, farmer and sometime pub landlord. Originally of poor farm labouring stock George and his forebears managed to save enough to buy a small farm and William looked back on his childhood years with great fondness working on the land and enjoying the countryside.

The parallels between the childhoods of Hunt and Cobbett are quite remarkable, both headstrong and rebellious. He attempted to leave home at 11 and at the age of 19 he went to stay with an uncle in Portsmouth and saw the sea for the first time, 'no sooner did I behold it than I wished to be a sailor'. He tried to get taken aboard a ship but was turned down, and 'happily I escaped, sorely against my will, from the most toilsome and perilous profession in the world'. In 1783 while on his way to Guildford Fair he saw a stagecoach and claims that purely on impulse he boarded it and made for London ending up spending nine months in a lawyer's office which taught him to write legibly and at speed. Having enough of such drudgery and once again on impulse, he attempted to join the Royal Marines at Chatham but ended up instead in the 54th Regiment commanded by Lord Edward Fitzgerald, Irish patriot turned revolutionary shot while resisting arrest in 1798.

By 1785 he was Corporal Cobbett and off to New Brunswick with his regiment. His time there seems unremarkable and involved a great deal of drinking, mainly rum at 7d per quart, he claimed, as would Hunt many years later, that 'not a single man out of 300 or 400 was sober for a week – except myself'. He proved to be so punctual and reliable that he became a clerk to the regiment and was promoted to sergeant major over the heads of 30 others taking him into the orbit of the higher ranks, 'whose profound and surprising ignorance I discovered in a twinkling'. His great intelligence

Corporal Cobbett off to New Brunswick 1785. (Gillray)

and industriousness which could be expected to cut him off from his fellows does not seem to have hindered him and he formed many friendships. His promotion gave him a broader view of how things were run, and from his familiarity with regimental accounts he could see that corruption was rife. In his naivete he expressed his concerns to fellow NCOs who urged him to keep quiet on the grounds that such things were widespread and perfectly normal. He was discharged from the army in 1791 totally disillusioned with the corruption and abuse that he had found there. It was these experiences which helped to mould his later political campaigns.

He made his way back to England with copies of the fraudulent accounts and instituted legal proceedings against the guilty parties. The court-martial was set to convene on 24 March 1792 but he heard that the accused were preparing to make counter allegations claiming that at a farewell party he had proposed a toast to the destruction of the royal family which could involve a sentence of transportation. Shortly before, on 5 February 1792 he had married Ann Reid known as Nancy the daughter of an artillery sergeant who had served with him in New Brunswick. Taking fright at the thought of having to leave her and of being imprisoned himself, he abandoned the prosecution and, in a move that was to become common in his career, the pair fled to Normandy.

> I went to that country full of all those prejudices that Englishmen suck in with her mother's milk against the French, against their religion; a few weeks convinced me that I have been deceived in respect to both. I met everywhere with civility and even hospitality, in a degree that I have never been accustomed to.

In August they set out for Paris but upon hearing news of the arrest of the king and queen and the massacre at the Tuileries Palace, Cobbett took fright once more and sailed for New York arriving when the newly independent government was but three years old. America was also contrary to his expectations,

> ... The country is miserable. Exactly the contrary of what I expected. The land is bad – rocky- houses are wretched, roads are impassable after the least rain... the seasons are detestable. The people are worthy of the country a cheating sly, roguish gang. The natives are by nature idle and seek to live by cheating...

Cobbett opened a bookshop and published a daily paper, *Porcupine's Gazette* and in support of the English cause which was widely read but too

Cobbett flees to America

provocative and in August 1796 he was convicted of criminal liable and had $5,000 awarded against him. This was a shattering blow and he began to find earning a living very difficult. The threat of yet more legal action prompted him to run once more and he returned to England in June 1800.

Cobbett had been away from his native land for sixteen years and upon his return he was treated as a hero by the Pitt Government, his American writings had been freely available and much admired at home and he returned a famous man. The government offered him money, work and pretty much whatever he wanted if he would continue to use his pen to support the establishment. He refused, and as he put it, 'From that moment all belonging to the government looked on me with a great suspicion.' A natural contrarian he was not to be bought and soon evolved his own radical course. He was not a revolutionary, but saw parliamentary reform as a way of avoiding the excesses of revolutionary France. Cobbett changed sides from Tory to radical reformer earning himself the derisory term 'weathercock' from his enemies.

Cobbett opposed 1802 Treaty of Amiens between England and France as he did not believe that it was more than a truce. The population of London were asked to show their enthusiasm for it by illuminating their windows. Cobbett kept his windows resolutely dark giving an assembled mob cause to break them. As his objections were no secret and expecting trouble he applied to magistrate Arron Graham for some protection which resulted in a patrol being sent from that office. Graham appears again later in the story. Despite this, windows were broken and attempts made on Cobbett's front door. Graham attended in person and arrested three of the mob himself but at Clerkenwell court the miscreants turned out to be clerks at the post office one of them barely 16 and all of respectable backgrounds. They were convicted with the jury recommending mercy and when Cobbett was asked if he was agreeable to this his reply was, 'Certainly not Sir, I came here for justice not for mercy.' The three received substantial fines but were set free. As regards the treaty he was proved right as hostilities resumed in May 1803 and continued until victory at Waterloo in 1815.

In October 1800 he launched a new radical paper, *Cobbett's Political Register*; it became a great success and ran from January1802 until 1836. Originally propounding Tory views, and costing a shilling, Cobbett changed his editorial line to embrace his new radicalism, advocating widening the suffrage, opposing political corruption, nepotism and the judicial system. It had a large circulation for the time of 6,000 copies but was read by many more often aloud to the illiterate in pubs and coffee houses. In the same year he began publishing *Parliamentary Debates* as a supplement to his *Political Register*. This he had printed by Thomas Hansard and in 1812, with his business suffering he sold the *Debates* section to Hansard in whose name it continues today. In 1805 he purchased a spacious house at Botley near Southampton along with a farm nearby living beyond his means and by now he had four children to support.

Enter Henry Hunt

IN JULY 1805 Henry Hunt called upon William Cobbett at his home in Westminster. They took an instant dislike to each other. The two men had as much in common as brothers, both brought up on farms, albeit of different social standing, lovers of the countryside and those who worked the land, passionate about exposing corruption and improving the lot of the common man. They both had wives named Ann who they addressed as Nancy. Cobbett met a fashionably dressed man ten years his junior with a marked West Country accent, Hunt was confronted with a tall robust man florid of face in an old fashioned coat, a master of his craft. Both were conceited, proud, arrogant and did not suffer fools lightly. Hunt was a great admirer of the older man and an avid reader of the *Political Register*. Cobbett was impressed by Hunt's intervention during the Melville affair – Hunt had sent a report of the meeting to Cobbett which was very well received. Despite this the lad had to learn his place and as Hunt recalls in his memoirs,' He addressed me very briefly, very bluntly, he never asked me to sit down but this might have arisen from there being no other seat in the room except the floor. I thought that of all the men I ever saw, he was the least likely for me to become enamoured of his society'. Hunt's entanglement with Mrs Vince was of course well known by now and this may have influenced Cobbett's initial judgement of his character.

Despite what must have been a great disappointment, Hunt was still dedicated to the *Political Register* and began to write for it starting with an article on enfranchisement addressed to the freeholders of Wiltshire during the general election of 1806. A freeholder was then defined as a man who owned property valued at 40/- per year and was allowed to vote as were those known as 'potwallopers' a borough in which the franchise was extended to the male head of any household with a hearth large enough to boil a cauldron – or wallop a pot. They were generally entitled to vote if they had been living in a house for six months and were not receiving any payment from the parish. The whole political system countrywide was arbitrary, corrupt and incoherent dating back to mediaeval times. This was the age of rotten boroughs that were able to elect an MP despite having very few voters, the choice of member typically being in the hands of one person or family, examples were the old deserted village of Sarum in Wiltshire or Gatton Park in Surrey both represented by two MPs chosen by a handful of voters. The landowners there would nominate candidates and sell the rights to the highest bidder while voters were bribed with cash. Ballots were held openly with threats or actual violence visited upon those who dared to vote the wrong way. Hunt's address was to those who owned their own properties and did not have to worry about eviction if they voted for the man of their choice. Cobbett printed Hunt's article in November 1806 much to the younger man's delight.

The following year saw the election of two reformers to Westminster, Lord Cochrane and Sir Francis Burdett. Hunt who was by now living in the

Looking for votes

Clifton area of Bristol saw it as the start of a new era of political reform and organised a dinner for 100 people at the Trout Tavern, Stokes Croft. The authorities found out about it and put up posters warning people off which encouraged half of the city to turn up but fearing violence Hunt asked them to disperse, as the military had been ordered to clear away any crowds at bayonet point.

Bristol 1807

HUNT TRIED TO involve himself in the Bristol election of 1807 but was disallowed as he was not a freeholder and the old guard was returned. Hunt claimed to have calmed a riot during the campaign by opening the cellars of his brewery and distributing strong beer amongst the populous. As 'Bristol Hunt' he began to campaign for parliamentary reform and as he put it later, 'Thus was I, in the year 1807, fairly drawn into the vortex of politics.' Despite his arrogance and cocky self-belief, a brief message describing some argument with a barrister shows that a little, if extremely rare, self-examination was not beyond him,

> A quarrel was excited and fermented by table bearers and go-betweens which commenced a paper war, directing all his talent against my views and objects. I replied: and a most vindictive political warfare raged for a while, in which we were both most magnanimously bespattered with the filth of our own creating. I was very young at this time, and where I failed in argument, I of course made up for it in abuse. In reality, there was very little argument on either side; and in default of it, downright abuse was resorted to, to the great amusement of the two contending factions.

It was during April of 1808 that Cobbett wrote his infamous letter to his publisher John Wright, warning him against associating with men of bad character and denouncing Hunt who he had not seen since their meeting in 1805 when the two had taken such a dislike to each other.

> There is one Hunt the Bristol man. Beware of him! He rides about the country with a whore, the wife of another man having deserted his own! A sad fellow, have nothing to do with him.

It was of course an unmerited attack on Hunt's relationship with Mrs Vince and Hunt was unaware of its existence until ten years later during the election campaign of 1818 when Wright and Cobbett fell out and the note was made public to devastating effect. The disclosure left Hunt shocked and bemused, as he says in his memoirs many years later,

> I must seriously ask the reader how I am to account for the scurrilous letter being written by Mr Cobbett to Wright, cautioning the committee of the electors of Westminster to beware of me? If this letter be not a forgery, Mr Cobbett was openly recommending me to the notice of the public, in his *Political Register*, while he was privately vilifying me by letter, and recommending the Westminster committee to beware of me, as I was a sad fellow. For the honour of human nature. I should yet hope that this letter was a forgery.

Cobbett's reasons for this note remain obscure and the rest of the text, which may have given some context, does not seem to have survived. Possibly it was at the behest of his wife Nancy who took extremely strong moral objections to Hunt and his relationship with Mrs Vince. The truth of its authorship did not emerge until many years later when John Wright successfully sued Cobbett over the matter and compelled him to admit that he had been the author. Hunt and Cobbett didn't meet again until April of 1809 when Cobbett was to speak at a meeting in Winchester and Hunt rode over to see him. He was invited to the dinner at the George Inn and the two got on famously with Hunt dating their political intimacy from this time. The treacherous letter as yet undisclosed.

The King's Bench, Newgate & The Tower

MEANWHILE, HUNT WAS having troubles at his home in Enford during 1807. His old adversary Astley, of the Eveleigh troop and the local landowners were determined to bring him to heel and conspired against him to the extent of organising a common fund to defray expenses incurred in carrying out actions against him – or so Hunt believed. Still determined upon revenge for his activities regarding the yeomanry and after several failed attempts to have him indicted for trespass and damage against which he successfully defended himself, Hunt was provoked into a fight with John Bennet's gamekeeper resulting in a conviction for assault in March 1810 and his second spell in the King's Bench Prison. He describes the affair in his own inimitable manner,

> …having given a good thrashing to a ruffian who was hired to assault me as I was riding along the high road, and who was proved to have actually assaulted me first, the Judge, Baron Graham, upon the trial at Salisbury, instructed the jury to find me guilty of an assault, though he admitted it to be clearly proved that the fellow had committed the first assault. His argument, if so it may be called, was, that I had given him more than an equivalent beating in return: had I, he said, only struck him once, I should have been justified; but, as I had struck him three times with my fist, it was an assault; and for this I was sentenced to three months in the custody of the marshal.

Hunt had of course spent six weeks 'within the rules' during 1800 and this time, he took some cheaper rooms over the coffee house within the confines of the prison itself. During 1809 there had been a serious incident at Ely in Cambridgeshire and reports of an army 'mutiny'. Accounts vary but it seems that a group of half starved soldiers demanded backpay that was being withheld to pay for their knapsacks and held their officers prisoner to press their grievance. The ringleaders were court-martialled and sentenced to 500 lashes each. Cobbett was outraged and gave vent to his feelings in the *Register* for 1 July calling for an enquiry which resulted in him being served with a writ for seditious libel. He was convicted and remanded to the King's Bench for sentence on 5 July 1810. Fearful of advocates fees he had defended himself which proved a disaster as he was extremely nervous and much of what he attempted to say was disallowed as irrelevant.

There was talk about a deal to avoid a prison sentence and in a state of shock he agreed to give up publishing and all attacks on the government. He was living at Botley in a house he couldn't afford with six children and facing a heavy prison sentence and bankruptcy. He wrote a farewell statement for the *Political Register* which he sent to his publisher but within hours changed his mind and pulled the article. In reality the authorities had never offered him any terms or guarantee that he would not go to prison and he knew that he couldn't trust them to honour any agreement. There was to be no deal and Cobbett was sentenced to two years in Newgate prison moving in on 9 July 1810. His attempt at a deal was to come back to haunt him at a later date. It must have come as some surprise when Cobbett turned up at the King's Bench prison on his way to Newgate on 5 July just as Hunt was settling in to his own prison lodgings. He immediately offered his hero his comfortable room which was accepted, Hunt confining himself to a damp cell for four days while Cobbett awaited his sentence hearing. Hunt received little thanks.

Despite his fears Cobbett managed to pass his sentence quite comfortably eventually moving out of Newgate altogether and into the prison keeper's house at the enormous expense of 12 guineas per week plus fees. As we have seen, he sold the rights to his *Parliamentary Debates* to raise funds to his publisher, Thomas Hansard and the publication continues today as the official record of events in Parliament. Despite the comparative comfort of his imprisonment, he felt the resulting financial loss keenly and the injustice of his sentence caused him great anger and bitterness, The experience changed him and he became short tempered being particularly outraged at the effect on Nancy and his children. Hunt and many of his other friends were to experience this sourness of attitude in the years to come but for the time being all was well and Hunt paid frequent visits to Newgate, one jailbird to another, and they became increasingly close. Cobbett was released on 9 July 1812.

By mid August Hunt was back in Wiltshire and in March 1811 his tenancies having lapsed he moved to a farm at Rowfant near Worth in Sussex where he received visits from fellow radicals Major John Cartwright, Burdett and Cobbett. Advancing further into radicalism and distancing himself from the mainstream and the Foxite Whigs, he joined Cartwright's radical Union for Parliamentary Reform.

Henry Hunt in 1810

The Candidate for Bristol 1812

THE CITY OF Bristol had only two seats and the two contending parties Whigs and Tories very sensibly saved money and effort by having one each. During July the Whig member, Bragge Bathurst, was standing down triggering a by-election. Sir Samuel Romilly was standing for the Whigs (he later withdrew) and Richard Hart Davis for the Tories. It was Hunt's first real attempt to test his abilities and popularity, he gave a long speech as an anti-corruption candidate in what had now become a three cornered race and no longer a formality. Bristol was on a par with 'the rottenest of rotten boroughs', to quote one of the resolutions adopted at the foundation meeting of Hunt's Bristol Patriotic and Constitutional Association in 1807. Hunt demanded an end to the intimidation and corruption of the electorate by the political clubs, and the right of freeborn Englishmen to choose their representatives freely. To achieve this locally meant having a third candidate genuinely independent and pledged to accepting neither bribes nor public money. Hunt knew perfectly well that given the wealth and power of the clubs, he had no chance of being returned, but if he could keep the polls open for the customary fifteen days he would force the clubs to use their 'machinery of corruption' and, so he hoped, by sheer exposure the system would be discredited and Parliament itself would be forced to intervene. Several hundred of Bristol's electorate of 5-6,000 voted for him. He was well received but there was trouble from the start. Davis was alleged to have paid 400 men as a sort of private police force armed with bludgeons painted blue. In retaliation, Hunt organised evening rides through the city, his supporters also picking up sticks to use as clubs. In this he was turning a blind eye to violent activity amongst his supporters and laying himself open to charges of incitement and violent conduct, it was not a mistake that he would make again. Troops were marched into town in contradiction of election rules causing some confrontation as they occupied key public buildings. There were riots and the military were engaged in a precursor of what was to come in a few years' time at Peterloo. In one of his speeches Hunt gave his opinion in characteristic style,

> You have heard of a large Army of 20,000 marching into the north of England, and for what forsooth? to subdue Buonaparte? To drive the French Marshals out of Spain? No, I say no, gentlemen, but to subdue your own starving countrymen. The next official news will probably bring us an account of a great Victory obtained by our Armies over the Workmen, or at least over those who used to work, in the potteries in Staffordshire, the reduction of the weavers at Manchester, the routing of the nail makers at Sheffield, the capture of the Lace-makers at Nottingham. Thus, are we approaching to a military despotism; we have been at War against Liberty for the last twenty years which appears likely to end in a civil war at home.

Every newspaper and publication was against Hunt but Cobbett continued to publish glowing reports of the campaign from his cell in Newgate even though both knew the cause was futile. Hunt's intervention cost Romilly and Davis a great deal of time and money to fight their corner and Hunt spent sixteen days in the city campaigning. He estimated that he had caused his opponents no less then £2,000 a day in bribes and expenses whereas he had expended a mere £30. The opposing parties threw whatever they had against Hunt including his relationship with Catherine Vince. Knowledge of the relationship was long in the public domain and Hunt, already portrayed as a dangerous Jacobin and ex prison inmate was now stigmatised as far worse, an 'unrepentant adulterer', proclaimed the opposition, seeking to discredit him through his personal life rather than his policies,

> Hunt has, by quitting his wife to live with another woman, broke his plighted vows to his own wife; a man who will break his promises in one case will break them in another case; and, therefore, as Mr Hunt has broken his promises to his wife, he will break his promises to the people of Bristol.

Cobbett was strongly opposed to adultery but put his personal feelings aside to defend his friend in print insisting that it was a private matter with no bearing on the election and asked if their moral outrage extended to peers and princes. The successful candidate was Richard Hart Davis a banker and Bristol merchant trading with the West Indies who polled 1,907 votes against Hunt's 235. The general election was held in October and passed quietly with Hunt gathering 455 votes against Davis with 2,910 in a four horse race. Hunt claimed that all parties had used improper means during the campaign and that the experience in Bristol had turned his hair grey and aged him seven years.

One of the main impediments to the growing friendship between Hunt and Cobbett was Nancy Cobbett's utter distain for Hunt brought on, it is assumed, by his continued relationship with Mrs Vince. In the same year Hunt sold his lease on the farm at Rowfant 'a poor, hungry, deceitful and barren soil', upon which all his sheep had died of foot rot and rented Middleton Cottage at Andover in Hampshire.

The Corn & Property Bills 1815

AGAINST THE BACKDROP of a strained post-war economy, Prime Minister Lord Liverpool's government passed the Corn Laws in March placing tariffs on cereal grain imported from other countries to favour domestic agriculture. The price of grain had to reach 80/- a quarter, – near famine inducing levels, before foreign imports would be allowed. Riots took place, barricades were erected, Cobbett and Hunt led protests and demonstrations but the bill passed, increasing the profits and political power of the landlords, raising food prices and the cost of living for working people and slowing the growth of other sectors, by reducing disposable income. Hunt's view was that it was a great 'injustice making the mechanic and the labourer pay a war price for his bread in time of peace'. The pair continued to campaign both in print and on stage but to no avail. The government was alarmed by the success of Cobbett's journalism and tried to prevent the mass circulation of his, and other radical papers, by adding a 'stamp duty' on all newspapers, putting them out of reach of all but the wealthiest. From November 1816, Cobbett published his *Political Register,* as a twelve page newspaper of solid text in a cheap 2d. pamphlet, which kept political comment but evaded stamp duty by removing news items. The price of the paper gave it the nickname *Two-Penny Trash* -a title that Cobbett cleverly adopted himself and soon gained a circulation of 40,000.

Hunt had achieved a reputation as an excellent speaker and was constantly being invited to public gatherings. During 1816 he spoke at large reform meetings at Birmingham (80,000), Blackburn (40,000), Nottingham (20,000), Stockport (20,000) and Macclesfield (10,000). Samuel Bamford a fellow campaigner met him at one of these meetings:

> Henry Hunt was gentlemanly in his manner and attire, six feet and better in height, and extremely well formed. He was dressed in a blue lapelled coat, light waistcoat and kerseys, and topped boots. He wore his own hair; it was in moderate quantity and a little grey. His lips were delicately thin and receding. His eyes were blue or light grey – not very clear nor quick, but rather heavy; except as I afterwards had opportunities for observing, when he was excited in speaking; at which times they seemed to distend and protrude; and if he worked himself furious, as he sometimes would, they became blood-streaked, and almost started from their sockets. His voice was bellowing; his face swollen and flushed; his griped hand beat as if it were to pulverise; and his whole manner gave token of a painful energy.

During a meeting at Bridgwater, Hunt described an annoying heckler and surely there can have been few better put-downs of a fellow human being than this description,

> ...a notorious Customhouse scamp of that town; a tall, lanky fellow, whose head was nearly half a foot above the rest of the crowd. From the visage of this worthy projected a cocked nose of a very peculiar kind, the nostrils of which appeared

to be two round holes passing horizontally, instead of perpendicularly, into his head. Upon this delicious proboscis (which was a sort of mixture between the pug-dog and a Chinese pig), was mounted a pair of silver barnacles, apparently placed there for the purpose of hiding a brace of things more resembling coddled gooseberries than human eyes. That feature which, in men, made as they ought to be, called a mouth, was in him not entitled to the name; it being a vulgar gash, with a pair of very thick lips, extending across two dumpling cheeks, and nearly uniting a brace of tremendous asinine ears. These altogether formed something like a half-decayed turnip stuck upon a mop-stick. Let the reader only imagine to himself a figure of this sort, constantly opening the slit that I have above described, and vomiting forth at once, from a fetid carcase, the most disgusting sound…

The Reformer's Dinner, Crown & Anchor 1809

During this period Hunt and Cobbett were at the height of their political collaboration and personal friendship. On 22 January 1817 a meeting was held at the Crown and Anchor to gather together petitions for presentation to Parliament when it opened on the 28th. Admiral Cochrane delivered them to Westminster with as many as one million signatures and about 20,000 people attending the event. The, by now, well-established double act of Cobbett and Hunt was ridiculed in the press and the butt of many cartoons which missed no opportunity to portray them as dangerous Jacobin revolutionaries involved in plots and conspiracies to overthrow the government by violent means. The brilliant caricaturist James Gillray produced a splendid set of cartoons lampooning the pair. Undeterred, from London, Bath and Bristol, with Cobbett's pen and Hunt's speeches they continued to agitate for the reform of Parliament holding meetings and organising petitions across the country. At one point nearly 600 petitions signed by over a million people were piled up on the floor of the House. As we have seen spies were everywhere inventing conspiracies to justify their fees and reporting back to Sidmouth and Castlereagh in February 1817 giving the impression that nothing less than total anarchy was the aim of every reformist.

Despite their close relationship there are many indications that Cobbett was jealous of Hunt, his attractive and intelligent mistress, his money and breeding, magnetism and charisma, personal bravery, ability to control a crowd and command an audience. Cobbett had arranged a meeting in Portsmouth knowing that Hunt would be busy at the third Spa Fields event on 10 February 1817 and attended himself with Lord Cochrane almost filling an entire issue of the *Register* with a report of its success and making no reference to Spa Fields which passed off equally well.

The suspension of Habeas Corpus in March had Cobbett running scared once more, his *Twopenny Trash* was too successful, and too widely read to be allowed to continue – he could feel the prison walls closing in and just as he had done in 1792 Cobbett made a run for it, in May 1817 he arrived back in New York. He had said nothing to Hunt, who was deeply shocked and described himself as 'thunderstruck' when he heard the news, in fact they had agreed to meet for a political rally in Devizes. His best friend, his hero, mentor and comrade had deserted him without a word. In his child-like naivete Hunt could not believe that this had happened and their relationship was never to be as close again. Cobbett's justification was that he would be silenced in England and could not bear the thought of being unable to write about the things he believed in. The rest of the reformist movement, nearly all of whom were to spend some time in jail, regarded it as pure cowardice. Political repression was perhaps not his only motive. Cobbett left behind a great deal of debt, his rented farm was repossessed, all his farming equipment and household goods at Botley had been seized and sold off; attempts to raise a subscription amongst his political friends came to nothing as they believed he had deserted the cause. There was no communication with Hunt for five months although Cobbett continued to laud him from afar in his *Register*.

The Westminster Election of 1818

IN JUNE 1818 Hunt put his name forward as parliamentary candidate for Westminster, 'recognising his duty to come forth from his retirement on behalf of the people', he pledged his campaign to universal suffrage, repeal of the corn laws, annual parliaments and opposition to all laws that curtailed the liberties of the people. He realised that, as before, he had no hope of success but, as always, could not resist an audience. Towards the end of the campaign the opposition produced with a flourish Cobbett's letter from ten years before referring to Mrs Vince as whore on horseback. Hunt was devastated, the opposition crowd hooted with delight and he was pelted with cabbage stalks struggling to maintain his dignity. Cobbett was still in America and unaware of the events and the dreadful consequences of his thoughtless note from many years before. Firstly, Cobbett had deserted his friend and run off to America and now this. Hunt tried desperately to contact him hoping that it was a hoax and when Cobbett eventually declared it to be a forgery Hunt was delighted to believe him. Hunt was the choice of the people but not of the electorate and after a 15 day campaign he received only 84 votes against Romilly with 5,538, Burdett 5,239 and Maxwell 4,808. He managed to console himself by stating that, 'I had the honour of being the first and only man who ever offered himself as a candidate for a seat in Parliament upon the avowed principles of 'Universal Suffrage, Annual Parliaments, and Vote by Ballot.' Not everyone was quite so enthusiastic, the *Commercial Chronicle*, produced the following on 27 June,

1818 Westminster Election

HUNT'S RABBLE. -The asses of reform had yesterday the misfortune to do some mischief while performing the drudgery of drawing their idol to his present home. Having thus usurped the labour of his hired steeds, they were proceeding most furiously down Southampton Street, to the Strand, when, owing to their zeal for freedom, some of the foremost fell down, and others tumbled over them, crushing those who lay prostrate. One unfortunate young man had his leg broken in two, and another had his skull fractured by the carriage wheels going over him. Several others were sadly bruised. The new 'Orator of the Human Race' did condescend to command his animals to stop, which order was complied with, but he himself did not alight from his elevated seat, or make the least inquiry as to the mischief which had been done.

Peterloo and Bail 1819

WHEN HUNT WAS dragged from the platform of St Peter's Field on 19 August of the following year Cobbett was still organising his return from America and unaware of the dreadful events. Hunt, was initially charged with high treason which could carry the death penalty, and was hauled off to Manchester's New Bailey prison with several others for 11 days solitary confinement before appearing in court to hear the charges reduced from treason to 'seditious conspiracy to overturn the government'. This was always going to be the case, a jury would be unlikely to convict knowing that they could be sending a man to his death for a comparatively trivial offence. The establishment would then be faced with riots and possible insurrection, or an acquittal would seem to trivialise the awful events of the day. Bail was granted but he was hurried off to Lancaster Castle under heavy military guard before sureties could be organised. He was back in London by 13 September welcomed by a vast crowd possibly as many as 300,000 bringing the city to a standstill. Whilst on bail Hunt engaged in a flurry of activity demanding that the charges against him be dropped and protesting against the illegal actions of the military. He engaged lawyers in Manchester and London addressed public meetings and attempted to bring charges in the King's Bench against all and sundry. He did succeed in getting the trial moved from Lancashire to York in the hope of a fairer hearing and proceedings opened on 16 March 1820 at the York Lent Assizes .

5
THE TRIAL OF HENRY HUNT

Trial, Transcript & Sentence

THERE ARE AT least three separate transcriptions of the trial and I have tried to take the most interesting parts from each concentrating on Hunt rather than the other defendants for reasons of relevance and space.

The case against Hunt began on Thursday 16 March 1820 at the York Assizes before Mr Justice Bayley. 'The doors opened early at 6:45 to allow gentleman from the London press to take their seats and by 8 o'clock all the boxes and galleries were occupied by gentlemen of the first respectability with no less than 20 reporters from London and provincial papers. The defendants seated themselves at the semi-circular table in the centre of the court. The ten defendants, Henry Hunt, John Knight, Joseph Johnson, John Saxton, James Moorhouse, Joseph Robert Jones, George Swift, Robert Wilde, Joseph Healy, and Samuel Bamford, were charged as follows,

> Having on the 1st of July conspired together, to call divers public meetings of the people and thereby to excite terror in the minds of his majesty's liege subjects and that in furtherance of their designs they had produced an unlawful assembly at Manchester on 16th of August last for the purpose of breaking the peace and exciting disturbances in the town. And it also charges them with attending the said meeting, at which 60,000 persons at least were present, many of whom conducted themselves in a formidable and menacing manner, and were armed with clubs and other weapons, having also flags with them on which were divers seditious and inflammatory inscriptions. This indictment contains two counts, one charging the defendants with a conspiracy and the other with riot.

The actual number of counts referred to seems to have totalled seven but these were not clearly defined in the published reports and other than the above the only comment seems to be that, 'There are several counts, varying

The Assize Court, York. (Nilfanion)

the form of the indictment, but in substance, implicating the accused in a conspiracy against the State'. Mr Scarlett opened the case for the prosecution in the usual manner by asking the jury to disregard what they had read or heard about the events and concentrate on the evidence before them. It was, he continued, the right of the people of England to hold public meetings for the purpose of taking into their consideration any alleged grievance and to petition legislature for redress of those grievances.

On 9 August Hunt was in Manchester to take part in a meeting that had been prohibited by the magistrates as illegal. He made a speech expressing his displeasure that people had obeyed the order and gave notice that he would hold a meeting on the 16th. Before that meeting the prosecution alleged that 'secret drilling had taken place in the dead of night, unlawful, and dangerous to approach, any who dared were beaten in a cruel manner'. On the morning of the 16th people were observed moving in large bodies upon Manchester in formation with all the appearance of an invading army. Mr Hunt arrived accompanied by persons carrying very large sticks and banners moving in perfect military order. Inflammatory banners contained such mottos as, *Equal Representation or Death, No Corn Laws, Universal Suffrage* and *Election by Ballot*. The meeting was convened for the avowed purpose of inspiring terror and alarm and he would, ask 'whether such an immense number of labourers and mechanics as were assembled together on that day could fail to produce the most serious alarm in the minds of men of property.' Could such a meeting be lawful in a country where laws were framed for the security of property? What could 200 constables have done against a mob of 60,000 men for the most part of desperate habits, fortune and character?' A number of witnesses were called to prove that various combinations of the defendants had been seen in each other's company before the 16th an essential element in any conspiracy.

One of the first witnesses was Henry Lomas a publican and member of the Cheshire Yeomanry, he didn't see anyone marching in battle array, and by the time he arrived people were running away, he saw no resistance made to the Stockport troop and nothing to call for the interference of his troop. 'Our swords were drawn before we came upon the ground by order of our officers'. Samuel Morton, fabric manufacturer, described a great number of people marching six or seven abreast keeping in step like soldiers which took about half an hour to pass. 'I heard trumpets blowing; people generally fight after they have done blowing trumpets. They had a black flag and others with *Liberty or Death; No Corn Laws* and *Hunt and Liberty*. I was alarmed by the black flag'. [it is as well to explain that historically a black flag symbolised 'that no quarter should be given' in any conflict and was only later adopted by the anarchist movement]. Morton says he was disturbed by the meeting to which Hunt responded, 'If you had been at home attending your business you would not have seen this procession'. The witness replied, 'Sir, if you had continued in London there would have been no one there'. Morton admitted having been discharged from Lancaster gaol under the Insolvent Debtors' Act, and that he had not since paid any of his former debts.

Shoemaker, John Chadwick saw night time training activities on the 15th at White Moss about five miles from Manchester. People were organised into companies belonging to the place they came from and every company had a person to command it. They are numbered two or three hundred people at first which increased during the morning, they were marching about the field for two hours with sticks held like rifles and when the word was given to fire they clapped their hands. The words,' make ready, present, fire! were given as if they had guns. He heard cries of *Hunt and Liberty,* but saw no swords, pistols or bludgeons. He was alarmed when the cavalry came in with their swords drawn at a sort of trot but not before.

Another constable, confectioner John Murray, found about 600-800 men being drilled at White Moss but was recognised as a constable and with cries of 'spy' 'spy' he was overtaken by 20 or 30 men who beat him with sticks and made him go down on his knees and swear never to be a 'king's man' which he did as he felt his life in danger. The people who beat him were not amongst the defendants. Under cross examination he denied that he had made statements like, 'If I had command of the troops I would put every b----rascal of them to death'. Or that he had said that he would rather be rowed to his own house in a boat in the blood of the reformers, than walk upon the pavement, but agreed that he had once said that if it was to come to an action he would not give in to the reformers, even if he were to fight up to his knees in blood. Hunt objected to the evidence of the drilling which he agreed amounted to 'grossness and illegality' but failed to see how the defendants were implicated. Justice Bayley said that the question was one of whether those assembled on the 15th were given a superiority which training gives on the 16th but concluded that he did not think it relevant. At the close of the first day Hunt was loudly cheered as he made his way to his lodgings.

On the following day William Morris, a weaver and special constable had also witnessed some training and claimed that on the 16th he saw men drawn into squares by the defendant Samuel Bamford who he heard say, 'You will march off this place quietly not to insult anyone, but rather take an insult; I do not think there will be any disturbance, if there is, it will be after we come back – there is no fear for the day is our own'. Bamford then spread laurel leaves among the men who were to command the sections, some put them on their chests, and others in their hats. The men were then marched off four abreast and joined other formations each with a cap of liberty. Some of the people had small sticks with them. Joseph Travis a grocer and special constable counted five divisions from various districts named on their banners and formed into marching sections; he had been sent by the magistrates to count the number marching in ranks which he put at 864 many divisions with bugles and flags. He saw people with a black flag, which had the words, *Saddleworth, Lees, and Mosley Union,* and something like two hands grasped, with the word *Love* but had not seen a bloody dagger on any of the flags as the barrister suggested. Time was taken up by other witnesses describing the various military style formations some putting the numbers of those in formation at 'at least 2,500 men'.

Publican William Standring claimed to be much alarmed for his property on the day but said that he did not remove it to any place of safety. Under cross-examination, he stated that, 'I was once charged for breaking windows one night when I was fuddled. I have had the misfortune of being confined in the lunatic asylum, but not latterly'. Manchester attorney and clerk of the local racecourse, Roger Entwistle described a large body of people marching in ranks from Stockport with very large sticks, totalling 4-5,000. He claimed that there were at least 100,000 people at the meeting, 'nearly all of them of the lower orders and many of them chanting, *Britons Never Shall be Slaves,* the meeting was most certainly calculated to inspire alarm and terror in the minds of the peaceable inhabitants of the town'. He said that after the military had moved towards Dickinson Street Hunt immediately pointed to them, and said, 'Your enemies are among you; if they attempt to molest you, get them down, and while you have them down, keep them down.' Entwistle gave further evidence to say that when the yeomanry were within ten yards of the hustings, they were assailed with sticks, stones, and brickbats. He saw a concourse of people with the flags, and one black one in particular which he thought resembled a pall more than anything else, this bore the inscription, *Equal Representation or Death*. He saw another with a bloody dagger painted on it in red and felt much alarmed because he knew that the minds of the crowd were very much inflamed by having read seditious works which he had seen them buying at the office of the *Manchester Observer*. The witness admitted having bankruptcy proceedings pending.

Francis Phillips a merchant and manufacturer who had acted as a special constable on the day claimed that he heard many taunting expressions amongst the crowd on the field aimed at every man who wore a good coat.. He had a stick shaken at him and considered the town of Manchester and the magistrates to be in great danger adding that few people could hear Hunt, he could not and he was about 75 yards from him. He saw very little of the battle, due to the dust and the number of constables. 'It appeared to me that they were disciplined troops who came to protect you, (Hunt) as they might be called upon, or as occasion offered. The crowd appeared to be ready to fight for you, if you gave them the command.' In his opinion the meeting was of a nature calculated to excite considerable alarm in the minds of the inhabitants of Manchester. There were a number of other witnesses giving similar evidence expressing alarm at the military formations of some of the participants. Justice Bayley again warned Hunt against asking questions with regard to the conduct of the yeomanry.

An accountant named Mathew Cooper made notes as Hunt began to speak, 'Gentlemen, I must entreat that you will be peaceable and quiet, and that every person who wishes to hear must keep order, and all I ask for is, that during the proceedings you will be quiet. We will endeavour to make ourselves heard but it is impossible for us to be heard by the whole. It is useless to observe upon the intended meeting of last week, only to observe that those who by their malignant exertions, in taking advantage of a few illegal words, expected they had triumphed, instead of which it has produced two-fold numbers (there were cheers), and now we have triumphed'. As Hunt was speaking, Cooper continued, some companies of foot soldiers appeared in Dickinson Street and formed into ranks. Hunt continued to speak but the witness did not take any more notes and gave the rest of his evidence from memory. Hunt said that they were only a few soldiers, and 'very few compared with us; we are a host against them'. Cooper claimed that in his judgment the meeting was such as to inspire very great fear in the inhabitants of the town and put the number of attendees at about 100,000. He said that he had written accounts of the events for London newspapers and admitted that he was once dismissed for using his employers money as his own but has since repaid it.

Mr Justice Bayley opened proceedings on the third day with a statement,

> Upon a question which arose yesterday, I stated that we could not here enter into a consideration of the conduct of the yeomanry cavalry on the 16th August. Whether that be proper or improper we are not now trying. But when I say this, I beg the defendants to understand, that it is open to them to shew the conduct of every part of the people collected at the meeting on that day, with a view to establish their peaceable character, or the tendency of their acts; also, with the view of shewing that there was no desire manifested by them to resist the civil authorities. Into all this they may fully enter, but not the conduct of the yeomanry.

Hunt spoke in response,

> My Lord, I was quite aware of your lordship's meaning yesterday. I know we are not here to try the conduct of the yeomanry cavalry...but whether the defendants are guilty of a conspiracy to form and attend an illegal meeting, and to inquire whether any illegal act had been committed by the people when assembled. I wish to show the *animus* of that meeting more particularly as the opposite side have travelled out of the record and attempted to shew that we were concerned in instigating some individuals to inspire terror into the minds of peaceable people, and have produced witnesses to identify us, as it were, with those who wanted to take a man's good coat off his back, who wanted to make Manchester another Moscow; and, thirdly, who wish to represent that I pointed to the soldiers, and then said to the people, 'There are our enemies get them down and keep them down.' If I can shew that instead of these statements being true they evinced a conduct exactly the reverse of that ascribed to them, and that their whole demeanour was orderly and pacific, then I imagine there will be an end to the indictment.

The prosecution witnesses continued with Henry Horton who had been sent as a reporter from London for *The New Times*. Horton claimed that he was able to place Hunt's, 'put them down' remark into context, 'Mr Hunt addressed the meeting and requested them to be quiet, and not to interrupt by calling 'Silence,' as that made more noise than anything else. He added, 'if any one attempts to destroy our tranquillity, I hope some persons will be found with courage enough to put them down, quiet them, and keep them down.' He believed that the meeting was calculated to create the most serious alarm in the town. When the cavalry appeared, there was some confusion near the hustings and Hunt said, 'Stand firm, my friends, they are in disorder already, let us give them three cheers.' After this the soldiers moved forward and Hunt and the others were arrested. Hunt read from Horton's report in the *New Times,*

> The soldiers advanced and surrounded the hustings, when Mr Nadin, with the utmost resolution, seized hold of Johnson first, and then of Hunt, and afterwards of several others, whom he handed to his assistants, and the latter carried them immediately to the New Bailey. The banners were the next objects to which the police officers directed their attention, and with very little resistance they got possession of the whole of them. The scene that now ensued was truly awful ! The shrieks of women, and the groans of men, were heard at some distance. Every person who attended out of curiosity, finding his personal safety at risk, immediately fled, and where was then the boasted courage of these mad-headed Reformers? They were seen retreating in all directions with the utmost speed. The crush was so great in one part of the field, that it knocked down some out-buildings at the end of a row of houses, on which were at least 20 or 30 persons, with an immense crush. As I was carried along by the crowd, I saw several almost buried in the ruins. Others, in their anxiety to escape, had been trampled on by the populace, many of them to death. A feeling of *sauve qui peut* [save himself who can], appeared now to fill the minds of everybody, and the dreadful result is not yet known.

Hunt read again from Horton's report, 'Had it not been for the interference of Nadin, the Deputy Constable, whom these men have particularly calumniated, it is certain that Hunt would not now have been alive, for the military were determined to cut him to pieces.'

Hunt asked the witness if he had seen him make any resistance to the 'constable's staff', to which Horton replied that he saw no resistance, but that it was rather a seizure than a surrender and that he thought it was Nadin who had seized him. He had seen Nadin take Johnson off the hustings by the leg, and it appeared to him he was about to do the same to Hunt. James Platt a Manchester police officer described an immense shout in which Hunt appeared to join and which he considered to be a shout of defiance to the constables accompanied by a waving of hats and sticks. Under cross examination Platt confessed that he was sometimes paid to give evidence against suspects and had once been involved with forged notes but had no convictions. Head Constable Jonathan Andrews claimed to have seen a great number of people marching like soldiers and carrying sticks shouldered like muskets which were very large and thick about four feet long. He calculated that more than one in five carried sticks and that the crowd numbered between 60,000 and 70,000 but saw no person struck nor any of the constables make use of their staves.

Next came the highlight of the prosecution case, William Hulton chairman of the bench of magistrates for Lancaster and Chester and in overall charge of events. Hulton was aged 29 and heir to a considerable fortune. He had been a magistrate since he 'came of age' but was thought by many to be too young and inexperienced for such responsibility on the day. He responded to Hunt's questions as follows,

> Hulton: The meeting did undoubtedly inspire terror in the minds of inhabitants. I received depositions on oath to that effect.
> Hunt: I desire that those depositions may be produced.
> Hulton: I have not got them.
> 'Many gentlemen stated to me that they were greatly alarmed, and, looking to all the circumstances, my opinion was that the town was in great danger. The population of Manchester and Salford, according to the census of 1801, was 100,000 souls. Manchester was a large place and contained many shops and warehouses. 'The magistrates, in consequence of these proceedings, deemed it necessary to issue a warrant for the apprehension of the supposed leaders, which was given to Nadin...he said he could not execute it without military aid. I wrote two letters, one to the Commander of the Manchester Yeomanry, the other to Colonel L'Estrange, requiring them to come to the house where the magistrates were, which they did. A troop of the Manchester Yeomanry soon arrived from the Mosley Street end. The troop came at a quick pace, and formed in a line under the wall of the magistrate's house. The moment they appeared, the crowd set up a tremendous shout. They groaned and hissed, and those men who had sticks shook them in the air. I saw those sticks lifted up in a menacing manner. I had a full view of the whole. I can positively swear that I saw the sticks flourished in this manner; and I even heard the expressions of some of the people who were near the military. Whilst the cavalry was forming, some of those persons who were nearest to them turned or advanced towards them. After the mob had set up this shout, the cavalry waved their swords. Then they advanced. From the appearance of the crowd, and from their general

conduct, I conceive it was totally impossible for the constable to serve the warrant without the assistance of the military.

I wrote at the same time to Colonel L'Estrange, and the commander of the Manchester Yeomanry, and I supposed the two forces would have arrived at the same moment on the ground but I was informed that from the appearance of the crowd, it was thought that it would be dangerous for Col. L'Estrange to lead his men through a narrow pass, where there was only room for a single soldier at a time. He afterwards brought up two troops of the 10th Dragoons, and two of the Cheshire Yeomanry. When the Yeomanry and the constables approached the hustings, I saw stones and brick-bats flying in all directions. I saw what appeared to me to be a general resistance. In short, when Colonel L'Estrange arrived at the magistrate's house, with the 15th and Cheshire Yeomanry, I conceived the Manchester Yeomanry to be completely beaten. The crowd closed in the moment the Yeomanry had entered and when Col. L'Estrange arrived, and asked what he was to do, so convinced was I of their perilous situation, that I exclaimed, 'Good God, Sir, don't you see how they are attacking the Yeomanry'. My idea of their danger arose from my seeing sticks flourished in the air, as well as brickbats thrown about. I believe the Yeomanry went in about four abreast, but their horses being raw, unused to the field, they appeared to me to be in a certain degree of confusion. They must penetrate through the crowd to get to the hustings, and as fast as they advanced, the crowd closed in around them. I saw distinctly from the window where I stood an immense body of people between the house and the Yeomanry, when they advanced to the hustings. In a very few minutes some of the parties were taken into custody. On my saying to 'disperse the crowd' he advanced, and the dispersion of the crowd took place. I am not sure whether Colonel L'Estrange advanced with the whole or only with a part of his force. Having spoken to him, I left the place. I do not know how many prisoners were brought in.

Q. Did your brother magistrates elect you to the chair on this occasion?

A. I was not elected chairman of the magistrates on this occasion because no one else would undertake the task; the situation was offered to no one else.

Q. Did any portion of the people, when I was advancing turn around, and give a shout of defiance to the constables?

A. Not that I know of. The shouts and applause that were bestowed on you had great influence with me in signing the warrant, because you brought with you a great accession of strength to the numbers already collected.

Q. Did the cavalry wave their swords?

A. The cavalry in forming waved their swords, and advanced to the hustings.

Q. Do you recollect the pace with which they advanced?

A. I would say it was something of a trot, or rather prancing, the horses were fidgeting in consequence of the noise, and they were not in good order.

Q. Did not some of them gallop?

A. I saw none of the cavalry galloping. The pace I wish to describe was between walking and trotting. I believe they advanced to the right of the constables, but the line of constables had, I believe, been previously broken. The space which the cavalry made in their approach was immediately filled up by the people.

Q. Was not the space blocked up with the constables?

A. I cannot say that it was filled up by the constables on the right, and the people on the left, endeavouring to escape. I only know the space was immediately filled up. I think decidedly that the space was filled up for the purpose of ... cutting them off.

Mr Justice Bayley—Do you think it was done to pull them off their horses, and injure them?

Witness—I certainly do, my Lord. The impression made on my mind, at the time, was, that the people closed in order to injure the Yeomanry.

A. I will swear that many of the people did not fly when the first body of cavalry rode amongst them. They fled when they saw the second. The moment Colonel L'Estrange advanced his squadron, the general flight, took place.

Q. Were there not many children in the crowd?

A. I saw very few children in the crowd. I cannot under take to swear that I saw one.

Q. There were many women?

A. There were a good many women, particularly noisy in hissing and hooting the cavalry when they first appeared. When the Yeomanry advanced to the hustings, I saw bricks and stones flying.

Q. Did you, or any of the other Magistrates, attempt to persuade the people to disperse?

A. Neither I nor any of my brother magistrates attempted to persuade the people to disperse.

Q. Why did you leave the window? [overlooking St Peter's Field]

A. Because I had given my orders to Colonel L'Estrange.

Q. Was the carnage too horrible to look at?

A. I would rather not see any advance of the military.

Q. Then you gave orders for that which you had not the courage to witness?

A. I gave orders to Colonel L'Estrange to advance to the support of the Yeomanry. I never thought it would be necessary to disperse them violently, as I thought they would disperse on the apprehension of those named in the warrant; and I will add, that we had no previous intention whatever of dispersing the crowd. I witnessed none of the scenes that took place after. I went downstairs just as Mr Hunt was brought in as a prisoner.

Nothing but a conviction of the existence of imminent danger could have induced me to order Col. L'Estrange to do what he did. I think that I ought to have been struck out of the commission if I had acted otherwise; I should not have discharged my duty if I had not done so. If the constables had not informed me that it would be impossible to execute the warrant, I should not have ordered the Manchester Yeomanry to advance.

On the following day, the first witness was John Walker an attorney and special constable who gave evidence that he had heard the defendant Wilde say, 'Stand firm to your post—if you have a leader of ever such strong nerve it is impossible that he can do it if you cannot stand firm.' This was addressed to the different columns or divisions ranged round the hustings… 'Every man who knows his neighbour, and who is staunch to the cause, by that means you will keep your enemies from the hustings.' Walker took this down at the time and saw the order obeyed, describing the people as about fourteen or fifteen deep when these words were spoken. He claimed that he could see the men were linked arm in arm. He heard Wilde say, 'I do not see any of our enemies amongst us; if I did I would tell you, and probably they might wish themselves in another place. Walker used an old letter to write down what he heard and was asked to swear an affidavit for several reasons, in the first place, his knowledge that large parties had been training in different townships round Manchester, and that those persons meant to march into the town with caps of liberty—revolutionary emblems, as he considered them— and that the meeting was calculated to overawe the town, to create disturbance, and to produce riot and confusion. There were 30 or 40 gentlemen in the police office at the time, all of whom agreed with him. He heard Hunt say, 'Don't cry silence, but keep silence, that will produce order: and, if our enemies endeavour to prevent order, put them down, and keep them down.' The military had not then arrived and he could not recollect whether Hunt pointed to any particular person, when that expression was used but he had no recollection of Hunt pointing to the soldiers as the enemies he wished to be put down and kept down.

The final prosecution witness of interest was Joseph Slater a publican who claimed that he had had a conversation about treasonous activities with the defendant Johnson as follows,

'Do you know, Mr Slater, there was a set of men at that time who intended to go armed to London, to disperse the members of the House of Commons?' I ridiculed the idea that such a set of ragamuffins could be allowed near the House of Commons. He said he knew it to be a fact; and that, if the subscriptions had been large enough to support their families while they were away, or in case they failed, they would have gone. I again ridiculed the idea, and Johnson said, 'Oh! but recollect, when Bellingham shot Mr Perceval, what confusion there was; Lord Castlereagh was scrambling to get out at one window, and Mr Canning at another; and when Bellingham was taken, they were near tearing him to pieces. They all strove to get hold of him.' He then observed, 'If one man could frighten them, he was sure it could be done'.

There had been a number of other witnesses giving similar evidence, and towards the end of the fourth day the defence opened its case.

The Defence Case

> The defendants' witnesses, in two bodies, amounting to one hundred and forty men, marched from Rochdale by the way of Huddersfield and Halifax. They joined at Leeds, where they slept. They carried two banners, inscribed *The Truth, the whole Truth, and nothing but the Truth*. They were all entertained on the road gratuitously by the Reformers and supplied with money to maintain them, in York, billets were provided for them on their return'. [Introduction to the transcript published by the *Observer* office, Manchester 1820. The journey was over 50 miles.]

Just before the defence case began there was another reading of the principal counts on the indictment in particular of the fourth which stated, that the defendants had *maliciously, unlawfully, and seditiously conspired, with other persons unknown, to cause discontent and disaffection in the minds of his Majesty's subjects, and to excite hatred and contempt against his Majesty's Government and the Constitution of the Realm*. The fifth charged them with, *having assembled for the above purposes*. The seventh count also charged them with, *having riotously and tumultuously assembled, to the terror and alarm of the inhabitants*.

After the various attorneys had outlined the case for his fellow defendants Henry Hunt gave his evidence.

> The learned gentleman set out with expressing to you his congratulations at the removal of this trial to your county from the neighbouring one, and in the pleasure it gave him to find it about to be tried in a place where local prejudices

were not liable to have particular operation. He made this congratulation, as he said, on the part of the cause of justice, as well as in behalf of the defendants. But with what sincerity, Gentleman, can you receive that congratulation, when I tell you that that Learned Counsel himself, with the Attorney and Solicitor-Generals, Mr Raine and the whole array of the Crown Lawyers, employed all their combined talents and legal acumen to deprive you of having the performance of that duty on which he now congratulates you, and to prevent my having this opportunity of obtaining an unbiassed Jury of the county of York? Has it also come to his knowledge that unfair means have been resorted to even with a Jury here? This Jury he knows were struck with the Sheriff at the side of the selector. Does he believe that no improper means have been resorted to? that no improper means have been used by the Under-Sheriff, or that no letter has been written to an individual called on the jury, but who has not attended ?

Mr Justice Bayley :-

Mr Hunt I must interfere, this is a quite extraneous matter. If any such interference were used, there is another way of investigating it. The party making that interference is answerable for it, but it is foreign to the present business.

Mr Hunt:-

My Lord, what I am informed I can prove. I am well advised upon it, and I do not hesitate to say, that it would form a good and valid ground of objection to any verdict tainted by such means. But I here confess that I have no such feeling. If any such attempt has been made upon any individual in your box, Gentlemen of the Jury, I am sure, that instead of creating an undue impression against me, it will operate in my favour and that you will feel no leaning towards the man who has dared to do it, and who shall hereafter, face to face, answer for his conduct. I must, however, say, that much prejudice has necessarily been imbibed against us.

Hunt asked why none of the banners and flags were produced. Why not a single witness to prove the existence of this bloody dagger? Where are the dreadful signs? Why not produce them here to see the effect they were calculated to produce? Where are the bludgeons that were shouldered like wooden muskets? They were part of the captured spoils, Mr Jonathan Andrews saw them four feet in length, where are they ? No, not one is here. I shall only say, that out of all the evidence brought forth on the part of the Crown, there had not been a single one whose cross examination did not elicit a contradiction of the charge brought against us.

Hunt explained that he did not call the meeting on the ninth it was the people of Manchester, 1,700 householders who signed a petition asking for the 'most legal and the most effectual means to procure a reform in the Commons House of Parliament, this was published in the papers and Hunt was asked to preside over the meeting.

The reporters who have been examined, all prove that I never used a single phrase but what was an exhortation for peace and order. Roger Entwistle alone says, I pointed to the soldiers and said, 'there are your enemies, get them down, and when you have them down, keep them down.' Mr Horton says, this was not addressed to the soldiers, and I will prove to you, that I could not, from my position, have seen the soldiers at the time.

The Riot Act. The prosecution did not bring a single witness to prove that it had been read—they knew very well that if they attempted to do so, the evidence of the individual would have been kicked out of court. They knew it was never read.

The purpose of the banners and drilling was to prevent the people from straggling about among other divisions, and staying behind in public houses instead of coming home. Then came the midnight drilling, yet, except in the case of the police runners' account, this was done not at midnight, but in broad day. We have found out that witness of all work, Chadwick, we know he is a character not to be believed upon his oath, and we have evidence to prove that in the presence of his fellow shop men he declared he would swear for any man who would pay him, we know him to be a manufactured witness. Thus, Gentlemen, to prop up the cause, you have a lunatic, [Standring] and a confessed thief. [Cooper]

[Hunt describes events after his arrest.] 'I was placed in solitary confinement; I was assailed even while in custody, with the most violent blows; and being immured for eleven days, while endeavours were making to trump up a charge of high treason, I demanded that the warrant under which I was detained might be shewn me; it was refused. At length it turned out that the charge against me amounted only to a misdemeanour; a bailable offence, Gentlemen of the Jury. I offered bail; two most respectable, men, a Mr Grundy and a Mr Chapman, the former an independent man, a person of the highest respectability, it was refused, I was hurried down to Lancaster, and confined unnecessarily for 24 hours. I can prove that few of those who surrounded the hustings were locked together, except at that part where an approach was opened for the constables. There was at the back a body of constables, from the public house, called the Windmill, up to the hustings. They kept a free passage, and there also it can be proved, that there was no locking of arms in such a way as could interrupt them in their approach. They passed easily up and down; I can prove, that any number of constables, however small one two, or three, might come up, and arrest whom they pleased without the smallest difficulty. They could come, at farthest, within 15 yards of the hustings, and any intimation of their intention communicated to me would prevent further trouble.

If I can bring forward men of the highest respectability, totally differing in politics, men who were as near to the hustings as I am to you, Gentlemen, who saw everything that occurred, my word is not worth a farthing, unless they prove that not one brick-bat, not one stone was thrown, unless they prove, as I stated, that the military cut to the right and left without any such provocation. They were even observed urging on their horses to jump over the heaps of unfortunate beings that were lying before them, and to force a way through a solid mass of poor wretches that were desirous to escape, but had it not in their power.

Here Mr Scarlett submitted that the conduct of the cavalry formed no part of the case but Hunt argued he had a right to state that the meeting was peaceable until the cavalry began to act, and that they were the aggressors. Justice Bayley responded once more that he could not allow Hunt to call evidence as to the conduct of the cavalry, as it formed no part of the present case, but he was free to bring any evidence to prove the quiet disposition of the people. Hunt continued. 'In asserting that right of freedom, I have done nothing that indicated any desire to destroy the Constitution or the Executive Authorities; I have used my humble endeavours in the sacred cause of my country's welfare, and will still continue to exert them to the utmost of my ability. As to the subject of Reform, we were told that it was confusion and disorder that we were seeking, the doctrines of annual parliaments and universal suffrage were ridiculed as wild and visionary, but I assert that every Englishman has a right to demand what we ask, we don't want equal representation of property, but an equal representation of right, what we demand is, that we may not be taxed beyond a fair proportion to the produce of the labour, and that in the imposing such taxes we may have a voice by our own representatives in the Legislature, chosen from the free voice of the people, and who will attend to the fair rights of the people.

Hunt was about to make some personal observations of Mr Hulton, when Justice Bayley stepped in once more, commenting that Hulton was in a situation of a very distressing and serious nature disallowing the observation. Hunt continued, saying that Hulton's evidence was totally unconfirmed by any witness, even a police officer, and yet with all its contradictions, it formed a large part of the prosecution case. Hunt claimed that he would be able to disprove every word

That was Henry Hunt's evidence, he now proceeded to examine his witnesses. Several gave evidence that participants had been asked to leave sticks at home and some recalled that the drilling had taken place in morning daylight and was quite public with many women and children observing. The idea was that, formed in companies, they would be conducted to Manchester as they were, and when they arrived they would remain in their respective groups and not intermix with others, returning in a body when the meeting was over.

William Elson a farmer, deposed that he didn't see any bludgeons, only walking-sticks in the hands of the old people. Bamford addressed the meeting, Elson continued, and advised the people that whatever was done on that day, to be peaceable, and not to molest any person upon the road, nor at the place where the meeting was to be held. He was well aware that there would be bad persons among them, and desired them to take care of them. 'If any person insults you', he said, 'show no resistance whatever, and if any person offered to take any of those who are called leaders, never let it disturb you. Let them be taken for what we have in view is a reform, and let us pursue it peaceably'. The junior editor of the *Liverpool Mercury*, John Smith stated that he had heard Hunt's speech, in which he congratulated the people on the effect of the postponement of the previous meeting which increased the numbers of the present; he thanked them for proposing him as their chairman, and hoped every person would keep the strictest order. He added that if any person shall be seen attempting to disturb the peace, those who were near him must put him down, and keep him quiet. In a short time the cavalry arrived and he was astonished at the circumstance but the general feeling was that they came to preserve the peace, the people gave three cheers and after a pause, the cavalry advanced hastily towards the hustings. He saw no resistance but thought that they advanced more quickly than he would have thought possible through so dense a crowd. He saw no attempt to resist, nor any encouragement to resistance given by Hunt or any other person, and saw no sticks lifted up against the military. No brickbats or stones were thrown until the close of the meeting when he saw one stone thrown. Up to the moment of the yeomanry reaching the hustings he did not feel any alarm and nor did those around him. He saw the people on the hustings seized without resistance after which the horsemen dispersed the crowd who were shrieking and weeping.

Hunt, 'Did you hear me say when the soldiers appeared, pointing to them, 'There are your enemies if they molest you put them down, and, having got them down, keep them down'? No, I conceive it impossible that anything of the kind could have been said. I must have heard it, that passage was uttered before the military arrived on the field. I saw the cavalry arrive at the meeting but I did not hear the crowd hoot and hiss, nor see them brandish their cudgels. The cheering with which they were received was of the same kind as that with which Mr Hunt was received when he arrived. I joined in this compliment to the military'.

John Tyas a reporter for *The Times* saw a black flag at the corner of the wagon near the house in which the magistrates met, and remembers Hunt saying, 'It is very foolish,' or words to that effect. He continued, 'The cavalry advanced, as far as I could judge, at a quick trot, Mr Hunt, ordered the people to give three cheers for the purpose of showing the military that they were not daunted by their unwelcome presence. The cavalry advanced and Mr Hunt told the people that it was a mere trick to disturb them, but he trusted they would all stand firm. He had scarcely said these words, when the Manchester Yeomanry rode into the mob, who opened for them in the most peaceable manner. The cavalry directed their course to the hustings, and, took a number of individuals into custody. I recollect an officer went up to you, with his sword in his hand, and desired you to surrender. You said you would not surrender to a military officer, but if any peace officer came up, you would surrender. You certainly incited no one to resistance. If brickbats, stones, cudgels, and bludgeons, had been hurled in the air in any great quantity, I must have seen them, I saw no such thing nor did I see a bloody dagger at the meeting. On Mr Hunt's arrest the people were flying in every direction and I was struck at myself twice on the hustings, and I was not resisting'.

Edward Baines of the *Leeds Mercury* gave the text of Hunt's speech before arrest. :

Friends and fellow-countrymen, I must beg your indulgence for a short time, and beg that you will keep silence. I hope you will exercise the all-powerful right of the people in an orderly manner, any man that wants to breed a disturbance, let him be instantly put down. For the honour you have done me by inviting me to preside at your meeting I return you my thanks-, and all I have to beg of you is, that you will indulge me with your patient attention. It is impossible that, with the most patient attention, we shall be able to make ourselves heard by the whole of this immense assembly. It is useless for me to attempt to relate to you the proceedings of the last week or ten days in this town and neighbourhood; you well know them, and the cause of the meeting appointed for last Monday being prevented; it is therefore useless for me to say one word on that subject, only to observe, that those who put us down, and prevented us from meeting on Monday last, by their malignant exertions, have produced a two- fold number today. It will be perceived, that in calling this new meeting, our enemies, who flattered themselves they had gained a victory, have sustained a greater defeat.

Robert Harrop, a spinner, was involved in making a flag but when the painter began to letter it in black, the lettering bled through, which prevented it being read and so they agreed that the flag should be painted black, and that the inscriptions and devices should be painted in white. It never occurred to them that a black flag was more offensive than a white one. There was a hand holding the scales of justice, and the word *Justice* under it. On the other side there were two hands clasped, with the word *Love* under them. The flag was produced, in court and was about six feet long by three or four broad. Other slogans on various flags were, *No Boroughmongering, Unite and be Free, Taxation without Representation is Tyrannical, Equal Representation or Death.*

Mr Scarlett complained that three quarters of the time during the prosecution was taken up in cross-examinations.

Mr Hunt, Yes, and very necessary ones.
Mr Scarlett, We have shewn that a strong alarm was felt in Manchester.
Mr Hunt, We have shewn the reverse.
Mr Justice Bayley, I must leave that to the Jury.

Prosecution Closing Speech

THE DEFENDANT HAD unjustifiably brought forward a charge against the under-sheriff in calling the jury; preparing himself, no doubt, for styling them, in case they brought in a verdict of guilty, a 'packed jury'. The defendant was most unfortunate in the number of his enemies, he was at war with, all juries, with all magistrates, with all constables, with all peace-officers, with all authorities, with all the House of Lords, and all the House of Commons. In proceeding with his personal attacks, he (Mr Hunt) had stated, that he (Mr Scarlett) had invented part of the charges against him, and that the bloody dagger of which he (Scarlett) had spoken, only existed in his distorted imagination. The statement was not indeed supported by the witnesses, as no dagger was painted on the banner, but the mistake admitted of easy explanation. The standard alluded to had not indeed a dagger painted upon it, but the top of the staff was pointed like a dagger, as had been stated by one of the witnesses, and painted red. He would leave the defendant all the advantages which might arise from this correction, which he did not think very material.

Whether the yeomanry attacked the crowd, or the crowd attacked the yeomanry, or whether there was no attack from either, had nothing to do with the question; the original formation and character of the meeting itself was the only point at issue. Though the motives of the law, in declaring meetings illegal, were grounded on the apprehended result of violence and riot, it was not necessary that that result should be consummated, to constitute its illegality: but the motives of the law were wise; for who could say what could be the consequences of such meetings? What power could restrain their violence, or repress their excesses? Was it safe; was it reasonable; that one man should be allowed to assume the power of commanding 80,000 or 100,000 people? and did the Jury think that Mr Hunt, whatever were his powers of oratory over a mob, should assemble 50,000 people, or that he should carry them about like a wild beast muzzled, to be let loose or not, as he should think proper. Could he, or could any man, however transcendent his influence over the minds of the people, be sure that he could always command them when they were excited, or calm their tumult, like the sage of the poet, [Virgil], by a look, by a word, or by the waving of his hand? The defendant did not possess that power, nor did any man and therefore, the law had wisely declared, that such meetings, creating such alarm, and tending to such dangers ought not to be permitted.

They had been occupied in hearing evidence foreign to the question. In a crowd of 80,000 people, the conduct of persons in one part of the people was not to be decided by what was observed at another. Was a witness to be proved perjured because he stated what occurred in one part of the multitude, and was not seen at another? Of the 400 of the Spa Fields rioters who went to attack the Tower, 300 would swear there was no violence intended. Besides, did anyone deny many things that the defendant's endeavoured to prove? Did anyone deny that the leaders of the party inculcated order? Did any one of the witnesses for the crown deny that Mr Hunt inculcated order'? or did any witness but one attribute to him any design of assaulting the military under the title of 'enemies' of the meeting. Yet all the witnesses called for the last two or three days for the defence only established negatives by assertions that had never been contradicted.

The broad question for the jury to decide was, whether this was, or was not, a lawful assembly? To that point he hoped they would give their most serious consideration. They were to say whether they thought it was lawful to assemble in such a form and with such banners as had been described. Mr Scarlett then summarised the evidence and main prosecution case against all defendants.

Mr Justice Bayley Sums Up

HIS HONOUR EXPLAINED that the indictment contained a charge of conspiracy, a charge of unlawful assembly, and a charge of riot, but on the charge of riot, he would not proceed because he believed the other charges to be sufficient. The circumstances of the conspiracy, as they were stated in the

Mr Justice Bayley 1763-1841

indictment, were these: *That the defendants conspired to meet, and to cause and procure other persons to meet, for the purpose of disturbing the public peace, and the common tranquillity of the King and realm.*

This was one count; and it would be for the jury to say, whether any conspiracy was made out, so as to find a verdict of guilty. The count further charged, that the defendants met together for the purpose of raising and exciting discontent and disaffection in the minds of the subjects of our Lord the King, and also to incite them to contempt and hatred of the government and constitution as by law established. Therefore, there were three aspects to be considered, First, that of a seditious meeting, to disturb the public peace; Second a purpose to raise and excite discontent and disaffection in the minds of the subjects of the King; and Third to incite the subjects of the King to contempt and hatred of the government and constitution of the realm as by law established.

Another count set forth, *That the defendants met and assembled, together with divers others, to a very great number, in a threatening and menacing manner, with sticks and other offensive weapons, and with divers seditious ensigns and flags on which there were various inflammatory inscriptions and devices, to the great terror of the peaceable subjects of our Lord the King.*

But, in an assembly so constituted, and met for a perfectly legal purpose, if any individuals introduced themselves illegally, in order to give to that meeting an undue direction, which would produce terror in the minds of his Majesty's subjects, although 59,000 persons out of a meeting of 60,000 were completely innocent, yet there might be 12 or 20 illegally met there, those 12 or 20 would be liable to be tried on the ground of having illegally assembled. It followed, that although a meeting might be perfectly legal as to the great bulk of the people attending it, if any persons, by a plan among themselves, introduced objects new to that meeting, by placards or any other means, which objects were likely to give to the meeting a direction not before contemplated, so as to produce alarm, or to endanger the public peace, and strike terror into his Majesty's subjects, those persons were liable to be indicted for illegally assembling together.

To show whether terror was or was not produced, he would state the testimony of both sides in this case. They would find in the evidence on the part of the prosecution, a great deal which imported that no apprehension of immediate danger existed and the circumstance of women and children being present would be worthy of their consideration in that respect.

Justice Bayley again rehearsed the evidence from the main prosecution witnesses and the defence case before asking the jury to consider their verdict.

He impressed upon the minds of the jury that the main question they had to try was, whether the meeting was, or was not, according to its manner, calculated to produce terror, either in the manner in which it was formed, or in the circumstances that ensued before its dispersion. If they thought it was so conducted, then the parties, with that view attending it, were criminal, and the Jury would find accordingly.

The Learned Judge concluded thus:

> You, I have no doubt, have considered throughout this arduous trial, and with patient attention weighed the evidence on both sides. Between the defendants and the public, I know you will impartially and justly judge, laying aside, as I implore you to do, all considerations of party or prejudice which may prevail elsewhere, and give your verdict, as you upon your solemn oaths are bound to do, upon the evidence alone. I have only one observation more, and I peremptorily require attention to it out of respect to the court, and out of deference to the laws, when your verdict is given, be it one of Guilty or Not Guilty, I require that no symptom of approbation or disapprobation shall be uttered within these walls; any such demonstration of feeling is a high contempt of this Court and such conduct would not only be highly erroneous but most criminal. Find no defendant guilty gentlemen whose guilt is not in your minds clearly established by the evidence – find no defendant innocent if you think the evidence establishes his guilt, whenever a doubt arises the defendant ought to have the benefit of it.

The Verdict

AT A QUARTER past twelve o'clock the Judge Bayley closed his charge and the Jury retired.

Shortly before five o'clock the jury returned into the box. The Foreman held a paper in his hand, and said the Jury had agreed upon their verdict, which he read as follows ;

> Moorhouse, Jones, Wilde, Swift, Saxton – Not Guilty.

> Henry Hunt, Joseph Johnson, John Knight, Joseph Healy, and Samuel Bamford, Guilty of assembling with unlawful banners and unlawful assembly for the purpose of moving and inciting the liege subjects of our Sovereign Lord the King to contempt and hatred of the Government and Constitution of the realm, as by law established, and attending at the same.

Mr Justice Bayley Do you mean that they themselves intended to incite?
The Foreman Yes
Mr Littledale-This verdict should be taken on the fourth count to which it more particularly applies
Mr Justice Bayley.- Let the verdict be so recorded.. You do not mean to find that they created terror, or incited it in the minds of the liege subjects of the King?
The Foreman, We meant, my Lord, to find on the first count, omitting a few words.

The Learned Judge then requested that they retire and look over the counts of the indictment again, particularly the fourth and fifth and say to which count they meant to apply their verdict.

The Jury withdrew for a few minutes, and returned with a verdict of Guilty generally on the fourth count, and Not Guilty upon remaining counts.

Mr Justice Bayley. I take it for granted the defendants are still under recognizance.
Mr Hunt. We are, My Lord.
Mr Justice Bayley.-Then let them now additionally enter into their own recognizances to keep the peace and good behaviour for six months, Mr Hunt in the sum of £2.000, Mr Johnson of £1,000, Bamford and Healy £500 each. The parties immediately entered into their several recognisances.
Mr Hunt.-What is meant by good behaviour, My Lord? – it is a very indefinite term.
Mr Justice Bayley.-The law defines it, Sir.
Mr Hunt.- I always, My Lord, wish to shew good behaviour to the law.
Mr Justice Bayley -Then you have only to continue to shew to it the good behaviour you observed in court.

It was near six o'clock before the court broke up on 27 March 1820 after ten days. Hunt was again cheered as he went home to his lodgings maintaining his composure and exciting much sympathy for his situation. Having been once more remanded on bail he returned to his rooms in London and on April 25 his application for a new trial was heard at the King's Bench during which Justice Bayley appeared and gave evidence by reading his notes. The application was considered in great detail in front of a crowded court before being refused on 8 May.

Hunt and his co-defendants appeared before justices, Bayley, Abbott, Holroyd, and Best again at the King's Bench on Monday 15 May 1820. They each gave their speeches in mitigation and once Hunt had had his say, 'In soft tone and gentle manner', trial judge Bayley sentenced him to be imprisoned for two years and six months in Ilchester jail as well as to find £1,000 as a surety for himself and two sureties of £500 each. His co-defendants were sentenced to one year each in Lincoln jail. In a final exchange Hunt had one more question,

> Hunt: I hope, my Lord, that the confinement is not to be solitary?
> Bayley: We make no order on the subject. I have no doubt that the persons to whose custody the defendants will be committed will show them every indulgence consistent with their safety. Their duty will be performed under the inspection of the magistracy, and we take it for granted that everything will be done to avoid aggravating the inconvenience of imprisonment'. The defendants were then taken into custody.

The tone of Hunt's description of his initial arrest was to become very familiar in coming years, 'I was confined in the New Bailey Prison at Manchester in a loathsome cell without candlelight on a bag of rotten straw without bedding of any sort, deprived of communication with wife or friend half poisoned by the non-removal for three whole days at a time of a pan, the receptacle of the voiding's of nature and treated in my native town, where my character has always been spotless, as if I had been a miscreant that had forfeited all claim to be considered as a human being. If I lose my life in prison with my last breath I will persist in the uprightness of my contact and will pray that my countrymen may be able to obtain that reform for endeavouring to assist in the obtaining of which I am now to suffer...' In his memoirs he describes events leading to Ilchester,

> I, and eleven others, having, by a mere miracle, escaped the military execution intended for us, were seized and confined in solitary dungeons in the New Bailey, for eleven days and nights, under a pretended charge of high treason. At the end of that time, upon a final examination, I was sent under a military escort, upwards of fifty miles, to Lancaster Castle, although bail was ready, and waiting to be put in for me. After this sentence was passed, I was sent to the King's Bench Prison, where I was confined till four o'clock on the Wednesday following, when I was conveyed in a chaise to this prison, where I arrived at ten o'clock the same night, being a distance of 120 miles. Thus, after having been confined in three separate jails since the 16th of August—the New Bailey, at

Manchester, Lancaster Castle, and the King's Bench, I am doomed finally to be incarcerated in a dungeon of this, the fourth jail, for two years and six months.

During his brief time on bail Hunt made constant attempts to bring the Manchester authorities to justice calling for an enquiry into the events at Peterloo but his unremitting efforts ended in failure. The government had stepped in early, legitimising the acts of the yeomanry and the Manchester magistrates by publicly congratulating them in the name of the Prince Regent.

6
HULK EDUCATED MONSTER?
WILLIAM BRIDLE 1779-1851

Birth and Family

GEORGE BRIDLE OF Evercreech, Somerset married Elizabeth (Betty) Melliar of Dodington by Banns on 20 February 1770 at Moorlinch 20 miles from Evercreech, both were able to sign their names and the family has been traced to Doulting in the early 18th century. William described his father as an industrious tradesman in failing circumstances and it appears from his burial record at St Peter's, Evercreech in 1830, that George was a tallow chandler or a tradesman who made and sold candles. His wife Betty had been blind for many years and when she died in 1833 aged 84 she had been an annuitant supported by the Rev. William Hetherington's Charity for the Blind at Christ's Hospital, London which had been operating since 1774. By 1829 the charity was able to pay £10 annually to each of 500 people. The stipulations were that the applicant must never have begged or received alms, must be over 55 years of age, and have lived in their present abode for three years with an income of less than £20 pa. They must also be totally blind meaning that Betty's condition alone must have made life difficult but with the ten children claimed by William and a business to run, 'failing circumstances' are perhaps not unexpected.

Their first child, a son named John was born in December of that year, he married a local girl Anna Cooke in 1794 and went on to become a grocer in Shepton Mallet. The electoral register of 1832 shows him living at Rock Terrace in Town Street, Shepton Mallet. He died of dropsy, a heart condition, in 1837 having done quite well for himself leaving various properties in the town and some parcels of land. Wife Anna was buried just two days before him and both were interned at St Peter's Evercreech. His son, also John, (b.1805) who seems to have had his own business in the town at Little London and is also on the electoral register. He inherited but was bankrupt by 1842 and moved to Liverpool where he found work as a looking glass silverer. By the census of 1871 he was living in London with wife Charlotte and family, now occupied as a clerk aged 66.

Their next child was a daughter, Mary born in January 1773 who married John Barber, described simply as a 'sojourner' or visitor in 1807. Elizabeth followed in 1775 and was always known as Betty like her mother. She married a Thomas Raines a bookbinder of Walcot, Bath in 1799. William was next in 1779, Andrew in 1781 but he died at the age of 5, Sarah Meliar of whom nothing is known but is possibly the one buried at Winsham unmarried in 1848. Ann followed in 1786, and was a witness at William's wedding in 1809 she married a Francis Cox from Shepton Mallet the following year, George 1788, married Jane Culliford at Ilchester in 1818 and the last born, Melliar christened in April 1790 may possibly be the woman using the name 'Amelia' to avoid having to constantly repeat her unusual first name in which case she married Robert Tite of Penselwood in Gillingham, Dorset a timber dealer and publican of the White Horse in Taunton who died in 1830. William and all his siblings were born and baptised at the church of St Peter, Evercreech and all who survived seem to have made good marriages and reasonable lives for themselves.

William was baptised at St Peter's on 5 October 1779, and by his own account left the family home at the age of about 16 'without a shilling in his pocket being unwilling to remain any longer a burden upon his father's industry'. Much later he was to describe himself as 'by misfortune cast upon the world, a poor friendless boy' [1836].

Somerset Fencible Cavalry

IN 1795 BRIDLE having left home, enlisted in the Somerset Fencible Cavalry which had been raised on 28 March 1794 and consisted of six troops under the command of Colonel Poulett, the fourth earl. John Poulett had succeeded his father to the earldom in 1788 and in 1792 he was appointed Lord Lieutenant of Somerset, a post he held until his death. He was also a Recorder of Bridgwater and a commissioned colonel of the Somersetshire Fencible Cavalry. On 1 February, 1793 the French Republic had opened hostilities with Britain once more catching the country at a disadvantage as it had disbanded most of the newly raised regular regiments of 1776-1783 after the last conflict had ended and reduced its own peacetime establishment to practically nil. Immediate steps had to be taken to recruit regular regiments for general service, and also to establish a force for home guard duties to augment the established militia. These became known as the Fencible Regiments, the word fencible is of uncertain origin but probably derives from 'defencible' – a defence force raised and deployed on home ground and described as, 'troops enlisted for service at home, and for the duration of the war only' designed to liberate the regular army for service abroad. It was proposed that the word 'Fencibles' should be included on their helmets but it was claimed that it was a, 'Scotticism' and therefore fit only for those regiments which had not volunteered for an extension of service. Later the following year the Somerset unit reportedly offered their service anywhere in Europe.

A Member of the North Somerset Yeomanry

Little has been discovered about the history of the Fencibles or its individual members, but in October of 1796 two troops from the Somerset Regiment arrived in Lincoln to be 'quartered for the winter with the rest of the regiment expected' and they spent the winter of 1798 in Weymouth desperately short of food and clothing and amidst the most severe frost in living memory. The majority of the companies were of short duration and in 1799, it was decided to disband them except for those who had volunteered for service outside of their own area. Bridle states that the troop was asked if they would volunteer their services to Ireland and, 'reference was made to me – the troop would do as I did; I commanded the volunteers to advance to the front, obeying the word as I gave it, upon which the troop joined me with much cheering'. It seems that movement to Ireland became unnecessary and by September they had moved to Modbury in Devon finding the accommodation less than agreeable, cramped and lacking in sufficient furniture.

Those troops offering to serve abroad had their pay raised and pensions for the disabled were introduced. Many men from the disbanded regiments joined the regular army and numbers of the former non-commissioned officers became officers in the militia. But the whole enterprise was not to last

The reduction of the Fencible Cavalry was announced to take place on the 25 March, 1800 and the remaining regiments were finally disbanded two years later at the Peace of Amiens. Bridle's regiment was 'broke up', he would have been about 21 having served for six years as private, corporal, serjeant, and acting quartermaster under Charles Procter Anderdon of Henlade House in Taunton. He could have continued his military service in the local militia or the regular army and carved out a decent career for himself, however, the rule was that non-commissioned officers must re-join as privates until an opening becomes available for them and this is dependent upon certificates of good conduct from their previous commanding officers, in all probability many would see this as demotion and look for other careers,

The following instructions were issued for the final disbanding of the Fencibles,

> Whereas we have thought fit to order our regiment of Fencibles, commanded by our trusty and well-beloved Mackay Hugh Baillie, Esq. Major General of our forces, to be disbanded and discontinued on the establishment of the army, our will and pleasure is, that you do disband our said regiment accordingly, and that in the disbanding thereof, the following rules to be duly observed.
>
> **1st**, Before such disbanding, you are to cause an exact muster to be taken by the regimental paymaster of the several companies of the said corps.
>
> **2nd**, Care to be taken that the arms delivered for the use of our said regiment out of our Stores of Ordnance, and indented for, to be returned thither again, and acquittance taken for the same from such person as shall be appointed to receive them.
>
> **3rd,** Care to be taken before the disbanding that the quarters of each company be duly satisfied; as also that the accompts of the men be made up, and all their just pretensions completely satisfied to the time of their being dismissed.

4th, Care to be taken that each non-commissioned officer and private man hereby to be disbanded be permitted to carry away with him his knapsack and his clothing for the present year, consisting of coat, waistcoat, breeches, cap and one pair of shoes, due 25th December last, and of the second pair of shoes due at midsummer next. But if the second supply of shoes be not provided in readiness for immediate delivery, each man is to be paid the sum of five shillings and sixpence, as a compensation in lieu thereof.

Each sergeant is also to be settled with for the sum of three shillings due him under the authority of our warrant of the 20th May 1801, as being the difference between the value of the former articles of half-mounting for a sergeant and a private man.

The greatcoats in wear by the regiment are to be disposed of according to such orders as you shall receive from our Secretary at War.

5th, And we being pleased to allow as our royal bounty each sergeant, corporal, drummer and private man, who shall be hereby disbanded, a certain proportion of pay beyond the day of his discharge, to carry him home according to the distance which he shall have to travel, viz.:--

In Scotland, 14 days

To England, 21 days

To Ireland, 28 days

and at the respective daily rates of,

1s. 6 3/4d. for a sergeant

1s. 2 1/4d. for a corpora

1s. 1 3/4d. for a drummer

1s. for a private

Payment thereof to be made to each of them respectively, and the charge thereof is to be inserted with the pay of the men in the pay-lists, care being taken to distinguish in the columns of remark the day, or days, on which they were disbanded.

6th, An account is also to be sent to our Secretary at War, attested by you and the Commanding Officer of our said regiment, of the names of such Commissioned Officers as may have been taken from half-pay, and are not, by law disqualified from receiving the same again, on the discontinuance of their services in our said regiment.

7th, And to that end, that the said non-commissioned officers and private men may be sensible of the care we have taken of them upon their discharge, you are to cause these, our directions, to be read at the head of each company and see that the same are duly put into execution.

Given, 10th August 1802 in the 42nd year of our reign. *George R*

The Prison Hulks

IN 1802 UPON the decommissioning of his unit and at the age of 23 Bridle chose what must have been a difficult and thoroughly unpleasant career. The rotting warships known as 'hulks' had been a feature of the English prison system since the American colonies revolted in 1775 and refused to take any more criminal transportees from Britain. The hulk system was legitimised in May 1776 when, *An Act to authorise, for a limited time, the punishment by hard labour of offenders who, for certain crimes, are or shall become liable to be transported to any of his Majesty's colonies and plantations,* (16 Geo.3 c.43), otherwise known as the Criminal Law Act, the Hulks Act, or the Hard Labour Act, was signed into law. One of London's leading merchants, Duncan Campbell whose business had been transporting felons to America while returning home with lucrative cargoes of tobacco, won the contract.

Imprisonment was not used as a sentence in itself during this period – there were very few jails and these were used mainly for those awaiting trial or execution. As those on the transport ships had no destination the prisoners remained where they were. Decommissioned warships were dismasted and made suitable for long-term incarceration with hard labour for periods of between seven years and life. The situation remained pretty much the same until Australia was opened up as a new destination and the first fleet sailed in 1787. The Australian solution did not relieve the situation to any great degree and the hulk population expanded with conditions and overcrowding becoming intolerable, but it was an option that suited the government as it was much cheaper then constructing land-based prisons and the enterprise was put out to private tender relieving the burden on the government still further.

How or why Bridle moved from the cavalry in Somerset to a prison hulk on the Thames we will probably never know and there is very little information about his time there but he does describe one of his adventures,

> I obtained an appointment as second mate on board one of the prison ships at Woolwich, containing at one time 560 convicts. Here, whilst only second mate, I obtained a premium beside my salary a thing before never heard of in the service. Being one day, whilst young in the service and second mate only left in command, the convicts employed to man the launch had observed a boat alongside a vessel on their way to the shore, and, considering the number of absentee officers, (who were absent for an escaped convict) they thought it a fair chance for escape; they, in fact determined thereon when they sharpened

every man his knife which they crossed, and bound themselves by a horrid oath to destroy all opposed them and that their motto should be *Death or Liberty*.

At the proper time I hailed the ship and ordered the launch to be sent on shore; and whilst directing my sub officers to bring up their men I was alarmed by the repeated fire of musketry, I ran to the wharf and observed my six launchmen in a strange boat and making their best way to the Essex shore, my launch being so left, was drifting down the river with the tide. I was here much distressed, 200 prisoners on shore and no launch to remove them, six men upon their escape before my face and no person at hand to relieve me so that I may follow in pursuit, finally, however, I arranged for the security of my working hands, when I jumped into a boat with a boy only as my companion.

On making the Essex shore I found two men dead in the boat and the others at a great distance in the marshes, we gave chase and when we had run a mile or so we came to a convict lying on the ground wounded, and *in each hand an open knife* these I took from him, left the boy in charge, and proceeded alone after the other three. After a long and tiresome chase, for they were a mile ahead at starting, I passed them, when turning on my heel, I presented a pistol and declared I would shoot the first man that advanced, no advance was made and, seeing the great odds, that my prisoners were provided with murderous weapons and that I had no visible appearance of relief I directed my men instantly to sit down and that no man should speak, nor move hand or foot for fear that I should suspect they meant to further to prosecute their attempt and I should be thereby be induced to fire upon them. My orders were strictly obeyed and when I had stood over at my prisoners for the long period of half an hour or more I observed some persons in the distance coming to my relief, finally I conveyed my men all safe on board, when I found that the arrangements I have previously made for the security of my working hands had been well attended to and that all were safe on board. In this excursion I had to pass through stagnant water and mud up to my middle the effect of which, and similar services prevents me now from the power of walking without support. [letter of 1836]

In December 1806 at the age of 27 Bridle was initiated into Freemason's Lodge No 304 at Woolwich, members met at the Prince of Wales Head on the first Monday of the month. His occupation is given simply as 'hulks' and his contribution of 5/-marked against his name. From January 1802 the English prison hulks had a new inspector, Aaron Graham a 49 year old Bow Street magistrate who had already had an impressive career as secretary to several governors of Newfoundland, a merchant ship's captain in his own right,

Prison Hulk 'Devonshire' at Sheerness

government spy during the mutiny at Spithead and played a large part in the defence of one of the mutineers from the *Bounty*. It was he that was charged with defending William Cobbett's windows against the mob during the peace of Utrecht. A brilliant administrator, Graham ran the hulk establishment until ill health forced him to resign in 1814. His appointment marked the change of convict management from private contractors to one supervised by the government but made little practical difference to the administration and life on the hulks as such. Perhaps the regime change involved the appointment of new staff in which case Bridle, at the age of 23, with a background of military discipline and service would have been an ideal recruit.

When Graham took over, the hulk establishment consisted of, the *Retribution* stationed at Woolwich, housing 450 convicts, *Captivity* at Gosport, with a similar number, the *Laurel* at Portsmouth docks, with about 300 and the *Portland* in Langston Harbour with about the same again. The *Prudentia* had just been retired from Woolwich and the newly acquired *Zealand* stationed at Sheerness with around 450 convicts making the Medway a permanent hulk station. The new inspector began to make reforms immediately, and had rations increased by rooting out some of the corrupt contractors and insisting that none of the hulks facilities were to be used for personal gain.

John Commins

ANOTHER STORY FROM this period, although he only played a tiny part took place at the Old Bailey in June 1808. Bridle was called to give evidence in the case of John Commins who was charged with escaping from the *Retribution* on 21 September 1802. The hulk lay at Woolwich on the Kent side of the river. In his evidence, Bridle describes his occupation as chief mate of the *Retribution* having held that position for about three years [ie 1805] before that, 'about five years ago' when Commins came on-board, he was second mate of the ship. In fact it was six years ago as Commins received his commuted sentence from the King's Bench in April 1802

Commins is of particular interest. He was a seaman, in fact, a Captain of the Forecastle which isn't as grand as it sounds merely meaning that he was responsible for a certain part of the ship. Built at Chatham Dockyard, *Temeraire* entered naval service on the Brest blockade with the Channel Fleet. Missions were tedious and seldom relieved by any action with the French fleet. In December 1801 *Temeraire* was off Bantry Bay, County Cork, Ireland awaiting orders for their next voyage. Several of her crew, hearing rumours that they were to be sent to the West Indies (which was true) at a time when peace with France seemed imminent, refused to obey orders, and demanded to know their destination. There was a little or no violence but a large number of the crew refused to weigh anchor unless it was to return home. Eventually the marines had them cornered and the attempted mutiny failed. Once word of the events reached the Admiralty the *Temeraire* was ordered to return to Spithead. There were a number of trials and Commins was amongst the first batch held on 6 January on-board the *Gladiator* at Portsmouth Harbour. The conspirators faced three charges,

1. Making, or endeavouring to make, mutinous assemblies.
2. Uttering seditious expressions; and for concealing traitorous and seditious words spoken, and tending to the hindrance of His Majesty's service; and not revealing the same to their Commanding Officer.
3. Being present at such mutiny and sedition, and not using their utmost endeavours to suppress the same, between the 1st and 6th day of December, 1801.

In his defence Commins, misspelt throughout the transcript as 'Cumings', read a statement,

Upwards of nine years have I served his Majesty with steadiness and loyalty; and every officer under whom I served has given me a good character. I shall call witnesses, and, with permission examine them as to the matters charged against me and trusting to the purity of my own mind and my innocence of the offences imputed to me shall conclude with appealing to the officers themselves of the *Temeraire* to say, whether during the whole time I belonged to the ships company, I ever upon any occasion incurred their displeasure or behaved unworthy of a seaman. I fought many of my country's battles; I was in the action of the 1st of June and that of the 23rd of June and behaved in all things as I hope I in all things became me.

It was to no avail. He was convicted of mutiny and sentenced to hang with the others. However, in April 1802 whilst awaiting execution his sentence, and that of six others, was commuted to hard labour for life on the hulks at Woolwich or at His Majesty's Pleasure.

He was sent aboard the *Retribution* one of the oldest and most decrepit of the prison ships, a 32 gunner captured from the Spanish. One of the largest and longest-serving hulks moored, close to the Woolwich Arsenal with up to 450 men kept shackled below deck. Of all the hulks, this was the one prisoners dreaded most. The death rate on board was more than double that of the others, and the number of attempted escapes was correspondingly high.

In good weather *Retribution* was a popular destination for tourists, who were curious to view its awful bulk and infamously depraved inmates from the safety of a small boat. From there they could also observe the multitude of convicts in chains working on the Warren. The men slept on straw, and it was said that no officers dared descend among them after dark, despite numerous reports of robbery, murder, suicide and 'unnatural crimes'. Several attempts to seal off each of the three lower decks to reduce the incidence of crime and disease had failed because the convicts tore down the carpenters' work every night. Efforts to erect a chapel on board were equally unsuccessful. Convicts of a higher social status did receive kinder treatment from the ship's officers, as they could seek help from influential friends in high places to gain a royal pardon, or permission to be transported on an earlier ship to Australia, but most were unsuccessful.

It didn't take Commins long to realise that that was not the life for him and on 21 September the same year he made his escape and remained free for about six years. The details of this time and his recapture are not known but on 11 May 1808 at the age of 27 he was 'found at large ' and arrested in the name of John Bley and brought before the Middlesex magistrates where he was sent for trial at the Old Bailey for perverting justice, ie being at large from transportation, a conviction which could easily result in the death penalty. William Bridle gave evidence which amounted to the fact that he didn't remember much about him. When asked if he had seen the prisoner come on board he replied, 'My memory will not allow me to say, ' and then asked if he had received any order respecting the prisoner, his reply was, 'I saw no order; it is about five years ago,' adding that Commins was only there for four to five months before making his escape.

Given that none of the witness's called by the prosecution could remember much about the case at all it was thrown out with a verdict of Not Guilty. A further twist in the tale is that at the Court of St James, 'in consideration of some favourable circumstances … His Majesty is pleased to extend our still further Grace and Mercy unto him and grant him our free pardon for his said crime.' What provoked this generosity we shall probably never know, possibly it was just part of one of the general amnesties that His Majesty liked to declare or possibly he was able to provide some information that they wanted. Commins was not a career criminal like most of his fellows and was perhaps guilty of nothing more than being easily led, he had a very lucky escape in any event.

The *Retribution*

As for Bridle's career on board, again, little is known. Some account books for the *Retribution* have survived, the earliest from April – June 1804 and show him as a second mate in receipt of £12/10/- for that period having been victualled for 92 days under the command of Captain George Reed. In the accounts for October/December 1805 he is listed as first mate, second in rank only to the captain and now in receipt of £15. Captain Reed was paid £75 for the same period. For October/December he slipped down the financial pecking order. He was still first mate but now fifth on the pay list as a chaplain and two surgeons appear above him, nonetheless his pay was increased to £18/7/6 for that period. In January of 1808 Bridle saw an advertisement in the *Salisbury and Winchester Journal* for the position of governor at the Somerset County Gaol, Ilchester and applies for the position along with 26 other candidates. The position offered a large salary while promising that,

> the strictest investigation will be made into the principles and moral conduct of every person who may think fit to offer for this appointment and a reference to persons in the respectable situation of life will be required to establish the character of such applicant. The superior education and the previous habit of command, where other qualifications are equal, will meet with decided a preference.

He was successful, and despite Aaron Graham's attempts to keep him at Woolwich – even to the extent of offering him command of his own vessel he chose to return to dry land, and a greatly increased salary. He was given glowing testimonials by Graham and, 'other gentleman connected with the observance of prison discipline'. He also claims that, 'On my leaving the ship, the convicts sent me a letter, expressing their thanks for my careful and kind of treatment and their sorrow at my leaving them'. A most unusual occurrence indeed. The surviving records show that Bridle left the hulk service on 31 May 1808.

Convicts at work. Woolwich c1800

One of the most famous accounts of life on board his former ship is contained in the memoirs of James Hardy Vaux who was imprisoned there in February 1809 the year after Bridle left. It pulls no punches and despite an obvious bias does not depart greatly from other accounts of life onboard the hulks at the time. Described as a gentleman thief and career criminal, Vaux was arrested in February 1809 and, under the alias of James Lowe, he was convicted at the Old Bailey of stealing three diamond rings and a brooch from a jeweller's shop in Piccadilly. As this was a capital offence, he was sentenced to death but this was subsequently commuted to transportation for life and he spent some months aboard the *Retribution* leaving a vivid picture of the conditions he found there.

There were confined in this floating dungeon nearly 600 men most of them double ironed and the reader may conceive horrible effects arising from the continual rattling of chains the filth and vermin naturally produced by such a crowd of miserable inhabitants…On arriving we were immediately stripped and washed in large tubs of water, then after putting on each a suit of coarse slop clothing we were ironed and sent below; our own clothes being taken from us and detained until we could sell or otherwise dispose of them, as no person is exempted from the obligation to wear ship dress.

Every morning at 7 o'clock all the convicts capable of work or getting into the boats are taken ashore to the Warren in which the Royal Arsenal and other public buildings are situated and there are employed at various kinds of labour some of them very fatiguing and while also employed each gang of 16 or 20 men watched by a guard. These guards are commonly of the lowest class of human beings; wretches devoid of all feeling; ignorant in the extreme brutal by nature and rendered tyrannical and cruel by the consciousness of the power they possess, no others would hold the situation, their wages being not more than a day labourer would earn in London. They invariably carry a large and ponderous stick which without the smallest provocation they will fell an unfortunate convict to the ground and frequently repeat their blows long after the poor sufferer is insensible.

As to the food the stipulated ration is very scanty, but of even a part of that they are defrauded. The provision is being supplied by contractors, and not by government and is of the worst kind such as would not be considered eatable or wholesome elsewhere. The allowance of bread is said to be about 20 ounces per day. Three days in the week they have about four ounces of cheese for dinner and the other four days a pound of beef. The breakfast is invariably boiled barley, of the commonest kind imaginable and of this the pigs of the hulk come in for a third part because it is so nauseous that nothing but downright hunger will enable a man to eat it. For supper they have on banyan days, burgoo of as good a quality as the barley and which is similarly disposed of, and on meat days water in which the beef was boiled is thickened with barley and forms a mess called 'smiggins' of a more detestable nature then either of the two former… the beef consists generally of old bulls or cows which have died of age or famine, the least trace of fat is considered a phenomenon and it is far inferior on the whole to good horseflesh. I once saw the prisoners throw the whole days supply overboard the moment it was hoisted out of the boat and for this offence they were severely flogged.

If I were to attempt a full description of the miseries endured in these ships I could fill a volume but I shall sum up by stating that besides robbery from each other, which is as common as cussing or swearing, I witnessed among the prisoners themselves, during the 12 months I remained with them, one deliberate murder for which the perpetrator was executed at Maidstone and one suicide, and all unnatural crimes are openly committed.

On 5 March 1809 William Bridle, 'Governor of Ilchester Castle', as the notice in the press described him, married Maria Webber daughter of Mr Martin Webber a cattle dealer, chapman and hawker at the church of St Mary Major, Ilchester, by licence. Financially the marriage was probably not a good bet as despite father Martin winning 20 guineas for a breed of oxen followed by the same amount for a six-year-old ox at the Smithfield Show in December

In Honour of His Majesty's Jubilee. Weymouth 1809

1808, Martin and William Webber were declared bankrupt in April of 1811 to appear at the Blue Bell Inn, Ilchester on 8 April but no further details have been discovered.

A possible birthdate for Maria is 1788 making her 21 at her marriage but unverified, William was aged 30. Witnesses were his sister Ann Bridle, Jane Maria Rees (?) and Mathew Hobbs, later to marry his sister.

Debtor Relief

THE YEAR OF Bridle's marriage, 1809, was also the 'Grand Jubilee' to celebrate George III entering the 50th year of his reign on 25 October. In Bath a Jubilee Fund for the Relief of Debtors was established with a great many of the town's residents and beyond subscribing and by the 28 November £1,151 had been collected from as far away as Frome and Yeovil. 'The Society for the Relief and Discharge of Persons Imprisoned for Small Debts', had been formed in May 1773 and fifteen months after its formation, 986 prisoners had been discharged at a cost of less than £2,900 (about £3 each). In December the *Bath Chronicle* issued the following appeal for their relief,

> The Poor Debtors in Ilchester Jail have for many years derived their chief comfort and support -fuel and food-from the benevolent visitors to the city of Bath. Once more, at this season of severity they earnestly implore their humane attention. At no period were the really distressed objects more numerous, or their calamities more severe. Pent in a dreary distant to prison far from the resort of the affluent, or the hope of casual bounty, the unfortunate prisoner has only this public means of making his sufferings known, and his wailings heard – and he rests assured that the humanely good will again extend their mercy, that the extremes of cold and hunger may not be added to that gloomy horrors of captivity. Donations will be received and duly applied... at different libraries in the city.

Amongst the donations listed in the *Bath Chronicle* were

Debtors in Ilchester Gaol, a gift from a friend £6/15/-
Charity box in Ilchester Gaol £5/-/-
A stranger at Mr Bridle's 7/-
Bridle Mr Wm. keeper Ilchester Gaol £1/1/-
Bryan Mr James surgeon to Ilchester Gaol £1/-
Rees Rev. TG chaplain to the Gaol 5/-

The fund was probably not entirely philanthropic but served to pay off the small debts of unfortunates without any hope of doing it themselves who were taking up room in the jails and had to be fed and clothed. Four years later the fund was enshrined in law as *The Insolvent Debtors Act 1813* (53 Geo. 3.c.102) in response to the burden on the prison system caused by the sheer numbers of those being incarcerated for debt, and some concern for their plight. The act created a new Court for the Relief of Insolvent Debtors whereby those imprisoned for debt could apply to the court to be released. Unless they were in trade or guilty of fraudulent or other dishonest behaviour an agreement could be reached with their creditors that ensured an agreed allocation of their present and future assets; regular assessments were held at Ilchester and other jails.

On 26 December 1811 having moved from his Woolwich Lodge 304, Bridle was accepted into the Freemason's Lodge of Brotherly Love 624 then based in Martock. In December 1813 he was elected as a Junior Warden and then as Senior Warden in November of the following year.

7
THE ILCHESTER BASTILLE

Early History

CIRCUIT COURTS HAD been held at Ilchester since 1166 following Henry II's order known as the 'Assize of Clarendon' which required that suspected criminals be named so that the sheriff could have them brought for trial before royal judges in the courts of their particular counties. In mediaeval times jail was a holding pen for those awaiting trial or settlement of a fine, various forms of physical chastisement, execution, or the payment of a debt. It was not until the 19th century that a term of imprisonment became the usual punishment for those convicted of a crime. Initially the jailer received no income other than the fees that he was entitled to charge those in his custody and their misery was compounded by the fact that the jailer was also entitled to charge a fee before their release which could delay their freedom by some time.

The jail at Ilchester would have been quite small and lay on the west side of the present High Street near the Market Place. It was moved to Somerton in the 1270s but returned in 1322 occupying a place on the west side of Ilchester Bridge. An Act of Parliament in 1576 supplemented the common jail by a, 'house of correction' or workhouse under direct administration of the local justices of the peace. Often known as Bridewells after the original in London, their purpose was the provision of compulsory employment with pay for beggars, vagrants and persons unemployed by a depression in a particular trade. As time went on the facilities were increasingly occupied by petty offenders.

By the early part of the 17th century the jailer was receiving £10 every three months for keeping the prisoners and a new building was begun on the north bank of the river at Northover probably used simultaneously with the lock-up remaining on the bridge. The new building seems to have been a disaster from start, built far too close to the river and continually flooded, sometimes putting the lives and health of the inmates in danger. The constant seeping of sewer water from the privies into the wells tainted the drinking water and spread disease throughout the prison, outbreaks of typhoid occurring with some regularity. During the civil war the house of correction was fortified by the Royalists but set on fire in 1645 before being quenched by the inhabitants of the town and restored in 1647 by order of the judges. At the Taunton Assizes in 1685 Judge Jeffreys sentenced 239 persons to death for their part in the Monmouth rebellion 12 were hanged at Ilchester. In 1685 there was an epidemic of typhoid during which many prisoners died, even at that early stage this was blamed on the seepage of sewer water from the privies into the drinking water.

In 1761 the following fees were approved,

> Fees to discharge every debtor and felon 13/4d plus 1/- to the turnkey.
>
> Single debtors, including a bed and bedding 1/6d unless two lodge together in which case each pay 9d. The jailer is not to compel any debtor to lodge single and if they have bedding of their own they are to pay 1/- a weekly. If the bed is his own he should pay nothing for it.
>
> Prisoners to be carefully shut up every evening at sunset; to be let out every morning between Michaelmas and Lady day at 8 o'clock in the morning and between Lady day and Michaelmas at six in the morning.
>
> To have liberty to buy their own victuals and drink in or out of prison.
>
> The felons to have 10 lb weight of clean dry wheaten straw every week.
>
> Each felon to have a two penny loaf of household bread each day.
>
> Felons men and women to be locked up separately from each other every night.
>
> A sick felon to be kept separate from the rest as conveniently as possible.
>
> The whole prison bog house sinks and gutters to be kept as clean as possible.

Joseph & Edward Scadding (1757-1808)

FROM 1757 UNTIL 1771 the jail was run by Joseph Scadding a yeoman farmer from Pitminster and sometime inn keeper; it was a strange change of occupation possibly the farm was not doing well. The jailer was appointed by the sheriff and the terms of his employment were that he had to be resident at the jail ensuring that no one escaped, he had to ensure that everyone appeared in court at the required time, pay the executioner's fees and the cost of any other punishments unless he inflicted them himself. Under the terms of his contract Joseph had to indemnify the sheriff against anything that went wrong, taking the blame and consequences himself, and if any writs, actions, law suits etc. were delivered Joseph would have to pay the fine along with full responsibility for any business relating to the running of the goal and the safe keeping of the prisoners. The prison salary was poor but there were many compensations. Scadding's reward for all this was that he, may take all such lawful fees, profits, and advantages during the time of his Shrievalty as to the place and Office of Goaler or Keeper of the Goal Ward or prison. Another bonus was that he was responsible for the quality and quantity of food and drink. Those who could afford it received the best but for others it was shared beds, overcrowding and inedible food. Aside from the fees the jailer was licensed to sell beer and wine to the prisoners and it has been estimated that this was in addition to around £54 obtainable from the prisoners by other means. A prisoner's comfort depended on how much money he gave the jailer for food, clothing and probably protection from the other prisoners where necessary, indeed, if a prisoner paid enough he could stay in the jail keeper's apartment in relative luxury compared to the hell holes below.

Joseph died in 1771 at the age of 57 and was succeeded by his son Edward who despite training as a goldsmith must have seen the advantages of the position. In 1774 the annual salary was increased to £25 and fees for the release of debtors were increased to 14/4d, 6/8d for felons with £3/12/0d for those under sentence of transportation. One way in which to increase profits was to remove the felon's allowance of 2d per day and change it to 2d worth of bread. Debtors received no allowance but had to rely on charity. One unpleasant little custom was that of 'gaol garnish' whereby prisoners demanded money from a newcomer; 'pay or strip' was the command and those unable to pay 3/6d were forced to hand over their clothes to that amount.

The Execution of Mary Norwood 1765

DURING HIS TENURE, in the early summer of 1765, Mary Norwood, of Axbridge, was found guilty of poisoning her husband and sentenced to be executed at Ilchester. She was brought from the prison at about three o'clock in the afternoon – barefoot, her legs, feet and arms covered in tar and dressed in a tarred cloth made like a shift with a tarred bonnet on her head. The summer heat melted the tar and it ran down her face. After being dragged on a hurdle to the place of execution Mary spent some time in prayer and singing a hymn before the executioner fixed a rope around her neck. She adjusted it to the right position herself and then the barrel on which she was standing was rolled away. The executioner seems to have been compassionate as he was reported to have pulled the noose tight several times to ensure she was dead before the fire was lit. Executions were public entertainment that drew large crowds but it was reported that great numbers felt unable to look as Mary's body burnt at the stake.

Prison reformer John Howard describes Ilchester after his visit of 1779,

The jail is near the river and has no offensive sewers. Departments roomy but the courts too little. They may be enlarged eastward. Women felons have no day room, a room which is fit and seems to have been designed for that use is taken by the jailer for a stable. Assizes never heard here. Prisoners are removed for trial to the Bridewell at Taunton or to Bridgwater where the prison is only one room or to Wells where there is no prison at all and yet at Midsummer Assize the prisoners were kept in that City eight days.

In the same year Ilchester had a total of 48 inmates compared to 12 in Bath, 19 in Shepton Mallet and 10 in Taunton. A new block was constructed in 1789 with 26 cells 8'8" x 7'8" with four staples and a ring fixed to the floor to which the prisoners were chained. It is reported that in 1784 30 prisoners died of the fever. Perhaps the jail's most famous prisoner of the period was Jane Leigh Perrot an aunt of Jane Austen. She was at a haberdashers in Bath in August of 1799 where she purchased some black lace whereupon, either by accident or design she also left the shop with a card of white lace for which she had not paid. What today would be the most trivial of offences was at the time of the utmost seriousness. The white lace was valued at 20/- when theft of an article over the value of 5/- from a shop was a hanging offence or a slow boat to Australia. Being a woman of great wealth, she was able to pass the seven months on remand in relative comfort by paying for a private apartment in the jailer's house accompanied by her husband. Sir Abraham Elton said that there was a report that Mrs Leigh Perrot was frequently out of prison whilst under sentence there, which was denied. The Leigh Perrots had properties in Berkshire and Bath and were more used to hosting large dinner parties than eating with a gaoler and his family.

The Assize Courts were held twice a year; the Lent Assize at Taunton, and the Summer Assize alternately at Bridgwater and Wells; the Leigh Perrot trial was held in Taunton. The defence managed to discredit the shop assistant who had wrapped up articles in error previously and Mrs Perrot was cleared in front of a packed court. Mrs Leigh Perrot must have appreciated the care she received from prison governor Edward Scadding because, instead of sending the two guineas she owed on her prison account, she sent a cheque for £25.

Attempted Escape by Ward, Maggs and Others 1786

CONVICTS OFTEN HAD very little to do and spent their time either gambling or devising methods of escape. On one occasion in early

October 1786, whilst Edward was at the Taunton Sessions, a number of them planned to get out together. A horse-stealer called Ward provided knives 'to get off their irons' so that they were free to sneak out whilst a party of them were to be posted in the passage. The idea was that the stoutest prisoners would be at the front, to fight their way through any opposition leaving the weakest to follow at the back. The attempt was postponed because one prisoner warned them that a Mr Pitman, who was generally in the gaol when Edward was away, and a debtor named Griffin were in a room overlooking the back yard where they would have to pass. Pitman and Griffin had access to firearms and would probably have been able to kill half of them from the window as they tried to get away. Ward wanted to carry on because, he said, 'if half escaped it would do, for the other half would die an honourable death.' The plan was discovered, however, because two of the weaker prisoners, Maggs and Sherlock, decided to confess rather than die an 'honourable' death and so the plot was foiled.

Ilchester by WW Wheatley 1840s

In 1800 there were various complaints about Edward's behaviour and conduct at the gaol. A Mr Gould asserted that a man committed under the game laws was in fact an employee on a farm owned by Edward and was freed ten days before his sentence elapsed. Edward admitted that this had indeed happened but that the man had been freed by the jail's turnkey without his knowledge. The average number of prisoners in the jail at any one time for the years 1795-1801 was 78, a report of 1806 lists 18 people imprisoned for debt. Edward Scadding retired in 1808 and died in 1811.

The 19th Century, Dr Lettsom

IN 1807 Dr John Lettsom a Quaker and founder of The Medical Society of London visited various prisons, including Ilchester, and wrote a report describing the jail and its buildings the year before Bridle took over.

The jail buildings and yards covered about one and a quarter acre and the jailer's salary had risen to £125pa. The jail itself was surrounded by a sixteen foot wall with the turnkey's lodge facing the river to the left of the entrance. To the right were the baths and over the gateway lay the jailer's house with a small garden and an area where the gaoler could grow vegetables. There were five courtyards one for petty offenders until they had paid their fines. The debtor's apartments were reached from this yard and the water pump which supplied the whole prison was in a yard adjoining supplying plenty of clean water There were arcades for the prisoners in wet weather and over these, two stories reached by a stone staircase. Each story contained five cells 8' x 7' and 8'6" high fitted with perforated iron bedsteads, straw, (for which the inmates were charged) a blanket and cover. Each cell had a double door, the outer iron grated with the inner made of wood which opened into a passage four feet wide. The cells each had a semi-circular window half glazed and half with wooden slats looking onto the keeper's garden with apertures in the wall for light and ventilation. Adjoining the arcades was the keeper's cellar with two storeys over it each containing six cells. The gaol was whitewashed at least yearly.

The woman's court was 18 yards x 6 yards separated from the male felons by a single iron palisade to which they could see and converse with each other. On the upper story were five cells with six over the chapel used by the most orderly of criminals having boarded floors. The chapel was segregated between male and female convicts and attendance was not compulsory for debtors. The woman felon's court was rather larger than that of the men and separated from it by a low wall with a single palisade. There was a pump in it but this was seldom used because the water was not good. On the ground floor were 14 cells 10' x 7' 6"and 8'x 6" with a day room on the other storey the 14 more cells and a lodge for a woman turnkey who attended to the female prisoners and was paid a weekly salary by the county.

Prisoners washed and shaved in the cold or warm baths near the main gate and had clean shirts each week. The county supplied clothing which was yellow with brown stripes but as it was not compulsory few of the men wore it, preferring instead to wear their own clothes as far as possible. If needed they could have a blanket, coverlet or rug but presumably they paid more for these luxuries. There were also some larger day rooms for the prisoners to use, a cellar and an infirmary As Ilchester didn't have a manufacturing industry to employ the inmates they occupied themselves with handicrafts or playing games – fives, skittles or tennis.

Although largely outside of the scope of this book it is worth making a few notes on the jail following Bridle's dismissal and Hunt's release. In 1822 it was recommended that £250 should be spent on improvements and that a permanent Sheriff's jail should be built at Shepton adjoining the present house of correction. A good site was made available for £10,000 by a Mr Morgan. Writing in the following year the coroner Peter Layng commented that having visited Ilchester on many occasions during the occupations of Scadding and Bridle he had always found the rooms in the jail to be perfectly clean but the buildings too confined and he recommended building a new jail on two acres of ground at Salisbury for about £30,000.

From Michaelmas 1832 to Michaelmas 1834 397 prisoners were admitted. At this time the prison could properly hold 67 persons in separate sleeping cells and 162 where more than one occupied a cell. During the same period punishments consisted of six whipped, five in irons and 68 in solitary confinement. There were nine solitary cells. The total expenditure for the year 1837 was £2,347 out of which the Exchequer paid £55 for transports leaving at a cost to the county of £2,292, the cost of each prisoner per week came to a little over 8/- and the greatest number of prisoners at any one time during the year was 143.

In 1842 there was a particularly bad outbreak of typhus at the prison which had become too antiquated to continue in use and everything was moved to Wilton jail in Taunton. The last prisoners left Ilchester at the beginning of 1843 and the site was advertised for sale finally going to the Tuson family in 1848. They owned the mill and their house adjoined the north outer wall of the old jail. When it was demolished much of the stone was reused locally and the house of correction at Wilton became the county gaol from February 1843, when debtors were admitted. Shepton Mallet jail continued as a house of correction, serving the eastern part of the county including some debtors. In 1884, the civil part of Taunton prison was closed, most of the premises continuing to serve as a military prison leased to the War Department. Shepton Mallet prison then became the county gaol. Between 1810 and 1845 1,400 people were executed at Ilchester.

1808 William Bridle Takes Charge

ON 19 JULY 1808 at the age of 28 William Bridle took up his position as governor of Ilchester jail at the vastly increased salary of £500pa and set to work reforming the place which he found in complete disarray. The following details are taken from his book, *A Narrative of the Rise and Progress of the Improvements Effected in his Majesty's Jail at Ilchester between July 1808 and November 1821*. This was published in 1822 some months after his dismissal in July 1821.

The total number of prisoners was 62 of all classes. There were just five wards, one for male prisoners under sentences less than transportation, one for those awaiting trial from highway robbery to the simple country boy jailed for stealing a few apples, one for all classes of female prisoner and one for infirmary purposes. The remainder of the site was occupied as a garden, piggery, stables and cow house for the use of the governor. There was no system of labour nothing to prevent the prisoners from spending their time as idly and dissolutely as they liked, visitors were permitted into the wards taking with them anything they pleased resulting in drunkenness and gambling. There was no laundry or supplies of clean linen, the bedding and linen was washed by one woman in the kitchen. There were no firearms in case of mutiny and the prisoners could easily have broken out of the jail with the minimum of effort.

Having secured the agreement of the magistrates Bridle set to work employing carpenters, masons and tradesman. He began to reclassify the prisoners dividing the debtors into those who could support themselves, 'gentlemen debtors', in the upper ward, and those in receipt of county allowances to the lower award. The exterior walls were raised, wells sunk, yards pitched and paved . All these endeavours were greatly helped by Sir John Acland who took a deep interest in the work. Constables and cooks were appointed to the respective wards selected from amongst the most orderly and best disposed inmates. Instead of the 'squalid misery, idle inanity, frenzied drunkenness, licentiousness and vulgarity,' that had prevailed, discipline and order ruled within six months. A new ward for boys was commenced to separate them from the men, and new drains were dug using prison labour resulting in a great saving to the county. By 1810 a laundry and a wash house had been built and work found for all the female prisoners in the jail some at sewing and knitting which produced articles that supplied the houses of correction in Shepton and Wilton. This was followed by the manufacture of gloves, mittens, worsted caps and eventually shoemaking. Bridle saw the opportunity for a business venture putting his own capital of £400 into it for two years until 1817 with many prisoners learning a trade for the first time and eventually weaving looms were

Sir John Palmer Acland in 1829

introduced. 'All our clothes and linen are worked in pattern stripes to prevent their being cut up by prisoners and taken out of the prison with a view to being converted to private use'.

Until 1811 executions had been held a half mile from the town on a common by Yeovil Road. Those to be executed were taken in open wagons traveling at about three miles per hour exposed to the jeers and taunts of large crowds. Execution days were known as 'hang fair days' many people would assemble from the surrounding parishes and after the execution many enjoyed drinking and dancing at the local pubs. Bridle put a stop to this by organising the executions within the prison having built a new 'drop' above the front lodge so that spectators had to watch from the bridge and river bank opposite which was occupied by a coal merchant who charged 1/- for admission to his land.

Sir Francis & The Loaf 1812

IN DECEMBER 1812 the jail was mentioned in the press when three people, 'decent hard-working tradesmen' were arrested during elections in Bath under the riot act. They had apparently demanded entry to the Guildhall which was refused and some windows were broken. They were denied bail, and dispatched to Ilchester where they were alleged to have been kept in solitary cells and heavily ironed. All offers of food, clothing and other articles from relatives were refused and despite excessively cold weather they were allowed no stove to warm themselves and had nothing to lie on but straw. Such were the conditions described by Sir Francis Burdett, a radical MP who brought a petition before the House protesting about the severity of their treatment. Burdett produced a small loaf from his pocket which he said had been sent to him as an example of the food that was provided at the prison, this he threw onto on the floor in dramatic protest proclaiming that it was disgraceful for any civilised country and asked that the House interfere in their favour. However, it was pointed out that once the riot act had been read bail was not available and that they will have to wait for the judgement of the jury at the next Assizes. The following exchange took place in the House on 9 March.

> Mr Dickinson MP for Somerset, recalled to the recollection of the hon. baronet, a petition which he had on occasion presented to the House, from some persons confined in Ilchester gaol, for a riot at Bath and who, in their petition, complained of ill-treatment. He also recalled the circumstance of his having produced a loaf in the House, which had been sent from the prisoners confined in the jail. He wished to know whether the hon. baronet meant to proceed any further with those complaints.
>
> Sir F Burdett replied, that his time had been so much engaged by an election committee, that he had not been able to proceed further in the business of these petitions; and that he had no intention of pressing the matter any further upon the consideration of the House.
>
> Mr Dickinson wished to know whether the hon. baronet had inquired into the truth of the allegations in the petitions which he had laid before the House?
>
> Sir F Burdett replied, that the causes of the complaints preferred in the petitions had been removed.

The petition was ordered to lie on the table making it extremely unlikely that anything further would be done. However, the following May an article in the *Taunton Courier* stated that,

> The loaf which Sir Francis, with indignation, threw on the floor of the House of Commons is now well known not to have been any one of those assigned by the rules of the jail. The Hon Baronet, agreed that it had been sent to him from

Bath not from Ilchester and thus in this particular, there was a miserable hiatus in his case, which, considered with the other unfound incidents of his dolorous story renders his interferences on the occasion almost ludicrous. The truth is that the petitioner palmed onto him for presentation to the House a complete tissue of inventive malignancy, base insinuation and groundless assertion which ought never have to polluted his hands... the Hon Bart. ought to have declared his conviction of the treachery and deceit practiced on him by the promoters of the petition or to have pressed it on the attention of the house... he has not, however, thought fit to do so...

What became of the rioters named as Hickwood, Taylor and Lovell is not known. In January of the following year a James Turle keeper of the prison at Wilton was dismissed from his office for misconduct and replaced by the head turnkey at Ilchester after investigations by John Acland Esq. There are no further details. Bridle's renovations were certainly being noticed as the following brief report in the *Bath Journal* for June 1816 shows,

The excellent regulations adopted in the jail at Ilchester have so far attracted the notice of the magistrates in Wiltshire, that the jailer of Devizes has very recently visited with a view to the introduction of corresponding arrangement in his prison. After a minute inspection for three days, he returned home with the fullest conviction of the admirable and good system he had witnessed.

On 22 October 1814 Bridle's brother-in-law Matthew Hobbs joined the Lodge of Brotherly Love 624 at Martock presumably introduced by Bridle himself. Hobbs was aged 34 and described as a Yeoman of Lymington. He and his wife were later to join Bridle's staff at Ilchester before falling out in spectacular fashion.

Bridle Expands the Jail

ADVERTISEMENTS WERE PLACED in the local papers inviting tenders for the supply of building materials and in November 1813 appeals were made for the following items, 'blue quarry stone, building bricks, freestone, lime, pavement stone, oak for the roof, deal for the floor, partitions, stairs, slate, cast iron railings for gallery, ditto for grating for windows, ironmongery for lengthening one of the buildings 13 feet and raising the same 8 feet. Further particulars from Mr Robert Anstice the county surveyor Bridgwater.' During 1816 a manufacturer in Frome was supplying cast iron the bedsteads to Ilchester and Wilton (carriage free) at £1/16/-per item. The building work continued throughout that year, with the jail requiring 12 wrought iron gates of various dimensions along with iron gratings for four windows. Other regular advertisements invited bakers to tender for the supply of wheaten loaves of three pounds each to be offered at prices per hundred weight, 700-900 loaves to be delivered three times per week for this period. During 1817 the price of bread supplied to the jail increased greatly, for the last quarter of 1816 it was 25/- per hundredweight and by Easter 1817 it had risen to 44/-. All goods and services seem to have been regularly tendered for with written bids. As the prison population increased more buildings were added, a matron's lodge, a misdemeanour ward and a kitchen built entirely by prison labour an activity which Bridle contends astonished many visitors from other prisons. His efforts were greatly admired by a select committee of the Commons in 1819 who commended his methods and the savings that prison labour meant for the county.

Bridle's balance sheet of his improvements reads in summary,

Increased five wards to 13 now containing 266 prisoners
Every prisoner willing to work is now able to do so.
Area formally occupied by the keeper now has new buildings.
The jail is now strong and secure.
Religious books are now available.
A caravan on springs constructed to transport the prisoners to and from court.
All building work carried out by prison labour.

At the beginning of 1815 a 'Steady Man' was required, 'capable of superintending the hemp and other manufactures and labour of the above jail. He must write a good hand be conversant in accounts and well recommended.' Bridle was rightly proud of his building work, and if he read a report in February 1819 that seven prisoners had escaped from the newly built part of Wilton jail by breaking through three walls constructed at great cost to the county he would probably have been even more pleased. When the magistrates inspected they asked the opinion of a very superior stonemason who remarked that, 'there was nothing resembling mortar in the walls, it was literally mud, not a particle of sand amongst it that he could discover, with a common knife a man could affect his escape through the garden wall and it was by far the worst work he had ever beheld'.

Daniel Lake, Taskmaster 1815

HAVING A NUMBER of men in his employ it is quite reasonable to assume that not all will be happy with their lot. This curious tale begins with

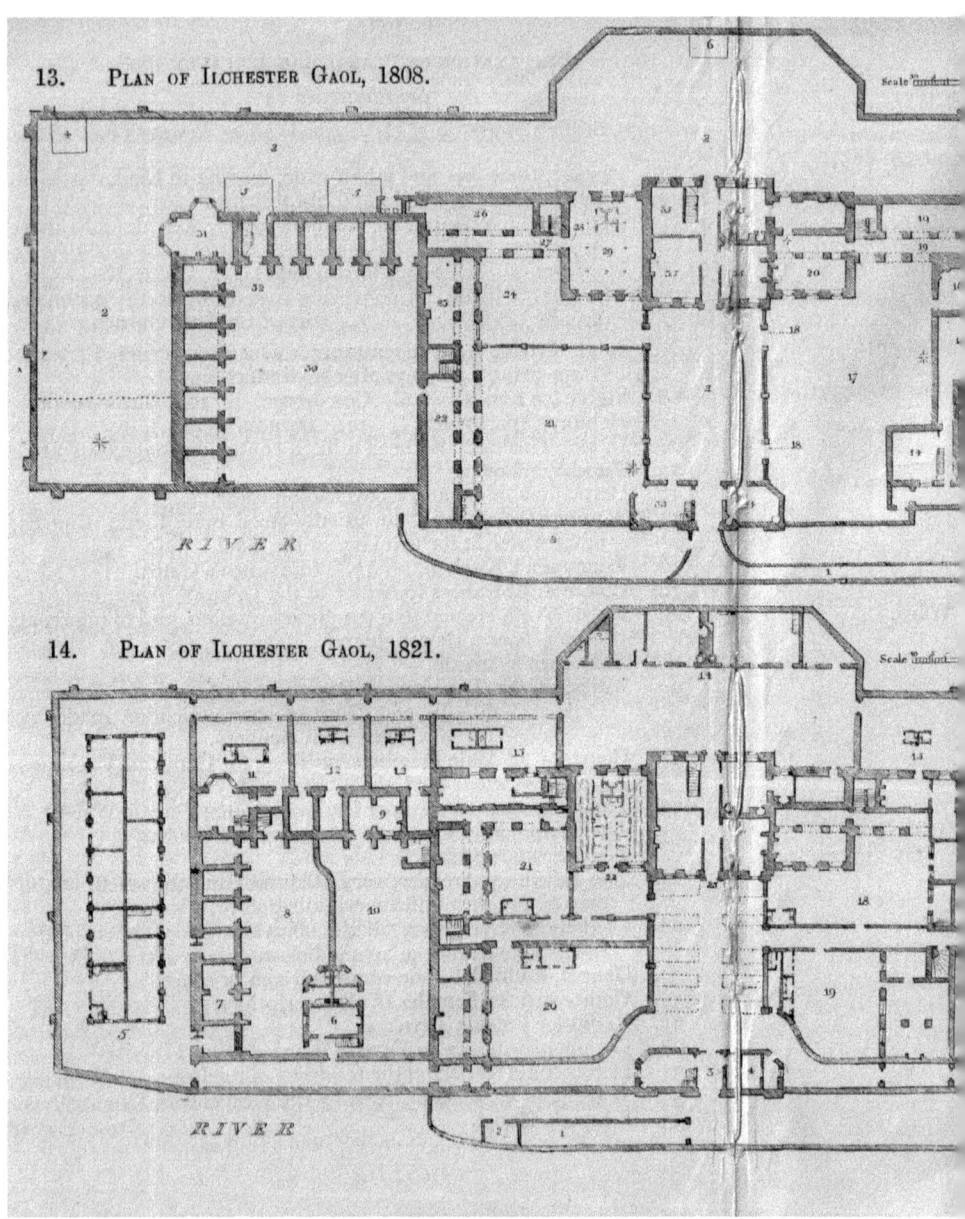

Plans of the Jail with key to numbers 1808-1821

the sacking of Daniel Lake the 'taskmaster' whose job it was to supervise the prisoners maintaining order and making sure that everything ran smoothly. The exact reasons for his dismissal are uncertain but having complained to the visiting magistrates about Bridle's behaviour he was requested to appear before the magistrates at the jail on 22 February and required to put his case in writing

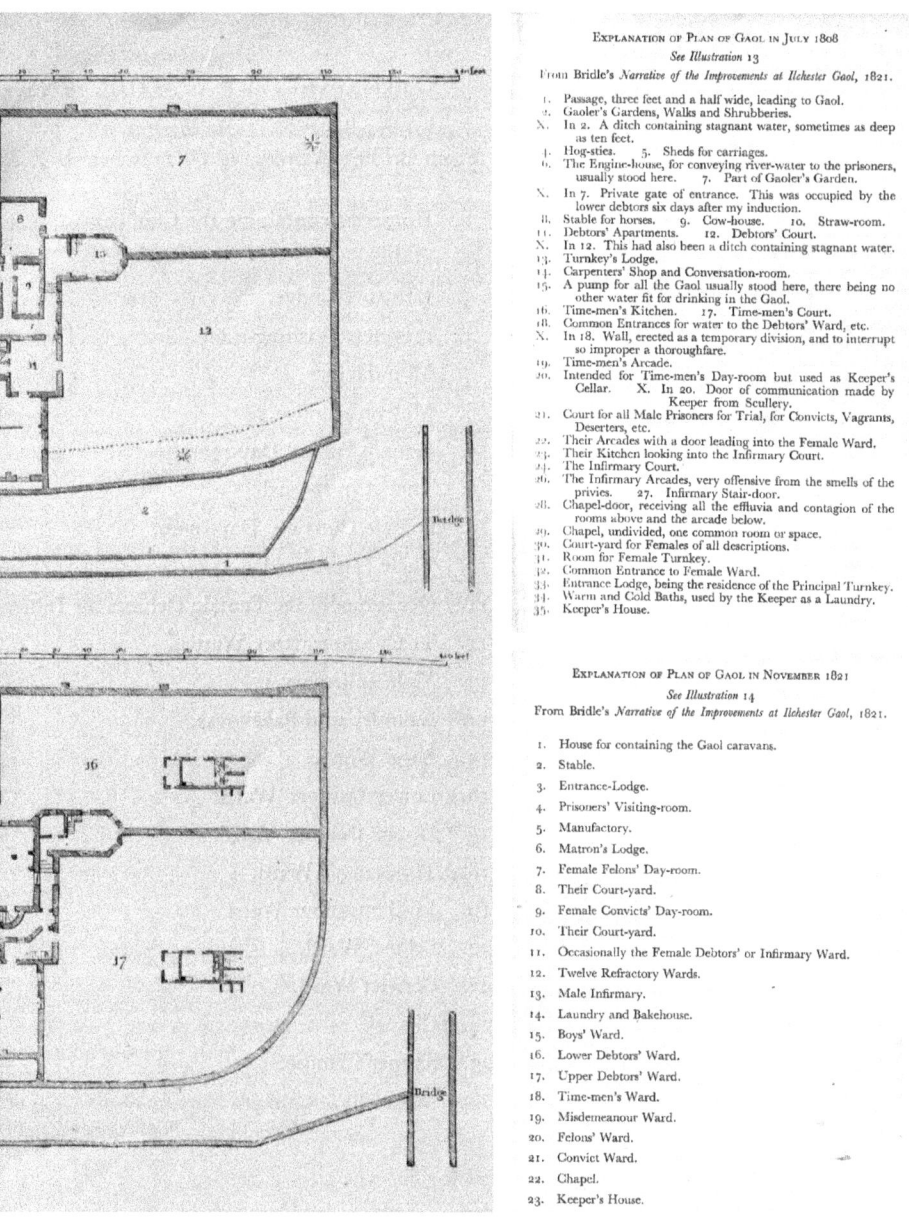

EXPLANATION OF PLAN OF GAOL IN JULY 1808
See Illustration 13
From Bridle's *Narrative of the Improvements at Ilchester Gaol, 1821.*

1. Passage, three feet and a half wide, leading to Gaol.
2. Gaoler's Gardens, Walks and Shrubberies.
X. In 2. A ditch containing stagnant water, sometimes as deep as ten feet.
4. Hog-sties.   5. Sheds for carriages.
6. The Engine-house, for conveying river-water to the prisoners, usually stood here.   7. Part of Gaoler's Garden.
X. In 7. Private gate of entrance. This was occupied by the lower debtors six days after my induction.
8. Stable for horses.   9. Cow-house.   10. Straw-room.
11. Debtors' Apartments.   12. Debtors' Court.
X. In 12. This had also been a ditch containing stagnant water.
13. Turnkey's Lodge.
14. Carpenters' Shop and Conversation-room.
15. A pump for all the Gaol usually stood here, there being no other water fit for drinking in the Gaol.
16. Time-men's Kitchen.   17. Time-men's Court.
18. Common Entrances for water to the Debtors' Ward, etc.
X. In 18. Wall, erected as a temporary division, and to interrupt so improper a thoroughfare.
19. Time-men's Arcade.
20. Intended for Time-men's Day-room but used as Keeper's Cellar.   X. In 20. Door of communication made by Keeper from Scullery.
21. Court for all Male Prisoners for Trial, for Convicts, Vagrants, Deserters, etc.
22. Their Arcades with a door leading into the Female Ward.
23. Their Kitchen looking into the Infirmary Court.
24. The Infirmary Court.
26. The Infirmary Arcades, very offensive from the smells of the privies.   27. Infirmary Stair-door.
28. Chapel-door, receiving all the effluvia and contagion of the rooms above and the arcade below.
29. Chapel, undivided, one common room or space.
30. Court-yard for Females of all descriptions.
31. Room for Female Turnkey.
32. Common Entrance to Female Ward.
33. Entrance Lodge, being the residence of the Principal Turnkey.
34. Warm and Cold Baths, used by the Keeper as a Laundry.
35. Keeper's House.

EXPLANATION OF PLAN OF GAOL IN NOVEMBER 1821
See Illustration 14
From Bridle's *Narrative of the Improvements at Ilchester Gaol, 1821.*

1. House for containing the Gaol caravans.
2. Stable.
3. Entrance-Lodge.
4. Prisoners' Visiting-room.
5. Manufactory.
6. Matron's Lodge.
7. Female Felons' Day-room.
8. Their Court-yard.
9. Female Convicts' Day-room.
10. Their Court-yard.
11. Occasionally the Female Debtors' or Infirmary Ward.
12. Twelve Refractory Wards.
13. Male Infirmary.
14. Laundry and Bakehouse.
15. Boys' Ward.
16. Lower Debtors' Ward.
17. Upper Debtors' Ward.
18. Time-men's Ward.
19. Misdemeanour Ward.
20. Felons' Ward.
21. Convict Ward.
22. Chapel.
23. Keeper's House.

beforehand. His first statement, sent to Rev. Whalley one of the magistrates and presumably composed soon after the request is quite remarkable,

> I Daniel Lake late of Ilchester jail, do most solemnly declare that in the absence of Mr Bridle the keeper, the jail is more like a common Bawd house than a Prison. I mean in the conduct of Mrs Bridle and Miss Culliford who admits

men in their bedroom while they are in bed (about May 1813). Mrs Lake went to Exeter … in the meantime Mr Bridle went from home one night. I was up at the house until late. Mrs B went up to bed and I was invited up by Miss Culliford but I did not go. Next morning I was in the front yard and Elizabeth Hillier, a transport, [ie sentenced to transportation] was at Mrs Bridle's bedroom window she beckoned me to come up, I went up, Mrs B and Miss C was in bed together and invited me to come into bed with them. They said take off your clothes and come in. I did not go into bed but lay down on the bedclothes. Another evening I had been drinking some grog, Mrs B went to bed and rang her bell shortly afterwards which was for Miss C and me (having been invited) to come up. I went up, undressed myself and got into bed between them both. And all three got a sleep and did not awake until daylight and Mrs Lake had been about the jail to look for me. Another time, Mrs L went to bed. Mrs B and Miss C went to bed and afterwards I went up. I was not invited up at that time that I can recollect, however I was in bed with them and Mrs L thought I stayed up late.

Another morning a young man named George Slade, an acquaintance, jumped into bed and Mrs B told me herself that she went outside the curtains to put her clothes on while he had connections with Miss C several times. Several times I have been in my own lodge and have been sent for as if Mr Bridle wanted me, and only Mrs B and Miss C and sometimes only Mrs B was there. They began their jokes with me and have even unbuttoned my breeches. I am sorry to convict myself. I have been to blame I must confess and have been guilty of a great crime. It is almost impossible for any young man who fills that situation to do otherwise, Mrs B is of that disposition that she would get Mr B to find some fault to discharge him if he did not comply with her wishes and it is my firm belief that Mrs B has been the means of my being discharged as I have behaved very cool to them for several months past. At the time the connection was carried on in that disgraceful way this is being used to do her endeavours to set myself and wife at variance. She would give Mrs Lake strong liquors on purpose to make her abuse me. At one time in the office I was standing before the fire, them one each side. Elizabeth Hillier came to make up the fire, Mrs B took hold of her hand and endeavoured to rub it down over my thigh. A number of such lewd practices have I been witness to in such a manner as I never saw in my life before and had not Mrs B invited me should never have thought of taking the liberty.

There is not a woman discharged from the jail but what is worse and more corrupted than when admitted. Mrs B takes a pleasure in talking her obscene discourse. Mrs Adlam was visited by Mrs B and Miss C who began such a discourse as Mrs A did not think proper to join. Mrs B was offended and said that she was so modest that she could not join in a bit of fun but could have a child before marriage.

More than once Mrs B I said if our connection was found out she would take her oath that nothing of the kind had occurred. She was very aware that Mrs Lake was acquainted with the transactions and wanted me to send her out of the town. The day after we left the prison I was very ill and Mrs B offered to let me have some money as I said I went out so suddenly it was a great injury to me and I must send to Exeter for some cash and Mrs Bridle lent me some money.

Sir,

When I took up this paper it was not my intention to have troubled you on the subject. I merely meant it to live with my wife who is perfectly acquainted with the circumstances and is ready to be examined on both before you or any other magistrate. My wife will inform you, Sir that it is a life that I was never given to before. Mrs Bridle was jealous for fear I should tell of these transactions. Sir, I feel I am duty-bound to let the magistrates know what kind of people they have to deal with. This day I am bound for London but I am ready to prove every word by witness on oath before any person at any time at any place. I wrote a letter to Mr Acland in defence of the several charges. I never received any answers nor heard nothing of it,

I am yours etc

Daniel Lake

At the same time, or very soon after, Lake writes in great haste to magistrate Moody informing him that at his lodge there is 62cwt of coal which he has not paid for. This is of course an oversight and not an attempt at fraud but he was rushed out so quickly that he did not have time to account for it which he values at £3/14/11d and which he will pay to the county.

What follows is a 14 page closely written 'List of charges preferred by Daniel Lake against William Bridle and Mrs Bridle his wife'. It contained 25 charges starting with drunken behaviour amongst the staff and wine being stolen while the master was away leading to breaches of discipline being ignored. Prisoners complaints were not entered in the occurrence book as they should have been; Mrs Bridle was heard to speak of magistrate Moody in a very disrespectful manner; Mrs Bridle instructed Lake to prepare to take Mrs Adlam to Wells as she was to be executed on the following Monday. This was done because Mrs Bridle was jealous of her, she also told the debtors that this was about to happen causing much distress after which she had a great laugh at the fun she had had with it. Mrs Bridle gave a pregnant woman a pint and a half of brandy and water the child afterwards died of, 'lack of proper care'.

In 1813, claims Lake, Mrs Bridle and Miss Culliford were intimate with a man since transported. Whilst in the hulk the man told someone who knew Mrs Bridle and he in turn wrote to Miss Culliford to ask if it was true. When Mr Bridle took some prisoners to the hulks Mrs Bridle was afraid that he might meet the object of her attentions. Daniel Lake's bedtime fun with Mrs Bridle and Miss Culliford was outlined briefly.

So far it is all been little but gossip and all occurring during Mr Bridle's absence. It is not until towards the end of the statement that he is accused of misbehaviour himself; not accounting for a tenth part of the time that he is absent from the jail; using prison staff to look after his cows and fields: not paying the prisoners their wages regularly which were sometimes three or four weeks in arrears; many things charged against the county were not used in the prison, including saucepans and soap; magistrate Colston had apparently brought some charges against Bridle who then bribed a prisoner with £3 and an overcoat to contradict the evidence, after a successful outcome Bridle took the coat away again; Mr Bridle considered Lake to be a spy as the prison bills all passed through his hands and plotted to get rid of him.

Everything was in place for a hearing on 22 February but Lake didn't show up and it was said that he had gone to London. Enquiries there turned up his brother, Samuel who explained that his brother had been waiting to hear about the case but nothing had arrived and so he had, 'left town'. He had not left any forwarding address as he did not want to risk his wife finding out where he had gone and that he could no longer live with her due to her improper conduct, and there the matter could have ended but for the following account, published in the *Taunton Courier* and other county newspapers,

> A short time since, one Lake, a man employed as task master at Ilchester Gaol, was dismissed from his appointment, in consequence of improper conduct. The charges against him were confirmed by Mr Bridle, the keeper of the Gaol, and this circumstance appears to have excited in Lake a determination to effect the ruin of Mr Bridle and his family. For this purpose, Lake addressed letters to several Magistrates of the county, containing a number of charges against Mr Bridle for misconduct in the execution of his office, and even Mrs Bridle was included in the calumnious imputations.
>
> 'Upon receiving these charges, Mr Acland (the Chairman), with his characteristic promptitude, immediately proceeded to institute an inquiry into the facts. For this purpose, a notice was left at the presumed residence of Lake,

in London (his brother's house), requiring him to attend on the day appointed, to give evidence. Instead, however, of making his appearance, he sent down a letter, containing a frivolous excuse for his non-attendance, and referring to

SOMERSET, TO WIT. AT the General Quarter Session of the Peace of Our Lord the King, held at the City of Wells, in and for the County of SOMERSET, on Friday the Seventh Day of April in the Fifty-fifth Year of the Reign of our Sovereign Lord GEORGE the Third, by the Grace of God of the United Kingdom of Great Britain and Ireland, King, Defender of the Faith, and in the Year of our Lord 1815, before JOHN ACLAND, RICHARD THOMAS COMBE, Esquires, and others their Companions, Justices of our said Lord the King, assigned to keep the Peace of our said Lord the King, in and for the County of SOMERSET aforesaid, and also to hear and determine divers Felonies, Trespasses, and other Misdemeanours committed in the same County.

ILCHESTER GAOL.

ORDERED,

THAT in Case the *Gaoler*, or any of the *Officers*, or *Prisoners*, shall hereafter have reason to complain against each other, they are hereby respectively required to state the Grounds of such Complaint to the *Visiting Magistrates*, the first Time they attend the Gaol, after they may feel themselves aggrieved, or to the *Magistrates*, who may be assembled at the *Gaol Session*, usually held *the Thursday preceding every General Quarter Session of the Peace*, to the End that such *Magistrates* may report the same to the *then next General Quarter Session* of the *Peace*; but no Complaint is to be received after the said *Gaol Session* for any Act done before that Period. And, it is also Ordered, that Notice hereof be affixed in the most conspicuous Parts of the Prison, that no Person may plead Ignorance of the same.

By the Court,

COLES, D.

Clerk of the Peace for the County of Somerset.

MARRIOTT, Printer, Taunton Courier and General Printing-Office, TAUNTON.

Prison Complaints 1815

several persons in the Gaol, whom he averred could justify his complaint.

Although the specific charges adduced against Mr Bridle were thus abandoned, the Magistrates, having assembled for the purpose of effecting a plenary inquiry into them, very properly resolved on examining the persons referred to in Lake's letter. A most minute examination of the different prisoners accordingly took place, but in no one instance did it appear that the accusations were borne out by the facts, on the contrary, it was satisfactorily shewn that the charges were wholly invented and the Magistrates, after a patient investigation, which lasted from eleven in the morning until five in the evening, unanimously declared their opinion, that the charges were malevolent and utterly destitute of foundation. Mr Bridle has in consequence instituted a prosecution against Lake for his atrocious conduct, but we hear that the latter has, or is about to quit the country, probably to avoid the legal consequences of the proceedings against him.

The care, the anxiety, and unwearied attention displayed by Mr Acland and his brother Magistrates in the administration of their duties, are as conspicuous as they are important, and in this instance reflect on them the greatest honour. Had the charges against Mr Bridle proved correct, their duty would have become imperatively obvious, but the reverse having appeared, the public mind is prevented nourishing a groundless calumny, and the integrity of a useful, though humble, public officer, is unequivocally certified by the result of their laudable investigation.

The Typhus Outbreak of 1817-18

JAIL FEVER HAD existed in the Ilchester neighbourhood for about six months and first came to the prison in January 1817 when there were 240 inmates. Everything was fumigated constantly and all unaffected prisoners were daily bathed in tepid water with a quantity of bay salt. The cells were fumigated with a pan of newly slaked lime followed by nitrous acid gas. Vinegar was profusely burnt in court 'and every necessary precaution to obviate the effects of this alarming circumstance have been judiciously adopted', said one report. The judges at Exeter were informed and a house of recovery was procured, a cottage at Lymington about a mile from the jail and on 2 April 17 infected prisoners were moved, later increasing to 23. The looms were removed and the manufactory fitted up as a hospital. When taking prisoners to the hulks Bridle had to start at two in the morning as he could not find a nights lodging anywhere. As the number of jail inmates increased Acland managed to get an extra vessel fitted out at Portsmouth to take those sentenced to transportation. The prisoners could not be housed in the jail at Taunton and so 85 were taken by water to an unfinished house in the fields at Bathpool a few miles from town, Bridle stayed there with them as they took their turn in court. He was of course used to outbreaks of fever from his time in the hulks. During the epidemic there were 60 cases and only two deaths due to what was described as the admirable treatment of doctors Woodford and Bryer.

Thomas Fowell Buxton was a prominent antislavery campaigner and brother-in-law to prison reformer Elizabeth Fry. He made a tour of various prisons around the country and abroad and in 1818 produced a book *An Enquiry, whether Crime and Misery are Produced or Prevented by our Present System of Prison Discipline*. He visited Ilchester in April 1818 and was very impressed by the reforms that Bridle had instigated in the previous ten years including much of the building and construction work being carried out by the prisoners themselves along with weaving, spinning and shoemaking. 'The laundry equals any of that institution in the kingdom and all the female prisoners are employed in washing the weekly changes of linen and bedding making all the dresses worn by themselves'. 'If a prisoner cannot read he learns to do so, if he knows no trade he is taught one, there is no filth, no disorder, no tumult.' Buxton did not meet Bridle but quotes the taskmaster as having said, 'I look upon it that a man's mind must be occupied with something if it is not taken up with a good thing it'll be a bad one'.

The following notice appeared in the *Bury Post* during April 1819,

> As proof of the admirable management and useful employment of prisoners in Ilchester jail the assize courts at Taunton afforded the pleasing exhibition of two cloth covers for the counsel and attorney's tables in each court, entirely manufactured by the prisoners in this jail through the different processes of picking, sorting, combing, carding, spinning, weaving, dying to the greatest perfection. The cloths are dark blue, and the centre of each bears the following inscription, 'Manufactured by the Prisoners in Ilchester Jail 1819'.

The General Election of June 1818

PARLIAMENT WAS DISSOLVED on 10 June 1818 and the new government was to be assembled on 4 August for a maximum term of seven years. Throughout the conflict between Bridle, Hunt and the magistrates there are numerous hints and obscure references to Bridle's character and reputation being of an exemplary nature until he got caught up in politics during the election of this year. The electorate consisted of inhabitant householders and was often quite openly corrupt, candidates gaining power largely through a combination of threats and bribery. In 1811 the population of Ilchester was

745 those entitled to vote during 1818 was 90 and the going rate for buying a vote was £30. The big landowners wishing to stand for Parliament expected their tenants to vote for them with eviction being the usual reward for not doing so. A large part of the town had been bought by Sir William Manners for £53,000 in the expectation that future elections would be secured. Manners main claim to fame is that on acquiring the land he took drastic action and had most of the houses demolished, thereby making the former occupants homeless and without a vote to sell, reducing the size of the electorate and the number of bribes he would need to pay. A workhouse was built in place of the houses and it is likely that many of his 163 former tenants ended up there. Things were a lot simpler in those days. In the end John William Merest and Sir Isaac Coffin sponsored by the 4th Earl of Darlington were returned for Ilchester with 64 votes against 24 votes for Manners. The town, according to one newspaper, 'was thrown into an enthusiasm of joy…' by the revolt against Manners. Coffin, who had been advanced to full admiral in 1814 held Ilchester until 1826.

Bridle was a supporter of the yellow party or Whigs whereas Manners was a Tory and so he would have been very happy to see Merest and Coffin elected. James West a messenger at the jail, was dismissed by Bridle at this time, as he had once been a supporter of Manners, and replaced by one of the yellow party. John Treganzer, the principal turnkey and Bridle's right-hand man until he left in 1819 gave evidence that there was a band of music with singing and dancing at the jail during the campaign. After the election the sheriff donated £10 and there was a large amount of meat, hams, veal, beef and bread leftover from the campaign donated by Henry Tuson the election agent. Treganzer made three trips in the trucks and Bridle said it needed some beer to go with it which he supplied. The meat lasted for almost three days and the Parliament about a year and a half, as King George III's death on 29 January 1820 triggered the dissolution of that government and fresh elections.

Thomas Oldfield in his six volume *History of the House of Commons* 1822 says, respecting Ilchester, that, 'this borough has been so imprudent in the exercise of its corruption, as to have had the whole system several times exposed before committees of the House of Commons. At the general election in 1802, a great part of the voters were bribed at £30 a man to vote against the proprietor. This caused the trial and conviction of Alexander Davison, Esq. and his agents, at the assizes for the county of Somerset in 1804; for which they afterwards received sentence in the Court of King's Bench to suffer one year's imprisonment'.

As well as the election in Ilchester there was one for the county of Somerset itself and this is where the problem arose. Bridle's practical involvement is unclear if – he had any at all, but he was very close to Sir John Acland, chairman of the quarter sessions who had supported the campaign of Sir Thomas Lethbridge when he stood as a third candidate in opposition to the sitting MPs, William Davidson and William Gore Langton. This caused a huge conflict among the magistrates, sheriff and others with Bridle being blamed for supporting Acland and Lethbridge. Acland resigned as chairman sometime later and there was a campaign by a group of magistrates against Bridle with Hunt used as a pawn to attack him, but none of this emerged at the time and was not discussed by Bridle until much later as we shall see.

Away from the prison, on 11 February 1819 Bridle now aged 31was elected once more as the Worshipful Master of his Lodge of Brotherly Love at Martock, an appointment lasting for one year. In the lodge register he is described as a 'gentleman' of Ilchester. He took the chair and invested his officers the same evening. On 1 July 1819 the Lodge applied to move from its base at the White Hart Inn, Martock where it had been since 1810, to the Mermaid Inn at Yeovil. 'for the convenience of our respective dwellings and other good reasons', which was agreed.

8
A PERFECT PARADISE

Hunt's First Impressions

HENRY HUNT ARRIVED at Ilchester jail at 10.00 pm on Wednesday 17 May 1820 and from the minute the key turned in the lock he began to write, starting with a new journal, *An Address to the Radical Reformers of England* the morning after his arrival and after, 'enjoying an excellent night of undisturbed repose... You must not expect to hear from me', he continues, 'the language of whining or complaint either in regard to the sentence passed upon me or the sufferings to which I may be exposed...' he then proceeds to whine for two pages about his arrest and sentence and lists the names of all those concerned in his prosecution. He states that he intends to write his memoirs and produce them in monthly instalments for sale charging between 6d and 1/-'depending on bulk'. Hunt did not date his entries but the introduction to the first part, begins on the 22nd in which he contrasts his situation with the desperate conditions of the poor in Kirkheaton, Yorkshire taken from a petition presented to the House of Commons,

> Talk of imprisonment indeed! why it is a perfect Paradise compared with the wants and privations which you are doomed to endure. The situation of a prisoner in this jail, let him be confined for anything less than high treason or murder, is heaven upon earth compared to your lot. Let us see; there is a prisoner who is appointed to wait upon me here, an old soldier, who has enjoyed rank in the army as an adjutant, but having a large family, and meeting with many reverses of fortune, he became reduced in his circumstances, and, in consequence of great persecutions, was at length driven to seek relief from the parish. The sufferings and privations of his wife and children daily stared him in the face, without even the hope of relief; and, brooding over his unmerited persecutions and neglect, he was driven to drinking, &c. In a fit of temporary delirium, he attempted to lay violent hands upon himself and wife, for which he is sentenced to be imprisoned here for twelve months.

His wife and family are supported by the parish; and I will now tell you what he receives for his week's allowance, exclusive of clothes, lodging, fire, and washing, all found by the county. He gets one pound and a half of good bread and one penny every day. Ten pounds and a half of good white bread, and seven pence to purchase potatoes and salt, or milk, per week. Bread and pence, at the very lowest, two shillings and six-pence per week. Now, if we reckon one shilling and six-pence, at the very lowest rate, for washing, lodging, clothing, and firing, which are all found in plenty and very good of the sort, he receives the value of four shillings per week. The bread, &c.is quite as much as, or rather more than, a moderate man can eat; and this person, who has seen a great deal of the world, seriously 'informs me that he enjoys here, happiness, ease, and comfort, compared to what he had to encounter out of prison; and as he professes to be very well pleased with waiting upon me, he dreads the approach of his release. Every person in the jail has the same allowance, and if they choose to work, the Governor enables them to earn from threepence up to one shilling a day over.

The poor 'old soldier' was John Wyatt who Hunt was later to savage as a 'maniac' at the Commission hearing. In his own inimitable style, he wrote an enthusiastic letter to an unnamed friend in Bath dated 23 May 1820 which was published in the *Sherborne Mercury* on 6 June.

I believe no man that ever lived was more happy than I am here, in fact I esteem this only a cessation from my labours, and from all present appearances I anticipate the pleasure, at the end of two years and a half, of leaving this prison, (perhaps even reluctantly), at least five years younger in my constitution then when I came in here. I am in the enjoyment of that tranquillity which I have so long in vain wished for, and I possess a serenity and cheerfulness of mind, which alone can flow from conscious rectitude of intention, accompanied by the most vigorous health arising from temperance and exercise, which, as far as the strict discipline of this prison will permit, I shall not fail to continue. Cleanliness, which is next to godliness, as well as the greatest regularity, predominate here, and all the persons employed about the place, at the same time that they perform most strictly several duties allotted to them, conduct themselves in the most to becoming manner. Although I am in a dungeon I have at present no reason to complain. Last night I began to write the history of my life, which I intend to publish in numbers monthly; the first number will be published in a fortnight.

In a further letter the following month and published in the same newspaper he describes,

>...a paradise, a heaven upon earth, that at the expiration of his long sentence he should quit the premises perhaps reluctantly and five years younger in his constitution than when he came to it that if all the men in England had sworn before he came to Ilchester jail, that, under this government, there was one general where all the duties were well truly and honestly performed he would not have believed them, he now knew by experience that there was one and Ilchester was the very one…

William Bridle copied the first into his *Narrative* of 1822 and the second appears in, *Letter to the Aristocracy* when trying to regain his reputation in 1836. Of course, Hunt's absurd delight at his new accommodation must be at least in part an exercise in bravado, showing those who sentenced him and his followers that he is not at all down or cowed by the sentence. Hunt also kept a prison diary which he began on 23 June 1820 opening with a visit from Sir John Acland (1756-1831) chairman of the quarter sessions with whom he took tea and discussed the alterations needed to replace his cold stone floor with a wooden one as well as the installation of cupboards, shelves, doors, windows and curtains. There was a big point made about access to the factory yard so that he could walk in the fresh air whenever the builders were not there in the week and all day on Sundays. It was also agreed that Hunt could dine at the governor's table for one hour only which he did on several occasions and that he could have any furniture which he may require at his own expense. A bell was to be installed 'to use when occasion might require it'. All this being agreed, the discussion moved onto the subject of visitors. Initially Hunt was bound by the normal rules of the jail which allowed visitors for three separate hours during the day but finding this inconvenient, he asked Sir John to have this amended which could only be done by order of the magistrates. Acland promised that he would do everything in his power to make his situation as comfortable as possible and left after about an hour. Bridle asked him for a list of what he wanted done so that he could get it approved by the magistrates.

Bridle's recollection of Hunt's arrival supports his enthusiastic first impression, and describes his new inmate being placed in a comfortable ward which was perfectly dry and airy. The rooms had for a considerable time before been inhabited by five a female debtors who were removed so that Hunt might occupy the space. All additional beds were removed and a good feather bed provided. A day room and courtyard where appropriated for his use. Two prisoners who were there for want of sureties to keep the peace were placed in the ward adjoining to act as servants and he was allowed to purchase provisions from the town and have his meals prepared in the kitchen. A larder and scullery with a new fire grate for cooking was installed and four hours were allowed daily to walk in the factory yard which was about 100' x 40'. Hunt declared himself 'well satisfied'.

He was not alone in his new accommodation, he shared it with a fascinating conman, John Kinnear who was by all accounts a remarkable character, on this occasion he was charged with conspiracy to defraud to the amount of about £50,000 and described in the press as one of the most celebrated merchants in Liverpool, thought to have handled many millions of pounds fraudulently or otherwise and had been made bankrupt in 1810 for a figure approaching £1 million. He transacted business in that city perhaps to a greater extent than any man in Liverpool before or since having agents for the receipt and remittance of goods in almost all parts of the world. In 1838 after a lifetime of fraud he was sentenced to be transported for life and sailed on the *Earl Grey* to New South Wales at the age of 58. Kinnear had been lodging at Bridle's house and Hunt applied for a similar indulgence but the magistrates ordered that the two should be placed together within the prison itself in their own ward. They seem to have got on well with Kinnear sometimes making entries in Hunt's diary. He was about halfway through a two year sentence and it is most unfortunate that Hunt never recorded any of their conversation which must have been fascinating. It made sense for the magistrates to put the two highly intelligent and powerful individuals together and make them comfortable. Kinnear's career was closely followed in the press and Hunt was a widely known celebrity with supporters in the House of Commons and throughout the country, the magistrates must have been in awe of his renown and influential contacts, the last thing they would want was to upset him…

The building work soon began in their rooms, as agreed, including a partition to screen off Kinnear's section from Hunt's with wallpaper to follow. On several occasions Bridle and his wife had tea in Hunt's rooms where temporary flooring was in place. Light and airy it may have been but Bridle admitted that he had felt the damp very forcibly himself even in the little time that he had sat there with his feet up on the stones. Hunt continued to write at great speed. An entry for 28 June records that he received a parcel from Thomas Dolby with '50 copies of the first numbers of my life'. Dolby was an enterprising publisher and supporter of reform who operated from 299, The Strand in London publishing radical books and pamphlets along with prints and caricatures, many by Cruickshank.

On 27 June a Mr Fryer came to see him from Yeovil with some material for his memoirs but was refused admission on the grounds that he wasn't family, 'I suffered a very considerable inconvenience'. At a meeting of the magistrates it was agreed that from 6 July he and Kinnear could have visitors at any reasonable time from 9 o'clock in the morning until sunset. Everything indicates that Bridle was supportive of this application and that he had 'an unqualified wish to make us as comfortable as the prison would admit'. Within weeks the first issue of his new publication, *An Address To the Radical Reformers...* was being printed dated 1 July he even invents his own calendar dating from the events at Peterloo, thus 28 August 1820 becomes, 'the 12th day of the second year after the Manchester Massacre without enquiry', although he soon includes the established calendar as well. The first number contains numerous pages in support of Caroline of Brunswick who wished to return to the country as queen at her husband's coronation, a cause popular with radicals, before his pen turns, inevitably, to himself and Peterloo. It is remarkable that he was allowed to communicate in this manner, he could not only write whenever and whatever he liked but have it sent out of the prison and sold on the open market, reaping the profits, an activity that would certainly not to be allowed today.

According to Bridle, from 31 July until 20 August Hunt was visited daily in his sitting room by Mrs Vince often accompanied by a Miss Gray her companion, sometimes described as Hunt's 'ward'. They would have dinner with wine and liqueurs sent from the local inn. In an entry for 6 July he records that, 'Bridle informed me that six of the magistrates sent for a number of my memoirs each' and on 11 July he received a parcel from Dolby containing 150 copies of the second instalment and 50 further copies of the first issue.

There is little gossip in the diary but on 26 July he records a serious argument between Mr and Mrs Bridle. 'Mrs Bridle has not sat at the dinner table for some days, in consequence we get not only cursed bad but a very unpleasant dinner. We understand that W Bridle insists upon his wife leaving his house and going to London to her father the following day for a month until it has blown over. Mrs Hobbs appears frantic to think that her sister should be used so vile in consequence of the malignant falsehoods of Mrs George Bridle who at all events must be an infamous and abandoned bitch'. 28 July reads, 'we now hear that Mrs Bridle is not going to London but is to remain here, I am very glad to hear of this for every reason, as I think her the most respectable and reputable person about the jail, but it is an old and very true maxim that those who interface between a man and wife is sure to make enemies of both. In my situation I wish to be friends with both'. Other entries include the fact that on 12 July there were 165 prisoners in the jail with 23 staff making a total of 188 people living on the site. During a visit on 31 July he records that Miss Gray played and sang beautifully, she and Mrs Vince seemed to be spending most days with Hunt who had the piano retuned and the following day received 100 copies of the third instalment of his memoirs from London. Things were going well and although he would have preferred his freedom his situation could have been much worse.

During August things seem to have cooled between Bridle and Hunt. Hunt is presented with a large bill coming to £20/18/- for all his food, bed, breakfast, dinner and tea since he first arrived. He finds this to be overcharged by eight guineas and begins to describe the prison as the 'Ilchester Bastille' comparing conditions with the notorious Parisian jail before the revolution. In an entry for 11 August he records that 'Mrs Kinnear came to the jail at 8:30 and was admitted, but Pike told Mrs Vince that it was too early and would not let her in. Mrs Vince had ordered a leg of mutton, vegetables and pudding, a bottle of wine and three pints of beer but Pike came to say that there was no order for my having wine or beer and that I could not have any. This I think the most infamous conduct towards me, when I dine with Mr Bridle he comes prepared to take wine and when I have my dinner from him here wine and beer was regularly sent down so that I may have his nauseous guzzle but I must not have good wine from the inn'.

The following day he sent a note to one of the visiting magistrates, 'Mr Hunt presents his compliments to Mr Moody and requests that he will favour him with an interview… Mr Bridle declines to have those little things done that were directed by Mr Moody and Dr Colson the last time they came to the jail unless he receives a regular order from the magistrates and he also enforces some old regulations towards Mr Hunt that he considers were originally only meant for felons and low offenders and which he understood were totally superseded… Mr Bridle having enforced some of these regulations in the most odious manner regardless of the liberal intentions of the magistrates which Mr Hunt will personally appeal as soon as he has the opportunity'. The note was sent to Moody via Bridle as regulations dictated it must be. He makes a list of his main points.

> Bad water, no wine or beer allowed for me from the inn.
> My friends turned out at chapel time without ceremony.
> Mr Kinnear's friends remained in.
> No butcher admitted.
> Shop people hurried through the jail.

Tripod [for the fire] and the bell unfinished as well as the portico.

'Mr Moody came about one hour after I sent the letter and was very surprised as the magistrates have been told that Hunt should have every indulgence that didn't endanger the safety of the jail'. Moody made an order saying that things should be put back as they had been. On Sunday, 20 August Bridle came to see Kinnear and Hunt to explain that an order had been issued at Wells on the 14th when the magistrates, including Rev. William Colston, Aaron Moody and the undersheriff, William Melliar issued an order signed by 20 of their number prohibiting all females from visiting Hunt and Kinnear in their private rooms except their wives and children because, 'inconveniences had arisen'. There was no further explanation and all he could learn was that Acland had resigned as chairman of the quarter sessions and the Reverend Sir Abraham Elton of Clevedon Court had been appointed in his place. Sir John Cox Hippisley of Stoneaston and Edmund Broderip snr. the undersheriff, were amongst those who had signed the order which the visiting magistrates had no power to alter. Hippisley was a wealthy Somerset landowner and member of the grand jury with responsibility for conditions in the jail who had long been a victim of Cobbett's pen and Hunt's jibes.

There were no further restrictions, they were still allowed to walk in the yard and retain their two servants. It seems a case of pure political vindictiveness to use visits by his long-term companion Mrs Vince, the 'wife of another man' as the means to provoke him. In all probability, the sitting Somerset MPs Dickinson and Lethbridge were behind a lot of this petty treatment resulting from Hunt's success with organising the freeholders in the county against vested interests, they were fearful of his influence and that he might mobilise the freeholders against them. The spectre of the 1818 election with all its divisions and fractions was almost certainly a contributory factor.

Hunt had been, 'perfectly satisfied with the original arrangement which had continued for seven weeks to the mutual satisfaction of all parties', and immediately fired off a note to Bridle asking for an explanation. Bridle said that he did not know the reason or what the 'inconveniences' could be. He and Kinnear had done nothing to cause him any annoyance. Having got nothing from Bridle, Hunt wrote to magistrate Colston asking for a visit from him and Moody but when they arrived they explained that there was nothing they could do to alter it and explained that there had been a great number of letters from all parts of the county complaining about the indulgences granted to Hunt and Kinnear. He could get no further, everyone was saying it was a great shame but there was nothing they could do. Everybody individually, claimed bemusement and could not understand how the new ruling had arisen or who had initiated it. The new rules altered his life radically and he describes the only way in which he was allowed to receive a visit from Mrs Vince in one of his petitions,

> All visitors were to be received at the double grating of the felons' cage, or felons' conversation room, as it is called, which consists of two small cells, about six feet square, placed opposite each other at a distance of four feet ; in each of these is a grated window: at three separate hours in the day, the visitors of all the felons, all the convicts sentenced for bestiality and unnatural crimes; all persons sentenced for housebreaking, and even those committed for murder, are all assembled in one of those cells; when there is room for them, all the prisoners are placed in the other cell, and they are obliged to hold their conversation indiscriminately and publicly in the presence and hearing of each other… a disgusting and revolting spectacle…

On 15 August Mrs Vince and Miss Gray arrived for a visit unaware of the new regulations but Hunt refused to see them under those conditions despite them having travelled 150 miles from Sussex, and they had to make the long journey back. Hunt was beside himself with rage at being denied access to the most important person in his life. His heaven had become hell. The authorities probably took great delight in tormenting such an arrogant and trouble making 'Lord of the Manor of Glastonbury,' and how better to increase his punishment than to deny him the company of his beloved Catherine Vince. What made the situation worse, was that the purpose of their aborted visit was to obtain some urgent advice as Gray had been left some estates in Ireland by her grandfather with a yearly value of £800 which had been seized by a person not entitled to them. She had arrived with the documents to obtain his opinion as her guardian and protector, but had been turned away at the door. Bridle declared to the magistrates that he had not the slightest cause of complaint to make against Hunt or his visitors but an entry in the magistrates journal for 16 October 1820, confirmed that no female visitors except his wife and children were to be admitted to him except at the grating. Was this a simple matter of small-minded vindictiveness or part of a campaign to use Hunt as a pawn against Bridle and his supporters? Hunt believes that one of the principal authors of his woes was Francis Drake, (1764-1821) a Wells magistrate and former diplomat during the Napoleonic wars, and his deputy, undersheriff Edmund Broderip who he further accuses of conspiring with Bridle to treat him 'in the most cruel manner'. Hunt never explains his reasons for believing that these two were amongst those behind his misfortunes but he was not afraid to express his feelings to magistrate Colston on one of his visits,

> Let me see my family.' This one simple, this one reasonable request, is all I have asked, is all I do ask, and it is all I shall ask. But, while you deny me this, talk not to me of conciliation. All your little, petty, dirty, mean tricks to annoy me I can and do laugh at; I should despise myself, if I could not despise and disregard them. But, like expert butchers, who, when they are about to cut the throat of their innocent victim, the bleating lamb, know well where to apply the knife, so do you know where to inflict a deadly wound in the most vital part. There is, to be sure, this distinction between you and the butcher; it is his business, it is his profession, by which he gets his daily bread; and, indeed, the sooner he kills his victim the more merciful he is: but as for you, your conduct is ten thousand times more brutal than that of the butcher, inasmuch as you inflict torture upon a human being, merely for the pleasure of inflicting torture'.

The response of the Reverend Doctor is not recorded.

> MEMOIRS of HENRY HUNT, Esq. written by himself, in His Majesty's Jail, at Ilchester, now publishing on the 1st of every month in shilling numbers. No 4. was published on the 1st inst: In Mr. HUNT's address, to the Reformers, (stitched in No. 4.) will be found some highly curious and interesting particulars of the New Torturous Regulations in the Ilchester Bastile; which regulations are supposed to have been made by the newly appointed Reverend Chairman of the Quarter Sessions.
> Published by Dalby, 299, Strand, London; and sold by all booksellers.

The Memoirs of Henry Hunt. September 1820

On the face of it, Bridle continued to take Hunt's side, but 'completely failed to convince me of his sincerity, although he professed a great deal of kindness towards me'. Hunt complained that he was now locked in his rooms with greater frequency. Pike says that the harsher regime regarding visits was following an order by Moody who visited once more and told Hunt in front of the turnkey, Thomas Davis, that it was not him but came directly from Bridle. On 4 September Hunt writes in his diary, 'it is four months this day that I received the infamous sentence of the Court of King's Bench to be imprisoned two years and six months. It was a fortnight yesterday since this sentence was doubled fourfold by the additional sentence of the famous grand jury at the Wells Assizes which cruel and infamous sentence was signed by the notorious John Wiltshire of Shockerwick and 19 other magistrates. I know them all, empowering their tool Bridle to inflict the greatest torture upon me which this HULK EDUCATED MONSTER executed with a premeditated cold blooded savageness never surpassed by the blood thirsty agents of the most cruel, unfeeling, remorseless tyranny'.

Despite these strong words, jailer and prisoner still continued to be civil to each other. On 14 September Hunt records in his diary that Bridle 'sent us a piece of salmon but as we did not have a fish kettle large enough he offered to have it boiled for us and a little later Hunt sent Bridle a brace of partridges. Bridle also agreed that he and Kinnear could have a flower bed in the yard for growing herbs. Still trying to regain his visits on 16 September Hunt wrote a personal letter to the trial judge, John Bayley which his son Thomas delivered to the judge's house. His plea was that the sentence was punishment enough without being deprived of the comfort of visits from his family. Hunt continually describes periods when he is denied visitors on his own terms as, 'solitary confinement', and asks that the judge to agree that he made no such order. Bayley explained that it was a matter for the magistrates but solitary confinement was certainly not part of the sentence – although throughout the ongoing debate there was no agreed definition of what the term actually meant. On the 1st September the forth chapter of his memoirs was published along with the latest edition of his *Address* stitched onto it and containing some 'highly curious and interesting particulars of the new torturous regulations in the Ilchester Bastille'. With a large part of the building work now finished Hunt had the furniture he needed shipped over from Middleton Cottage the painting and papering is now in progress and 'the new grate draws very well'.

The General Election of 1820

IN EARLY SEPTEMBER Hunt made notes of the aftermath of the general election caused by the death of George III. The new Parliament was assembled on 21 April 1820 resulting in the re-election of Sir Isaac Coffin and the election of Dr Stephen Lushington both Whigs and the occasion for another party in the jail. According to Hunt's jail diary for 2 September the 'horseradish' or bribe money was being handed out, £45 for those who had supported the winning candidates in both elections and £30 for those voting in the recent one. Charles Marshall, who rejoiced in the title of 'deputy turnkey's servant', was apparently handed the full £45. In an edition of his *Address* Hunt is at pains to exclude his friend Dr Shorland from any hint of wrongdoing,

> It is a matter of notorious fact, that every elector of Ilchester who voted for Sir Isaac Coffin and Dr Lushington received £30 for his vote. When I said this, I meant every elector who chose to receive the money; of course, I did not mean that such a man as Mr Shorland, the surgeon of Ilchester, received that sum. I believe Mr Shorland is far above a bribe, nor do I believe for one moment that he was so incautious as to be in anyway concerned in bribery, although a wretch has been found to swear to the fact before the Grand Jury of the county, at the Assizes, upon whose oath a true bill has been found against Mr Shorland, notwithstanding the Grand Jury at the last quarter sessions threw out the said bill.

There had arisen a great argument between prison surgeon Dr Shorland and local butcher 'Big Jim' Culliford who supplied the jail with meat. Shorland had apparently stood bail for Big Jim in the sum of £40 and as he had not been repaid he grabbed Culliford's election money as payment. 'I believe that every elector in the Borough of Ilchester, on both sides, both Darlingtons' and Manners', are bribed and paid electors for their votes, with the exception of Mr Shorland, and perhaps one or two others', continued Hunt.

Ilchester Jail in 1820

William Bridle's brother George had married a Jane Culliford of Ilchester in March of 1818 and although no family connection has been established, when two of the Cullifords were arrested for assault over the affair, Bridle refused to supply the sheriff's officer with handcuffs and had them placed in the debtor's ward which allowed them much greater freedom and privileges. James was painting the governor's house and was allowed his wife with him at all times. 'These are Bridle's cronies which he plays off upon Shorland,' claimed Hunt. When undersheriff Broderip discovered this, he had them put on the felon's ward. The Cullifords supported the yellow party. In the same month Dr Shorland, 'the surgeon of Ilchester', was found guilty of posting obscene and disgusting letters around the town defaming Mrs Stainer landlady of the Castle Inn. He was ordered to pay Mr and Mrs Stainer £100 in damages.

Jail Matters

ON THE GOSSIP front, in early October things were looking up for the governor and his spouse. 'Mr Kinnear informed me that Bridle and his wife have made up their quarrel and that they slept together for the first time last night for two months although a bed and other things were packed up for Mrs Bridle to take with her; she was to have gone positively on Sunday. However, it is all well and it is to be hoped that things will go on more compatible in future but what will become of Mrs George Bridle? It is impossible that Mrs Bridle and her can live in the same place together after what has happened in fact Bridle could never stay here and be on good terms with his wife, but we shall see'. 'We understand that Bridle and his wife are kissing and cooing like to turtledoves, it is quite like another honeymoon'. Whatever happened to cause the problem between them Hunt does not explain and we shall probably never know.

Hunt had applied to have a meat cleaver in his room which Bridle declined on the grounds that his servant, Wyatt, 'was mad before he came in and that he might take up the cleaver and hit a man's head, he appeared to think Wyatt a very dangerous fellow, and forgot that he wished to put Wyatt to sleep in my room the first night I came'. 'The sitting room was papered but not yet dry so he and Kinnear dined and drink tea in my bedroom' On Sunday 22 October, 'Bridle came down and brought the infamous order made at the Taunton sessions on 16 October, I saw the line which begins, '…and it is further ordered that no female visitors except the aforesaid be admitted to the said Henry Hunt… I threw down to the paper and told Bridle that I had seen quite enough, for me one line was enough and that I would not spare any exertion to get such cruel restrictions taken off and that nothing on Earth should deter me from using every endeavour to gain redress'. Despite his hopes judgement had once again gone against him.

Hunt applied to have the restrictions lifted at the King's Bench in November and an order was issued to 'show cause why Mr Hunt should not be treated in the same manner, and be allowed the same privileges, as other persons in custody for a misdemeanour'. Nothing happened and so Hunt wrote to Sir Charles Bampfylde the high sheriff of Somerset asking for the restrictions to be lifted and received a reply in Bampfylde's name from his undersheriff William Melliar saying that there was nothing he could do. It should be remembered that Bridle's mother's maiden name was Melliar but like the Cullifords no direct link with the undersheriff has been discovered.

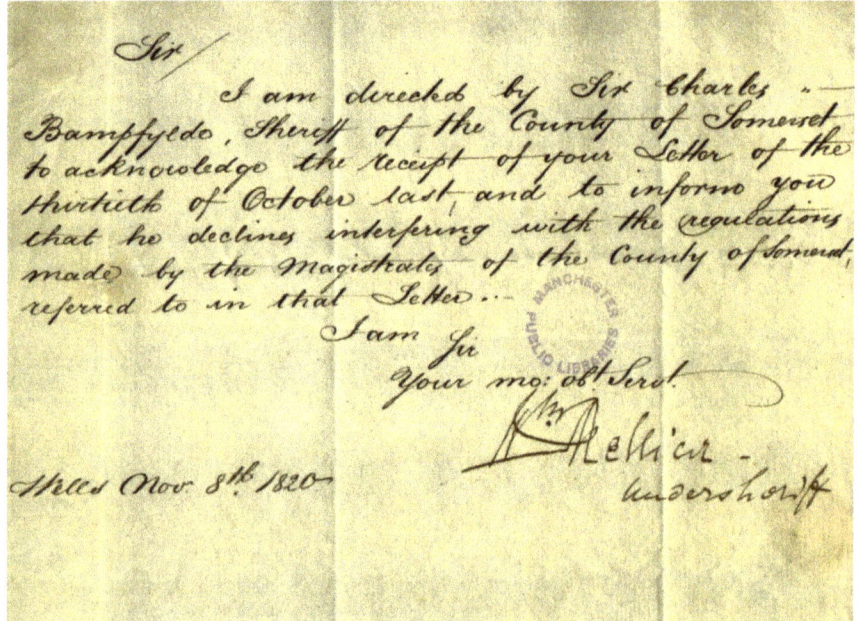

1820 letter from Melliar

It soon emerged that Bampfylde knew nothing of the matter and that the letter was written without his knowledge and he hastened to the jail in December immediately ordering that 'Mr Hunt is allowed to receive visitors of his female as well his male friends from nine in the morning till four in the afternoon'. Bampfylde's term of office ended in February and under his successor, William Hanning, the visiting magistrates, Dr Colston and the two Thrings, [father and son magistrates] re-imposed the October restrictions. In a statement sometime later Thring the younger explains the reasons for this,

Our conduct having been severely arraigned for having, at the expiration of Sir Charles Bampfylde's Sheriffalty, given directions for the re-enforcement of the order made at the preceding Michaelmas sessions, with respect to the admission of female visitors to Mr Hunt, without the authority of the Sheriff, I beg to offer the following explanation.

It is true that we had no direct authority from the Sheriff, but it is also true that we had his virtual consent. He was one of the twenty Magistrates who signed the original order dated Wells, August, 1820. He was subsequently a Member of the Court of Quarter Sessions, held at Taunton, 16th October, 1820, on which day the aforesaid order was confirmed. At the following Epiphany Sessions, at Wells, the interference of Sir C Bampfylde underwent a discussion, and it was very apparent that the feeling of the Court was in direct opposition to his conduct, although it was thought prudent to avoid any conflict with him on the occasion, and I well remember that a Magistrate, whose opinion carries the greatest weight (Mr Combe), then turned to Mr Hanning, and said, that he had no doubt when there was a new Sheriff that everything would be set right; to which Mr Hanning expressed no dissent, but signified that he should always hope to act in conjunction with his brother Magistrates, or something to the to the same effect; thus, for the third time, testifying his approbation of the original order made at Wells the preceding August.

In November 1820, several Magistrates some of whom had acted from ten to fifteen years, made affidavits before the Court of King's Bench, that, to the best of their judgment and belief, the said order was essential to the good government and regulation of the Gaol. We certainly, therefore, understood, and I am convinced that it was the opinion of a great majority of the Court, that soon as Sir C. Bampfylde should be superseded in his office, the authority of the Magistrates, was again to be enforced and by so doing, we had every reason to believe, as must be evident from the above statement, that we were executing the intention of those Magistrates who had always taken the active and leading parts in the county business, and with the virtual concurrence of the then Sheriff.

It is true that my father and self were of private opinion, that it was neither just or decent that Mr Hunt should be permitted to receive his mistress in his own apartments; an indulgence which was never granted to a debtor with his wife, by the regulations of the Gaol. This class of prisoners, the least peccant in the eye of the law, would have had ample reason to complain of the partiality manifested in his favour, he had already been made an exception to the discipline exercised towards them, inasmuch as he was permitted to receive his male visitors in his private apartments for four hours, during the day, and his wife and children, of both sexes, without restriction. All other female visitors he had permission to see in the conversation-room. This is the substance of the order respecting his visitors, which we directed to be enforced.

February, 1821. R Thring

It was a source of great annoyance to Hunt that his co-defendants had only received sentences of one year and that Bamford, was serving his time at Lincoln where his wife lived with him while the anchor of Hunt's life was forbidden even to meet in his rooms. The situation sent an already hyperactive, arrogant and obsessive man into overdrive. His whole view of his, 'heaven upon earth' changed and he gives a dramatically revised view of his initial confinement,

> On my arrival here, I was thrust into a cold damp unoccupied dungeon by the jailor where there was a bag of musty oat straw placed upon a jail truck not fit for the resting place of a hog. A stool and a table were the only furniture of my day dungeon which had a northerly aspect where the sun never deigns to show its rays for six months in the year. For the first fortnight I was neither allowed fire-irons nor fender of any sort, but as fingers were made before either of these I contrived to do without them... Within the pestilential air of these walls I was immured for seven weeks without once taking fresh air and which... has occasioned rheumatic pains which I shall be more than fortunate if I get quit of while I remain here.

For much of the time Hunt still believed that he was kept in what he called solitary confinement, which was certainly no such thing as would be commonly understood. He had servants to cook his meals, access to the open air and a fair degree of freedom. This entry is from Volume 1 of his memoirs, undated but from the honeymoon period before visits from Mrs Vince were banned after which he was at great pains to describe the horrors of 'solitary confinement' at every opportunity,

> The time that a man spends in a prison is not always thrown away, as I have found by experience; and I shall, I trust, be able to prove by and by, to the satisfaction of my numerous readers, that the time I have spent in this Bastille has been the most valuable part of my life. I never before knew what real leisure was. I have enjoyed retirement as much as any man in England; but then I have

been always surrounded with my family and friends; I have never, before now, known what it was to have seven or eight hours of a day exclusively to myself. I am locked up in solitary confinement in my dungeon every night, at six o'clock, without my having the power to go to any one, and without any one having the power to come to me, excepting the turnkey, which, thank God! never happens now after locking-up time, though it used to be the case very frequently when I first came here. It is considered a violation of the rules to go near a prisoner, unless upon a great emergency, after he is locked up; but it was not deemed any violation of rules for the turnkey to be constantly coming to my dungeon, and, with an authoritative rattling of the lock of the door, marching in to say that Mr Bridle, the gaoler, wanted a newspaper, &c. &c. However, that is all at an end, and I am never interrupted. I can sit down with a book or a pen at six o'clock, almost with a certainty of not being interrupted by any living creature, for six, seven, or eight hours at a time. My keepers think this the greatest punishment that can be inflicted upon me but, on the contrary, I contrive to turn their malice to advantage, and make this the most valuable time of my life. Few men can boast such a luxury. I really enjoy it beyond description.

The Campaign Begins.

HUNT BEGAN COMPILING evidence of what he considered to be every single indignity or vindictive act against him personally which he soon expanded to cover his fellow prisoners. Desperate to exploit any chink in the armour of his oppressors he sought out what he considered to be the most unjustly treated inmates and organised petitions which were eventually to lead to the appointment of a Commons Commission. In Bridle's words Hunt 'revolutionised the jail'. By November 1820 he had adopted an idea some way beyond ridiculous. Copying Queen Caroline who had established the order of 'St Caroline of Jerusalem', and made her alleged lover and former secretary Bartolomeo Pergami the grand master, he decided to create one in his own honour. The order of St Henry of Ilchester was bestowed upon all 'true radicals' who came to visit him, they were to become 'Knights of the Sublime Order of the Cross of Ilchester' and issued with a diploma. It seemed like a rather feeble joke but he was deadly serious wanting to establish two knights in every large town throughout the kingdom. Unsurprisingly, little seems to have come of this idea.

One of Hunt's servants, William Chidley who had moved to Taunton when discharged in January, is alleged to have told Bridle that Hunt was determined to ruin him, explaining that he had been asked if he could contact other recently released prisoners, 'I will give you some money to drink my health and ask them if they have any complaint to make against the keeper or the turnkeys and if they have to let me know and I will *work them for it*, they all met in the town but he did not hear any of them say that they had any complaint to make. Chidley further states that he met Shillibeer an associate of Hunt who gave him more money, got him drunk and to sign a document which he later discovered to be a petition attacking Bridle against whom he had no complaints at all. In early February Hunt complained to Bridle about his seemingly devoted servant Wyatt, saying that so far from being of any service to himself or Kinnear he had been quite the reverse, 'if he would have remained quiet and not interfered I should never have complained. I have been for some time obliged to make my own bed and clean my own room and would very readily dress my own dinner but his violence has become insupportable he has had frequent passions but they have now become intolerable'. Hunt gives no further details but it seems that he had decided that Wyatt was a spy placed by Bridle who promised to get him replaced. Another cause of their falling out is Wyatt's evidence that Hunt caught Miss Gray sitting on his lap when he returned expectedly to his room...

Mr and Mrs Hobbs

During the same month the jail was awash with rumour. The sheriff and a party of magistrates arrived and Mrs Bridle stood accused of acting improperly by receiving company to play at cards with the prisoners, gambling and keeping the jail open to visitors sometimes until three in the morning during Bridle's absence. Bridle had first blamed his wife for such lax behaviour then charged Mathew Hobbs and his wife Jane for allowing this to take place. Matthew was Bridle's brother-in-law, married to his wife's sister and employed as the task master; Jane was the matron and his brother Samuel Hobbs had been a servant in the house until he fell out with Bridle over money he claimed that he was owed and was dismissed in March 1819. Perhaps this was the start of the family conflict. The Hobbs's protested that they did not think they had any power to prevent Mrs Bridle from having parties in his absence as they had often happened while he was there. They were dismissed by the magistrates within the hour and trundled out of the jail that night with Hobbs further accused of drunkenness, which, as Hunt pointed out, 'there was no specific rule or regulation against' [!] Hunt described Hobbs and his wife as two, humane, kind hearted people who had been very civil to him. When Hobbs first became employed at the jail he was indebted to Bridle, for about £600 including interest without the means of paying it off having had to give up his farm at Lymington. Presumably Bridle had rescued his brother-in-law from bankruptcy by paying his debts and giving him a job. Bridle retained a portion of Hobbs salary and as much as two thirds of the debt had now been repaid and so it was of little consequence to Bridle what became of the pair with whom there had obviously been a very serious falling out with Mrs Hobbs swearing vengeance as she left the jail.

Hunt's constant letters and complaints about his personal inconveniences having fallen on deaf ears he continued to attack the prison system itself investigating stories told by fellow inmates,

> When I first came to this gaol, one of the poor prisoners, who was assisting to repair my dungeon, was telling me of an act of cruel injustice and torture that had been inflicted upon him by one of the turnkeys. Upon which I said to the man, "Did you not make a complaint to the magistrates? I am sure they would not suffer a prisoner to be treated in such a way with impunity." The poor fellow looked at me very steadfastly, for some time, to see if I were in earnest; at length he replied, "Lord, Sir! you will know better after you have been here a little while. I have been here nearly two years, and I never knew any prisoner make a complaint even to the gaoler, and much less to the magistrate, without being punished for it. I never knew a man make a complaint who was not locked up, in solitary confinement, within a week afterwards, for something or other. A prisoner is sure never to get any redress, for the turnkeys will say anything, and what one says another will swear; and the gaoler always believes them, or pretends to believe…

In March 1821 Hunt's son Thomas came to see him with a small pistol in his greatcoat pocket which was discovered by one of the turnkeys who confiscated it until Thomas left. The son claims that he threw it into the river after leaving but this had put the turnkeys on alert and they took to searching all Hunt's visitors upon arrival. Bridle in his *Letter* of 1836 states that Thomas returned to see his father three days later and upon being searched another pistol was discovered and he was refused admission. Hunt's writings continued apace. He had finished the second instalment of his memoirs by June of 1820 and written numerous petitions concerning jail conditions on behalf of himself and others, as well as writing his monthly *Address*. His memoirs were published in 46 parts eventually to became three volumes which ended with his arrest and being bailed after Peterloo, he may have produced more during his last six months in jail but it has not come down to us. The jail diary ends 3 April 1821 at the bottom of the last page in the notebook, if he continued onto a second volume it does not seem to have survived.

1821 Sketch of the Jail

Hunt 'Peeps' at the Jail

His *Address*, as the name would indicate, was for his followers and fellow radicals nationwide and a great success but Hunt needed something comparatively short and hard-hitting to publicise conditions at Ilchester. In the issue for March 1821 he announced the publication of a new 24 page pamphlet, *A Peep Into a Prison, or the Inside of Ilchester Bastille*, to be published by Thomas Dolby at 299 The Strand on first of April 1821 which he cheekily, *'Dedicated without permission to William Hanning High Sheriff and the Magistrates of the County of Somerset'*. Upon publication the *Peep* was distributed amongst the inmates and caused great disturbances sometimes bordering on mutiny.

He began his attack with a description of the jail, its damp conditions with some parts being below the bed of the river and built of porous stone. The river frequently overflows its banks and had recently placed the jail under 14 inches of water throughout with the prisoners wet to the knees. Of the buildings themselves about one eighth is occupied by the manufactory, which Hunt calls a 'toy or bauble', one eighth by the jailer's house and yards and one eighth by the chapel. There are three houses for the turnkeys and their families which with the prisoners and officers makes a total community of about 300 persons. The general sewer runs close by the wells and it has lately been discovered that its contents had burst into some of them. There is not infrequently on the sick list as many as 15 to 20 people but there is no hospital despite land having been set aside for the express purpose of building one four years ago. The chapel is not large enough to accommodate 100 people and sometimes has to take 200 or more; men and women are separated by a lattice work partition and, 'it is not to be wondered if indecencies occur'. There are no facilities for the 20 or so juveniles to be taught to read and write or give them religious instruction. The manufactory has no one to superintend it who has a knowledge of the practical part of weaving. The prisoners have part of their earnings given them for subsistence and part reserved for them until they leave. The washing for two to three hundred prisoners is nearly full time employment for the women here but the principal part is taken up with washing for the jailer, the staff, their family and friends.

The debtors have two wards allotted to them, one is occupied by those who can afford to hire their beds from the jailer at 2/6d per week and buy other necessities, the other, which is called the poor debtor's ward, is for those who have no money and subsist on the county allowance; they are restrained from buying any quantity of wine beer or cider. Debtors are permitted to see their friends and family at three separate hours in the day in the conversation room and their wives are allowed to visit them in wards common to all from nine until five daily. Men are often surprised in the privy having connection with their wives. There is one general sitting room for the whole and five or six sleeping rooms with sometimes as many as 16 or 20 persons sleeping in one room where a night stool is placed at one end.

The county allowance of one penny per day and one half pound of bread is distributed every morning and the prisoners are supplied with provisions by persons taken around the jail known as, 'the shop'. The weights and measures are supposed to be checked by the jailer but this has not happened for many years. The jailer's fixed salary is £500 per annum plus many expenses, income from the hire of beds etc. Hunt details many 'drunken frolics' at the jailer's house involving card games. 'The most eminent carousels here have been at the time of electing Members of Parliament for the borough, in which the jailer for many years has acted a principal part including people from the town, a numerous train of electioneering fashionables male and female with the singing of bacchanalian and lascivious songs'. Classification is hardly recognised. 'Boys from 7 to 15 are by day the associates, and by night the bedfellows, of men convicted of every variety of wickedness that is on record in the catalogue of human crime'.

Two women, Sarah Lawrence, now of Mere, and Sarah Hewitt became pregnant whilst in the jail. An 'occurrence book' or daily diary kept in the jail is a tissue of falsehood and misrepresentation from first to last and has been a great means of deluding and deceiving the magistrates. Punishments are excessive as in the cases of Hillier and Hill whose petitions are reprinted below. The prisoners are allowed one pair of stockings by the county, there is no opportunity of having them washed, with dirty feet in them until they are rags rendering jail fever more frequent and more dangerous. Very few prisoners have any opportunity of knowing anything of the rules of the place and are in constant danger of offending against a law about which they know nothing. The regulations are not exhibited and for contravening such unwritten authority some prisoners have suffered severe punishment. Hunt includes an illustration of the forms of chastisement used in the prison. Miss Smith, 'a poor Irish girl', is depicted in the stocks and Gardiner and Hillier are shown in irons. After the publication of the *Peep* Hunt admits that, 'The stocks here for the females are not such clumsy things as represented in the engraving, although there are holes in them to manacle a woman's legs.'

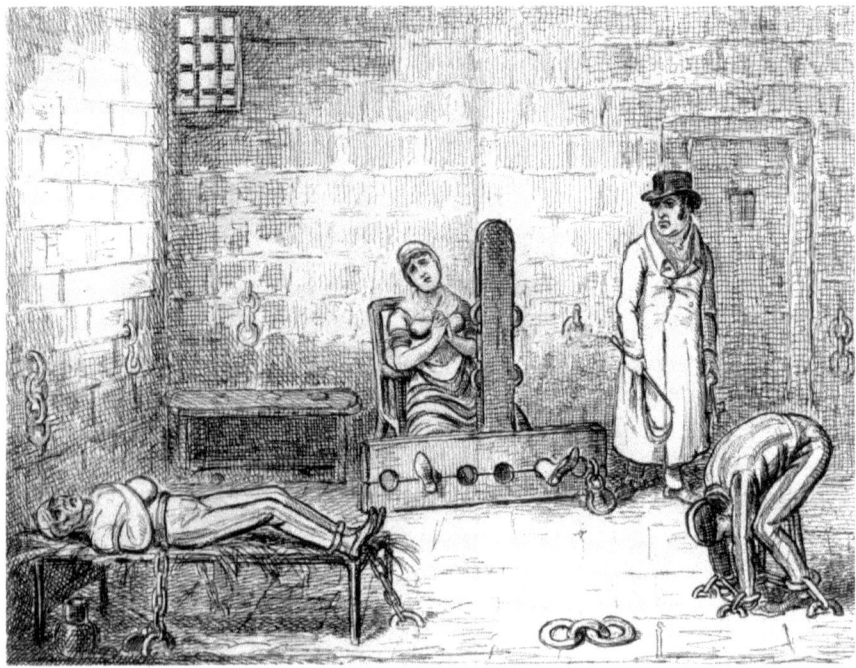

1821 Prison Cell from the Peep

Hunt also reprinted the petitions of two inmates who claimed to have suffered particularly badly under the present regime,

Petition of Charles Hill

Hill's Petition was dated 19 February 1821 and introduced to the House by Alderman Wood on 9 March. Hill was a former tax inspector from Bridgwater who found himself in prison for debts amounting to over £719 which had been partly paid by the seizure of his property leaving him owing just over £34. He had been in Ilchester since May 1806, a total of 15 years and was now 74 years of age. Hill had petitioned before in June 1815 applying for release as he had been in solitary confinement for a long time on bread and water and was not allowed to communicate with his friends. Somerset MP William Dickinson commented that if he really was in solitary confinement he must have committed some very serious offence as it was impossible for a prison to be better superintended by magistrates than this one. Hill continues,

> Your petitioner some years back ventured to send a petition which was presented to the House of Commons but instead of gaining any redress your petitioner was removed from the ward which he had before occupied. The jailer caused your petitioner's boxes to be searched and took away his letters, writings, papers and other documents which have never been restored from that time to this and which has proved a serious loss and a great injury to him. Your petitioner has ever since been treated with great hardships and cruelty'.
>
> These and many other privations your petitioner has been subject to for many years having been totally bereft of all property, he has been an inmate of the lower or poor debtor's ward. Your petitioner begs further to state that he is now upwards of 74 years of age; that is constitution is greatly impaired and broken down, and his body emaciated by such lengthened imprisonment and rigorous treatment which must hasten him to the grave unless he obtains relief… such privations and sufferings could never have been meant to have been inflicted by the legislature upon a defenceless prisoner whose only crime is the misfortune of falling into debt.

Other than that, Hill's main complaint seems to have been that the amount of beer or cider he was allowed had been reduced over the years and that he was not allowed to see visitors in private. In the Commons debate which followed, Dickinson, claimed that he was under the impression that Hill had appeared several times before the insolvency court but had been sent back because he owned certain properties that he would not give up. Captain Bennet, who had presented the petition admitted that he had been misled and was now satisfied that the allegations were false.

Writing in 1836 Bridle states that during George III's jubilee year debtors owing a total of £1545/12/8d were released under the insolvent debtor's scheme, claiming that over £48 was raised by his own efforts. All were freed except Hill who refused the charity preferring to remain in the jail where acting as an unofficial attorney he had made such considerable profits that he thought it worthwhile to remain there. The Chancellor of the Exchequer answered that he must first ascertain whether the Crown had the power of remitting the debt in question and secondly whether under all the circumstances the case was one for indulgent consideration. (*Taunton Courier* 14 March 1821).

Petition of James Hillier.

ANOTHER PETITION WAS that of James Hillier who was serving a sentence of 18 months for stealing from a shop in Bristol. He was engaged in a game of pitch and toss known as 'hussel-cap' with another prisoner when a third-party intervened and reported the game to the governor. His petition was introduced to the House by Alderman Wood on 11 April 1821.

> ...your petitioner was placed in heavy double irons, twice doubled so that he could not move his legs more than nine inches apart, handcuffs were then placed upon him and a chain passed from the fetters through the handcuffs so that he was literally chained down neck and heels together. He was then dragged away and thrown into a cold damp dark dungeon or cell where he remained until the next day, when he was led down before the visiting magistrates and other gentlemen who after lecturing your petitioner and scoffing at his humiliating and degrading situation of being so chained and ironed ordered him back again into the solitary cell where he remained in the whole for the space of nine days and nights in this deplorable state without being able to put his hands to his mouth, to stand upright or lie straight unless it was when the chain and handcuffs were taken off for about an hour every night to allow your petitioner to take his bread and water and ease the calls of nature; for the remaining 23 hours he continued in this distressing and painful situation with the exception of having the handcuffs off once to go to chapel and once or twice for a few minutes when he prayed to be suffered to go to the privy.
>
> Your petitioner never saw a magistrate during the whole time after although the turnkey informed him that Dr Colson and other magistrates had been at the prison on 22 February but they cruelly neglected to visit or relieve your petitioner from this horrible situation. Thus your petitioner lay for nine days and nights without once being allowed to have his clothes off or any relief whatsoever with his arms swelled with the pressure of the handcuffs to such

a degree that the iron rings thereof were almost buried in his flesh and they were obliged to use considerable force to get them out of the flesh and when the turnkey took them off towards the latter part of his time they were obliged to use considerable force and violence to get them out of the flesh! This only excited the merriment of Pike, the turnkey who laughed at your petitioners sufferings.

Your petitioner therefore most humbly prays your Honourable House to take his case into consideration and if not afford him any relief for his past sufferings he most earnestly implores your Honourable House to take such measures as will protect him and his fellow prisoners from such cruel and inhuman treatment in future.

James Hillier makes his mark. **X**

The two petitions were ordered to lie on the table which meant that nothing was to be done immediately – if at all. The final few pages of the *Peep* are taken up with a letter dated 27 March 1821 to Thomas Fowell Buxton the Weymouth MP to whose book Hunt took strong objection. 'I denounce you as the most bitter enemy the prisoners of this jail ever had; and that you have done more to sink this jail to its present lamentable and disgraceful state of irreligion, immorality, and irregularity with all the hideous and deformed train of vices than any other man could have done…'

There is much more in the same vein. Buxton's crime was to have paid a visit to the jail in April 1818 reporting favourably on the involvement of prisoners in construction work, manufacturing, and education. His failure in Hunt's eyes, was to send his seven page report to Bridle for his approval and not investigating further. 'I was not so fortunate as to see the jailer, but the aspect of the prison convinced me that he had well performed his duty to the magistrates who employ him, and that they had nobly discharged theirs to the county in which they reside'.

Hunt reported that the *Peep,* 'caused a great and general sensation throughout the county particularly at the Spring Assizes at Taunton'. Before publication he had taken the precaution of packing up all his papers and documents and sending them off to a friend in London, in case, 'others might be implicated or injured,' by their seizure. He also noted that the locks and bolts to the *interior* of his bedroom door had been removed although there seems nothing sinister in this, the bolts had been installed for the benefit of the five females who once occupied that ward and were just removed as part of the general refurbishment. As Bridle points out, 'internal fastenings being inconsistent with the proper management of the prison, and might be used by the prisoner confined, to prevent the ready access should it be deemed necessary'.

Placards had been posted around the town advertising the new publication but these were swiftly torn down. Bridle tried to get the new high sheriff William Hanning to have it suppressed threatening to prosecute Hunt and 'have him in jail for another two years' but, upon receipt of his copy, Hanning ordered an immediate magistrates enquiry into the allegations. The *Peep* was to go through at least five editions…

9
HUNT v BRIDLE

There seems little doubt that Bridle had seriously underestimated not only his opponent but those behind him. He had been master of the jail since 1808, he had practically rebuilt it, he employed his own people, sometimes family and friends, he had been on intimate terms with visiting magistrates for many years, he participated in local politics and was a prominent Freemason, he must have thought himself well respected and above criticism. What could some egotistical prisoner possibly do to hurt him no matter how well known he was? Nonetheless, the two petitions presented to the Commons in April 1821 had the effect that Hunt was hoping for. Alderman Wood quoted extensively from the descriptions of the jail conditions in Hunt's *Peep*, and after some discussion it was proposed, 'That a humble address be presented to His Majesty, that he will be graciously pleased to issue a commission to inquire into what has been, and now is, the condition and treatment of prisoners confined in Ilchester gaol, the conduct and management of the said gaol, and the site and buildings of the same', all of which was agreed to by the House.

[comments in square brackets are my own].

The Magistrates Inquiry 19 April 1821

On 10 April sheriff Hanning gave orders to Bridle that he was to permit whichever prisoners Hunt thought appropriate to be brought to his room so that he could take their 'informations' having first delivered their names to Bridle in theory giving him an opportunity to tamper with the witnesses but Hunt declares that he 'only succeeded in one case'. Hunt spent every waking minute assembling his evidence in great detail for both the magistrates and the Commission. The magistrates were asked to consider 13 charges and opened the proceedings at the magistrates committee rooms in the jail itself beginning on 19 April and lasting for 14 days until 17 May, one year to the day since Hunt first entered Ilchester.

According to Hunt, on the third day of the hearing the sheriff and magistrates offered a deal whereby they would discharge Bridle if he would agree to stop the hearings all together but his response was,

> No; it is your province to determine upon the conduct of the gaoler as you shall think proper, and to decide upon the facts as they shall appear in evidence. I charge your public officer with being guilty of great public abuse and I am ready to prove that charge and let you see the nature of his conduct. I must call for inquiry, not only with a view to his punishment, but also to secure future prisoners from the recurrence of such cruelty, it is for you to conclude the matter, I shall not consent to its suspension.

There is no official transcript of the proceedings but it was reported in the press, and in general the same witnesses were called and the same questions asked as at the following Commission's enquiry considered in detail below. It emerged later that Hunt had to pay for all the expense of procuring his witnesses as the magistrates had no power to apply the, 'county stock' for such purposes. Appeals and collections were held amongst radical groups and readers of his publications up and down the country. Where expenses stopped and bribery began is an interesting question but the same applied to both sides.

At the conclusion of the prosecution case Bridle asked for a month to prepare his defence – he was given a week until the 24th, 'and not an hour longer'. Bridle went at once to London to get the best legal advice and his counsel gave a very strong opinion on this investigation taking place just before the Commission held theirs, 'it would be a departure from the known principles of justice to require Mr Bridle to disclose to the party accusing him, the nature and proof of his defence before such investigation legally commences.' They advised Bridle to decline any defence before the magistrates and commentated adversely on the attempt to put him to such unnecessary expense. He took their advice preferring to save what he had to say for the Commissioners rather than repeat it. With that, the magistrates retired to consider their findings; their report was not to appear until August after the Commission had finished their own investigations. At 4.00 o'clock that same day as the magistrates prepared to leave, 'before I had time to wash my hands', as Hunt to put it, the Commissioners arrived at the jail and occupied the rest of the day inspecting the building, its water supply and facilities.

The Commons Commission.

THE NEW INVESTIGATION was held within the jail as before, the three Commissioners were Thomas Grimstone Estcourt MP, Charles Godfrey Mundy and John Delafield Phelps Esq. They were unpaid but allowed the services of one clerk and sat from 24 May 1821 until 2 July often working for eight hours a day six days a week conducting the enquiry with scrupulous thoroughness being allowed unlimited access to both premises and inmates. In a later petition to the Commons, Hunt makes the point that Bridle and the magistrates had now seen all of his evidence and witnesses before the Commission sat and were thus better prepared for their defence.

The evidence was recorded by Henry Blatchford Shillibeer a land surveyor of Taunton who operated as Hunt's clerk, a close friend and a supporter who shared his political views. It should be borne in mind that the transcript was produced and published by Hunt and cannot be considered an official court transcript. Shillibeer gave his services for nothing and was also responsible for the amusing caricatures of some of the defence team and witnesses reproduced below. In September he became honorary secretary of the Taunton Committee, 'formed for the purpose of paying a tribute of respect and for indemnifying Henry Hunt… from the expenses lately incurred in the arduous investigation into the contact of Bridle… and for his indefatigable exertions in the cause of humanity'.

Hunt had the resulting 300-page transcript, *Investigation at Ilchester Gaol into the Conduct of William Bridle, the Gaoler before the Commission appointed by the Crown.* published by Dolby and prefaced with an address to George IV in which he lectures the king about failing to live up to his oath in the application of 'justice and mercy' to the victims at Peterloo. Commenting further that, 'I have seen with extreme pain your majesty's *approbation of* and *thanks for* the performance of deeds committed at Manchester, as foul as ever sullied the page of history…[which] has done more to weaken the force, and to destroy the moral character of your Majesty's Government than any or all the other public acts of your Majesty's life'. He goes on to advise the king that his name is being used, to 'authorise every species of oppression and cruelty' via the magistrates appointed in his name and that he should be aware of what he calls, 'political judges' before declaring that, 'I have no right to expect that your majesty will retire from the busy round of pleasure and those scenes of gaiety and luxury that are the constant guests of your palace to read this evidence; yet I, as one of your prisoners, have a right to demand that you will order some of your servants to do it, that they may take such measures to rectify the enormous evil that exists in this jail'. Hunt finishes his advice with, 'should I be the humble means of causing such an enquiry to be instituted to all jails in your majesty's dominions, I shall think nothing of the injustice of TWO YEARS AND SIX MONTHS imprisonment in this Bastille for having attended a peaceable and legal meeting at Manchester, for I shall have laid in a stock of pleasurable reflections for the remainder of my days, sufficient, I hope to compensate for the persecutions I have endured'. Hunt follows this with some advice to the judge Mr Baron Graham of the western circuit on how to organise the jail and the magistrates in future.

The preliminaries over, Hunt and Shillibeer record the evidence of the various witnesses called before the Commission. Hunt opened his case against Bridle on 26 May and didn't finish until 13 June calling over 70 witnesses. What follows is a summary of the main evidence and the most relevant testimony avoiding repetition when several witnesses give the same accounts. Hunt was determined to paint Bridle us the most brutal fiend that had ever lived and Bridle was determined to show himself as an enlightened and humane guardian of the poor souls in his charge. The old saying that 'there are two sides to every story – and then there is the truth' could have been written for this case. Hunt had improved upon the list of charges since the magistrates hearing, increasing the number from 13 to 21. The complaints that Hunt brought before the Commission were,

1. Gross neglect of duty, and disregard of the orders of the magistrates.
2. Drunkenness within and without the jail.
3. Gambling within the jail with some of the prisoners for pounds and inflicting torture upon others for playing for pence.
4. Swearing horrid oaths within and without the jail.
5. Absenting himself from divine service and selecting a wicked and abandoned debtor as his clerk, who never attend divine service.
6. Opening the jail doors during the elections and at other times, and admitting the populous with flags, colours and bands of music, dancing himself, in the presence of the prisoners, with the women of the town, giving them liquor and encouraging drunkenness, debauchery and riot within the walls of the jail.
7. Cruelty and injustice to the prisoners male and female; and amongst other things during sickness and fevers, meat, wine and other necessities allowed by and charged to the county, and appropriating them to the use of himself his family and visitors.
8. Permitting at other times such necessities, charged to the county purchased for sick prisoners, to pass through the hands of his brother and sister-in-law, the task master and mistress, who had a large family of children

that he knew were deprived of the common necessities of life in consequence of his having stopped back and withheld half their salary which the county had allowed them and applied it without their consent to pay off a real or pretended claim of his own.

9. For embezzling the property of the county, candles, soap, straw, meat, wine, groceries etc. intended for the sick.

10. For inflicting torture upon prisoners male, female and infants, unknown to the magistrates.

11. For compelling boys and men, for misdemeanours, to associate with, to work and even sleep with felons, convicts, housebreakers, coiners, and even making boys sleep with a man convicted of bestiality.

12. For compelling women of all classes of crimes, as well as debtors to mingle together in the same ward, and sleep together in the same cells.

13. For licentious conduct towards female convicts, to having become with child in his own house, being himself the father of one of the bastards and strongly suspected of being also the father of the other; which bastards have been kept at the county's expense, and the county deprived of the labour of their mothers.

14. For placing debtors in solitary confinement, and depriving them from seeing their wives in private without an order from the magistrates.

15. For conniving at the prisoners being imposed upon by the shop people, and imposing arbitrary and partial rules, without their being sanctioned by the magistrates or the judges of the Assize.

16. For making interlineations, erasers and false entries in a book called the occurrence book of the jail in order to deceive, impose upon, and hoodwink the magistrates, so that he might be better and abled to carry on his infamous and cruel practices in the jail without detection.

17. For breaking open the letters of the prisoners contrary to law and in direct violation of the circular letter from Lord Sidmouth entered in the magistrates journal.

18. For compelling the prisoners to wear one pair of stockings for many months together without any change or washing, also their linen for many weeks together without washing, thus endangering the health and safety of the whole establishment by pestilence and fever.

19. For employing some of the prisoners to work at hard labour on the sabbath day and continuing to do so the whole of chapel hours, himself and his clerk setting the example of a total disregard of all religious duties, while he caused other prisoners to be locked up in solitary confinement for not attending chapel.

20. Illegally and inhumanly placing prisoners in heavy irons before trial, and causing them to take their trials so manacled and shackled and constantly executing criminals in irons.

21. For concealing from some of the magistrates that the water of the jail was bad and unwholesome and that the prisoners were suffering great bodily pain therefrom and conniving with other magistrates and the firm of perpetual Under-Sheriffs, Messrs. Broderip & Co to debar the prisoners particularly the debtors from receiving milk, water, beer and other necessities in reasonable quantities at reasonable hours of the day time, and, in fact of being instrumental to all those atrocities enumerative in a publication called, *A Peep into Ilchester Gaol.*

Mr White, Bridle's Solicitor from Yeovil

Bridle claimed that he had not seen a copy of Hunt's *Peep* which is rather hard to believe as it had been widely distributed since April, and so a copy was sent for. Possibly underestimating the seriousness of the situation, he was not represented, and a short adjournment was agreed for him to summon his solicitor, Mr White of Yeovil, with Charles Williams as his barrister, Hunt then proceeded to call his witnesses.

Sarah Hewitt married to a William Hewitt and a prisoner for four years having been convicted of grand larceny [stealing wearing apparel; discharged 30 April 1822 with a free pardon] and sentenced to seven years transportation. She gave evidence that she had given birth after having been in the jail for two years and while she was a servant in Bridle's house. She admitted that in a recent statement before the magistrates she had claimed that William Bridle was the father but now denied this and stated that his brother George, a turnkey at the prison, was the father. [The occurrences book entry for 26 March 1819 reads, 'S Hewitt delivered of the female child at 2 am']

Richard Pike turnkey at the front lodge for three years and Bridle's righthand man [described by Hunt as an 'unwilling witness'].Pike agreed that there was a rule which stated that, 'No person whatever but the prisoners committed to the jail, be permitted to lodge therein except the governor, his officers and their wives and families', and that this rule was frequently broken. There are many rules which are neither written nor printed which make it very hard for prisoners to obey regulations of which they are unaware. Despite an order allowing debtors to be supplied with pitchers of fresh water from the river by their wives this activity was often blocked by Bridle.

Pike let the election band and dancers into the jail as well as people from the town during the middle of the day, they were there for about an hour. [presumably during the time of the general elections which had taken place on 17 June 1818 and again in March 1820].He gave evidence that a prisoner was employed to maintain Bridle's horse and that county straw was used, Bridle had always asked for it to be weighed and an account to be drawn up but he had never known the straw to be replaced; there was much surplus straw from the prisoners beds which may have been used. Various other petty infringements of the rules were agreed by the witness.

Pike gave evidence regarding a prisoner named Thomas Gardiner [many press reports and transcripts have his name spelt as Gardner but as all legal documents have Gardiner that is the spelling used here] serving 18 months commuted from a death sentence for stealing.[With his brother James and two others he broke into a watchmaker's shop in Bath and stole 50 silver and six gilt watches.] He was ordered to be placed in solitary confinement having had his head shaved and a blister [mustard plaster], put on it, this he managed to rub off and Bridle ordered it to be replaced. Gardiner was also confined in a straight waistcoat, [jacket], he had claimed that he was too ill to work. Pike claimed not know if the blister was for medical or punishment reasons but it was applied about a week after the prisoner had claimed to be ill. He was in solitary confinement for about a month before being released and had been convicted of many offences whilst inside, his character was described as very bad, swearing heavy oaths and often in a deranged state.

Pike remembered a prisoner named Hillier having his wages suspended and being double ironed with his hands and feet chained together, his hands cuffed behind him, for gambling and striking a constable. The irons weighed about ten and a half pounds. Hunt asked Pike how long Hillier was ironed in that state to which the witness replied, 'About nine days and nights' [Pike was giving evidence on the second day of the Commission's investigation, 26 May and despite Hunt having published in his *Address* dated 11 April that Hillier was confined in that position for *four* and not nine days he allowed Pike's reply to stand without comment.] Hillier makes his mark on his petition and so presumably could not read.

There was another boy called Wheeler in a similar situation for a week or ten days. Bridle was not in the habit of visiting prisoners in solitary confinement. A boy named Holbrook was set to sleep with a man named Stillman convicted of bestiality with a mare for five or six nights due to the crowded state of the ward but neither he nor Bridle claimed to be aware of this until the *Peep* came out. When asked if he opened the prisoner's letters he replied that he opened all of the letters apart from those of the debtors, 'and yours Mr Hunt'. [Hunt comments later that this was the point when Bridle's solicitor, White, offered Bridle's resignation if the proceedings were stopped. An offer which Hunt declined]

Thomas Gardiner prisoner. 'A good looking lad of about 18 years and about 5' 8" who had been incarcerated for about for 14 months and been punished for various offences whilst he was there including a striking a fellow prisoner and impertinence. He was accused of stealing a purse from a fellow prisoner's pocket, which he denied but his wages were stopped and soon after he said that he was feeling very ill and could not work. He claimed that Bridle said to him, 'I can see the fever is quite strong upon you, I shall be your doctor, I shall find you a hospital by yourself for fear that you should infect other men'. The prison doctor declared him perfectly fit and he was taken to a solitary cell, had his head shaved, a blister applied to it and was placed in a straitjacket, 'the pain which I felt was like needles pins and knives running into my head'. 'I was obliged to eat my bread by kneeling down and pushing it with my head against the bedstead and gnaw it, I drank water like a beast'. 'They would not let me see the magistrates'. 'I begged Bridle to forgive me but he would not and ordered that another blister be applied'. As a demonstration to the Commissioners, the witness was placed in a straight waistcoat, he fell down on the floor, rolled about and picked up his cap to show how he had taken off the blister'. Even Bridle appeared to be affected as the witness gave evidence.

[According to Hunt Bridle later admitted instigating this treatment to the Commissioners and said that, 'he had suffered more in his mind ever since, than Gardiner had suffered in his body at the time.']

Thomas Davis turnkey, [as Pike, described by Hunt as an 'unwilling witness'] gave evidence that he saw Bridle dancing with young women of the town when the band were allowed in at the general election dinner for an hour or so and he was employed to hand out the cider. [Bridle was a keen supporter of the 'yellow' or Whig party].Davis stated that men had been double ironed for refusing to work due to the lack of adequate clothing in very cold weather, some had stockings without feet. He had known boys to be placed in the stocks from eight until one or two without any means of resting themselves. Mr Hobbs was the taskmaster in charge and the boys feared the punishment very much. There is no hospital nor one being built that witness knew of. Shop people are allowed in every morning except Sundays for three quarters of an hour bringing goods into the prison ready weighed, they were not weighed in the prison but some prisoners have their own scales. All men and boys are placed together – all classes of crime.

When Mr Kinnear first came here he lived and boarded with Bridle and after Mr Hunt came here he was sent to lodge in the misdemeanour ward to board with Hunt.

John Wheeler prisoner. 13 year old orphan, 'a handsome open-countenanced lad'. A weaver convicted of stealing a pair of stockings as he passed by a shop valued at about 18d at the age of 11 who was sentenced to two years hard labour and gave evidence to say that his hands were cuffed behind him for long periods for being saucy which resulted in him being unable to raise his hands to his head and caused violent pains in his shoulders. He had passed his time being educated by the most cunning of professional criminals. Whilst in custody he was accused of stealing onions and punished by eight days and nights solitary confinement and placed in the stocks.

John Southward prisoner. Described the milk brought in as very bad but when the men refused to drink it they were deprived of milk altogether. He said that his jacket had been washed only once in 18 months and that he had worn a pair of stockings for a similar time.

James Hillier prisoner of about 23 years of age. Gave evidence as to his petition to the Commons. Admits having struck a fellow prisoner which resulted in him being double ironed and put into solitary confinement for nine days and nights, his wrists were very inflamed and swollen. [Hunt was aware that this was not true see above, the period was four and not nine days.] Hillier had his hands and feet chained together which he re-enacted for the benefit of the court. He had appeared before magistrates, Dr Colston, Rev Thring and his son who allowed the punishment to continue. Hillier agreed that his petition to the Commons was taken down by Hunt and read over to him. [later sentenced to death for housebreaking *The Beacon* May 1822]

John Tresur & **Esau Whitcombe** prisoners 'We are Mr Hunt's servants, he has free access to us'. Reference is made in the magistrates journal to Mr Hunt's scullery where they cook his meals. Hunt had a bell to summon them to his room from theirs. They gave evidence that prisoners have been kept for up to four months with only one pair of stockings and double ironed when they complained that it was too cold to work. The men became a very filthy and stinking. The butter and bacon sold by the shop people was bad, sometimes full of maggots.

Samuel Hobbs [Brother to Mathew Hobbs below] First employed as a messenger then a servant in Bridle's house from 29 June 1818 to 9 March 1819. He looked after Bridle's horse and gave evidence as to articles paid for by the county being used by Bridle, straw, soap, candles, wine, meat etc. He fell out with Bridle over money when he was not paid his expenses of 7/6d per day for travelling to the assizes and the sessions. Eventually he was owed £5 and discharged without notice, the money was only paid after he sent a threatening note. Hobbs was paid £20 per year to be a servant in the house plus expenses. Mr Bridle's friends regularly stayed at the house, he would often not rise until 10 or 11 o'clock. Bridle was much in the habit of swearing in the jail. Straw for the stable and pigs was taken from the county stock and never replaced. Hobbs kept copies of some of the orders as he thought it a great injustice. Vinegar intended for the sick was used for pickling walnuts, tea and coffee for the sick was also used in the parlour. He remembers Bridle borrowing 10cwt of coal from the county stock but does not know of it being repaid.

Jane Hobbs matron, Matthew Hobbs, her husband, was the task master. [Jane Hobbs was formally Jane Webber and sister to Bridle's wife.] 'We left together about three months ago after 4 ¾ years. Sarah Lawrence was a servant in the house and was delivered of a child after more than a year in the jail and was dismissed. Sarah Hewitt was the next house servant, she also had a child delivered in the jail. 'Was there any attempt by the magistrates to ascertain the father or fathers of the children? There was not'. Both children were kept at the county's expense. Hobbs did not know if they had been baptised but had heard that a former prisoner, Thomas Palmer was the father of Sarah Lawrence's child he was at work in the house putting up bedsteads. 'Mrs Bridle wanted to get Hewitt out of the house… I was to detain her and put her in the jail dress, but she refused saying that she knew it was his [Bridle's] wish she should never wear it again. My husband put her back onto the ward'.

'You and Hobbs were dismissed from the jail by the magistrates?' Yes. One of the magistrates told me… we were dismissed through Mr Bridle making a complaint against us'. He said he was not the means of doing it, he had not made any complaints to the magistrates. I told Bridle that I considered him to be the greatest enemy I ever had as he was the means of getting me and my children thrown out onto the street'. What do you now understand you were turned out for? ' Me for having allowed Mrs Badcocks clothes to be washed in the laundry… she stayed three or four months at a time in the house, and both of us for not informing Mr Bridle or the magistrates of Mrs Bridle having had the company at the jail in Bridle's absence'. Have you ever known of drunken parties in the house? Yes when Bridle was at home'. 'Did you not understand that part of the charges against your husband was for getting drunk in the jail? 'Yes I know of no other charge'. 'Have you known Bridle, from negligence, keep prisoners in jail after their time expired?' Yes.

[According to a petition by Jane Hobbs dated October 1821 the pair were induced by Bridle to leave their farm at Lymington and work at the jail at a joint salary of £130 of which Bridle took £50 to cover their debt which did not leave enough to support themselves and their eight children. Matthew also had debts in the town. Bridle got them both dismissed and Matthew went to seek work in London but was imprisoned for debt. In July 1821 the family applied to his Masonic Lodge for relief as Mathew was in jail and his wife and children were in great distress, 13/6 was collected and sent to them. Jane Hobbs sent in a petition which was successful and they were awarded £10 by chairman of the quarter sessions William Dickinson who added that he, 'cannot concur with the correctness of some of the particulars'. The Lodge gave a further £2 to Mrs Hobbs in 1823 as the family was still in 'great distress.'

Jeremiah Hodges carpenter, serving two years and five months, made a sofa and tables for Bridle out of county wood, beech and sycamore worth about £6-£7 including labour. Hodges had done a great deal of painting about the house for which he was paid 2/- per week. When he arrived at Ilchester he could not drink the water at all but never complained to the magistrates as the officers said they would make it known to Mr Bridle and he was afraid that he would be punished.

Elisabeth Cox niece to Mrs Hobbs. A dance party two or three years ago included Maria Hobbs, Sarah Hewitt, Miss Jane Culliford who afterwards married to George Bridle, and Mr Bridle himself.

John Chapman former turnkey. Gave information on the prison before Bridle and evidence of Bridle beating prisoners. Bridle's father-in-law, Mr Webber's clothes were washed in the prison laundry, he occupied the principal farm near the town at the time. Bridle kept late hours, playing cards and gambling with the prisoners till early in the morning and was in the habit of cursing and swearing. County timber was used to make his furniture. Chapman claimed to have seen Bridle drunk, and beat a man with a horse whip until the blood ran over the stones.

Mary Cure [sometimes spelt Cuer] former prisoner. Imprisoned with a three month old child. She was fighting with another woman in the gaol a little before Christmas and the weather was very cold with snow on the ground. She was locked up from Thursday until Sunday, and claimed that she was not allowed a fire until Saturday about 11.00 o'clock and had nothing to eat or drink but bread and water which she had to drink out of a bucket .'The baby and I suffered very much from the cold. 'You were placed here for having a child?' Yes, it died about seven months afterwards. I was in for stealing turnips before that and fined 10/-. Mr Bridle paid a shilling towards the fine to get me released, he was not cruel to me, I don't know if he knew I didn't have a fire. You walked past the water pump could you not of had water if you wanted it? Yes, I suppose I could. I passed the pump twice a day with Mr Treganzer'.

Parmenas Mathews prisoner, a weaver who had been sentenced, 'about some pigs'. He had had his hands bolted behind him for two nights but the handcuffs were not large enough which made his hands swell very much and he was in so much pain that he could not sleep. He and others found the tobacco short of weight.

Charles Hill a debtor and previous petitioner, who has been imprisoned for debt for 15 years told the enquiry that the water was very bad when the river rises and he had been ill with the gravel [kidney stones] and costiveness [constipation]. The water has been complained about for the last 15 years and the bread was of very poor quality being made from damaged corn but he didn't complain in case it was taken away altogether. The debtors are prevented from receiving a pint of small beer as a gift without the doctor's orders and he lives at Somerton five miles away. The bedrooms go two months or more without being washed. The debtors are prevented from seeing their wives in private, there are there 12 or 13 in his ward and in consequence men have connection with their wives in the privy. The high walls were erected about seven or eight years ago and before that time the jail had never been visited with fevers. Hill was in the habit of writing for prisoners and assisting them. He complained that the constables were appointed by the jailer from amongst themselves, and they are compelled to pay him 2d a week each for keeping the rooms clean and making the fire. Constables are prisoners charged with keeping the place clean and seeing that the men are orderly.

Edward Sheppard a debtor who once kept the stamp office at Wells now clerk to Bridle who he claimed swears very much and is a notorious liar who hardly ever attends chapel. During 16 hours out of 24 we have no access to the 'necessary'.[privy] 15 have been known to sleep in one room without access and in cases of complaints or illness have no means of easing themselves but in the presence of each other, It stank enough to knock any person backwards and take their breath away after coming from the open air'.

'Sir John Acland was chairman at the sessions and attended the jail frequently. I had made many complaints to the magistrates but have had no redress. I sent a petition to the House of Commons. Has Mr Bridle ever assisted you in preparing your accounts for your discharge? Yes, I understand he is paid to do it. I applied for discharge during the King's Jubilee but it was denied. Have you ever remembered the poor box to have been opened or any money divided amongst the poor debtors? I do not remember the box ever having been opened except the other day since this investigation has taken place.

James Bryar surgeon at Ilchester for 15 years at a salary of 100gns per year visited the jail at least once a week. In his evidence he claimed that Bridle came to the surgery and said that a man was very outrageous and seemed to be disordered in his head but didn't recollect Bridle saying that the man was very ill, just that his head was disordered, but he did not go and see what the complaint was himself. Bridle asked for the blister Carter the constable applied it. Bryer claimed not to know what Carter was convicted of as he never asked about the character of those sent to assist him. He was told later that the blister had very good effect on the man's behaviour. Bryer did not provide the blister as a punishment but to cure his outrageous behaviour and knew nothing of the straight waistcoat until after the prisoner had been released.

The doctor gave evidence that there was no hospital as such, and that they used the boy's ward but it was certainly not a fit place for an ill person to be sent. Ground for a hospital had been purchased over a year ago but no work had been done. Kinnear's ward was once the men's infirmary and Hunt's ward was the women's.

Hunt asked Bryer about deaths in custody, which he sought to prove were due to inadequate care and resources including that of Edmund Treble for whom Bryar had prescribed meat and beer as he complained of general weakness. 'I said he needed nourishment more than medicine, he agreed and I was surprised to find him dead on my next visit, I cannot say what he died of, there are no marks on his body and I assume he died a natural death. Hunt, 'I mean to prove that this man died of want'. Dr Bryar replied that he found very frequently that a cook was required more than a doctor.

The condition of the water was complained about a very frequently, the men claiming that it gives them the gravel, and that it had a generally brackish taste. Overall, he did not think that the prison was unhealthy and he described Hunt's ward as very good with a yard open to the sky.

James Marsh prisoner, shoemaker who had worked for Bridle repairing his boots but was not paid until the Commissioners came. Some of the materials came from county stock. He had a boy of 13 and three others working and sleeping with him. When not working the boy is in the yard with the experienced convicts.

Edward Coles Clerk of the Peace since 1810 who kept the bills of the county after they had been passed by the magistrates. Coles gave details of materials supplied by the county despite claimed shortages within the jail. i.e. candles and soap but the Commission was of the opinion that this was a matter for the magistrates and that line of questioning was discontinued.

Henry Child ex debtor. There were about 20 debtors in the lower ward denied access to the garden and any sunshine. The debtors had nowhere to take their wives in private other than the general room which was crammed or the conversation room which was just as bad, there were sometimes between 60 and 70 people. They were prohibited until about a week before the Commission commenced from seeing their wives in the bedrooms. Child stated that George Treble died through lack of proper nourishment and that he wanted to let the magistrates know that this was an improper place for a sick man. He told George Bridle who said that he would let the magistrates know that I wished to see them but he did not.

John Chamberlain ex-prisoner and constable, formerly a leather scraper. A prisoner named Ford was a 'foolish' man, not in his right senses, he put his shoes on very slowly one day which provoked Treganzer the turnkey, a stout, strong, powerful man. Ford was not violent but he was shoved into his cell banging his head against the wall and found dead at breakfast time. The coroner's inquest was held in Bridle's house that afternoon and he was buried the same day. Chamberlain did not mention Treganzer striking Ford as he still had about 12 more months to serve. He claimed that Bridle was never cruel to him and never saw him cruel to anyone without some fault.

William Wells ex-prisoner and shoemaker. As Wells was not set to hard labour he could work for pay if he wanted to. The mechanics were entitled to 6/- a week but he was told that some will be withheld until he left. Mr Acland came around with the other magistrates and told Bridle that this would not do, 'whatever this man earns he shall receive half of it a week so that he may know what he has coming to him as well as you when he goes out'. 'When my time was up I received £5, out of that I paid 30/- for shoes which I wore out whilst there. I was at work about 100 weeks and never lost a day'.' I worked as foreman and learned four apprentices and had nine hands under me at once'. Wells told Mr Bridle that he thought there was a mistake about the money, 'he asked how much I have received I told him £5 he said he thought there must be a very great mistake if I had received as much as that'. Bridle said he would go to his books and see if I was owed more then wrote to me and told me I was not. In fact, I was due £17'

Dr Kinglake, Wm Shorland and **John Robertson** were asked to report on the health of the jail for the Commissioners and having gone through the various buildings they made the same comment on each one which was that the rooms were too small for their allotted purpose, given the number of inmates, and that there was a chronic lack of ventilation. The problem would seem to be a classic case of overcrowding. There was great concern about the contamination of the water supply by the drains particularly when the river floods which they described as an insufferable evil which might be removed by sinking fresh water wells in part of the jail securely distant from any drain and contained within lead pipes another problem was the lack of a suitable building as an infirmary for the sick.

John Hutfield Sherry Attorney, former crown debtor who spent two years and six months in the jail. Sherry complained that the water smelled abominably and that they were unable to see their wives except in the presence of other prisoners; indecency frequently occurred and they had to bribe the constable to go upstairs. He discussed this with Bridle pointing out that from the battlements the debtors could be seen with their wives in a very indecent position. Bridle seemed to find this very amusing. He had known 16 or 17 people to sleep in a bedroom at one time. The debtors take a vote to decide which alehouse to get a beer from. Sherry favoured obtaining it from an inn owned by the Blue party [Tories] but Bridle was of the Yellow [Whigs] party which caused a great dispute during election time, 'some yellow fellows from the town came up and abused me through the bars'.

James Johnson. Shared a bed with James Stillman for five weeks. 'Did you know his crime? Yes, bestiality. Did he ever behave indecently to you? Yes, frequently. Nobody sleeps with him now. Did you complain? No I thought it was useless and thought he was foolish or else he would not have come here for such as crime as that. How old are you? 18'.

Nicholas Collard, shoemaker and former debtor, who had been confined in the jail for 60 weeks complained about the quality of the water and his wife not being allowed to bring a pitcher of better water up from the river or the town. He claimed that the bedrooms had not been washed from the Friday before Christmas up until the time the magistrates began their inspection the 19th of April last. When called to give evidence at the Taunton Assizes he paid the expenses on the road for eight days and should have received £3/11/- but Bridle only gave him a guinea. He had not known the poor box to be opened until the late investigation before the magistrates when the money was divided.

Charles Lindo. debtor. Gave evidence that debtors were not permitted to see their wives in the bedrooms, married men can see their wives only in the ward, necessary, or conversation room. It is understood that they have a connection together in the privy or in the kitchen which is a general room and very unfit for such purposes. A fellow inmate, Drake was exceedingly ill with a bowel complaint in a room where two others slept beside himself. In the night he had occasion to make use of the close stool four or five times. Two or three days afterwards Thomas West complained that he was taken ill in consequence of the stench. 'When I first came here the night stool had not been emptied for 14 days'.

Joseph Smith. a debtor who acted as a cook having been chosen by his fellow debtors, a position which was balloted for. He provides a dinner for 6d a head and is well supplied with meat but vegetables were very expensive. Whenever a prisoner is brought in Bridle's clerk calls on him for 4/6 coal money and if there is not enough they have to have a collection amongst themselves.

John Bussell debtor and constable. 'Did Bridle ever give you anything out of his own pocket?... He gave us a quart of beer a piece at Christmas, we understand it was his gift. Are you sure it was not bought with your own money taken from the poor debtors box? I know nothing of that'. I have never seen Bridle inspect the beds to see if they were clean.'

James West. Former jail messenger. West was a follower of Sir William Manners of the 'blue' or Tory party and was sacked by Bridle once this became apparent. Bridle, being a supporter of the 'yellows', replaced him with one of his own persuasion.

Rev Richard Whalley visiting magistrate for about eight years. Has never found the bread bad enough to be returned but there have been complaints from the prisoners that it has made them ill. The jail pays about 12/- per hundredweight taking the cheapest tender. Goods like shoes are made and sold in the jail the witness had bought some himself but knew nothing of credit for the sales being given to the county as he knew nothing of the acts of the jailer. He agreed that the jailer's salary was £500 per year.

John Newman visiting magistrate for eight to ten years. The magistrates tasted the water about a month ago but could find nothing offensive in the taste.

Hunt: Do you understand as a visiting magistrate, that I am still prohibited from seeing my female friends except in the conversation room? Yes, I do, I believe it was ordered by Dr Colston and the two Thrings and sanctioned by the sheriff in February and he has not counter ordered it'.

William Pitcher former prisoner and former attorney's clerk. Mr Broderip has been undersheriff for 25 years. The women prisoners were compelled to witness an execution in front of the jailer's house and some of them fainted but the debtors were not compelled to watch unless they chose to. Pitcher and a fellow prisoner, Edward Shepherd wrote to all the debtor's prisons in England, Scotland and Ireland at the instigation of Mr Evill a solicitor of Bath who at the time was a debtor here in order to ascertain their rules. They received a great many replies but none had rules as severe as the rules at Ilchester. Pitcher said that Bridle had never treated him badly.

John Wilcombe prisoner. Complained about his letters being opened, which is illegal according to Lord Sidmouth, a letter from Sidmouth explaining the rules was read out.

Aaron Moody visiting magistrate for 15-16 years re sale of prison goods. 'I see there is no item whatever, in the cashbook where the county has had credit given for goods sold'. Magistrates journal, …'Mr Hunt maybe allowed to have a bottle of wine every two days and three pints of table beer every day'. Wells Assizes 14 August 1820, 'in future no female visitor except the wives and children to be admitted into the private room'. Signed by 20 magistrates. Wm Mellior undersheriff [Mellior is sometimes spelt Melliar throughout].

Do you remember making sundry orders for alterations and improvements in my ward to add a porch to the doorway, was this this ever done? 'No. Mr Bridle said it would be a step ladder to get over the wall'. Two respectable bakers had examined the bread and agreed that it was adulterated possibly with potatoes.

William Barnard debtor had quarrelled with Francis Drake of Frome, he had ordered some cabbages, from a woman named Honor China, they fought and Barnard had a tooth knocked out, 'I threw the contents of my chamber pot over him, he deserved it'.

Robert Gibbs prisoner and mason who had been cleaning the drains out claimed that the surveyor had never been down there and knew nothing about them. He described the drains as nearly level with no fall, some parts upwards of two feet deep in filth, and some of the wells were situated within two feet of the drains.

Dr William Shorland aged 46 surgeon of Ilchester. I was close to Bridle for about two years. I attended his family and we were concerned in a business. I degraded myself by having an acquaintance with him, we have played cards and drank at the jail with Webber, Bridle's father-in-law and others possibly 15 to 16 people. What broke off the intercourse between you and Bridle? An atrocious and gross act of injustice towards me in a private transaction. This ruffian (Bridle) hired two men to break into my house and murder me and when they were apprehended he refused hand bolts to secure them and sent bail for them before the magistrates. He swears abominably. He takes his glass freely but is not what I should call a sot'.

Henry Warren prisoner and stonemason who was working outside the jail last Christmas. Describes the men's hands being very cold and they had to beat them together to keep them warm. Many men found it too cold to work and laid down their hammers. Warren was put in irons for asking Bridle if he could work inside '.[Later sentenced to transportation *The Beacon* May 1822]

John Robertson. surgeon. Have you ever seen the gambling game *gobbo* or *three card loo* played in Bridle's house when a prisoner was present? Yes, I have seen it so highly played as to withdraw from the table. Have you seen £5 on the table at one time? I have seen £5 at a time.

I recollect [Bridle], saying that a prisoner had had his head shaved and a blister put on it by way of punishment'. What was the nature of Mr Hunt's complaint? ... indigestion, and a violent determination of blood to the head, I have been obliged to pursue repeated bleedings to a large extent due partly from want of a free and pure atmosphere. I have found Mr Kinnear affected by the state of the atmosphere so much that if he had not used medicine very frequently he would have been subject to a serious indisposition.'

William Marshman prisoner. weaver. Sentenced to seven years transportation. Stated that Bridle had asked him whether he would rather be imprisoned, or transported giving him to understand that he would be released after three and a half years and told him several times in a threatening manner that he could send him off whenever he chose. Marshman learned his trade as a weaver in prison but was sent to help clear the drains because he had a long sentence and he supposed that they would have locked him up or sent him off if he had refused. He declared that he was afraid to do anything or say that his soul was own for fear of being transported. [Marshman was given a free pardon at the end of August but apparently sentenced to death for a later offence *The Beacon* May 1822]

John Trayt prisoner. Sentenced for attempted rape and was caught gambling, he was double ironed for seven weeks but never saw a magistrate.

Jane Hobbs wife of Mathew who kept the occurrence book entries on a piece of paper when Bridle was away. She stated that when Bridle came home he would look at them and when convenient send for her husband to enter it in the book; she claims to have seen many lines altered and pages with some of the occurrences struck out.

Elizabeth Wilkins prisoner for the past four years for having a stolen ring in her possession. Describe how eight or nine women had their hair cut off, and that one made such a fuss about it she was put on the horse (stocks). Sarah Hewitt told her that William Bridle was the father of her child and she talked about the child with him. 'I said the child was like him and he laughed and said that the child was not a disgrace to any father, he did not say anything which led me to believe that he was not the father'.

Charles Williams barrister of Stone Buildings, Lincoln's Inn, had known Bridle for 11 or 12 years and described his general character as that of an exemplary and efficient officer. Williams found the prison, so strikingly clean as to draw the attention of all present.

W. Bridle Gaoler of Ilchester.

Bridle by George Cruikshank 1821

He had been to visit Hunt who said firmly on one occasion, 'I don't regard my imprisonment not this, (snapping his fingers), but on speaking of the exclusion of his female friends, Mr Hunt felt greatly agitated and the tears run down his cheeks'.

Hunt 'I believe Sir, you are employed here professionally for Mr Bridle? I am; but I hope you do not think that would influence me in what I say', Hunt, 'Certainly not'.

Bridle's Defence 15 June 1821

[Once again it should be emphasised that this transcript is written and published by Hunt and Shillibeer and should not be thought off as an official or impartial account of the proceedings.]

B RIDLE'S SOLICITOR, MR White, read out a paper written by Bridle's barrister Charles Williams in which he admitted some of the material charges particularly that of applying the blister as a punishment to Gardiner's head and threw himself upon the indulgence of the court. According to Hunt's account in his *Investigations* the paper was an attack upon the conduct of the sheriff and magistrates for allowing him [Hunt] an opportunity to prove his charges by permitting him to have access to the prisoners for that purpose. Hunt continues that, 'some very ingenious insinuations as to the motives which induced Mr Hunt to prepare those charges against the jailer instead of the magistrates who, it was pretty clearly hinted were more culpable than even the jailer himself implying that some of them, must have approved of the torture that he was in the habit inflicting upon the prisoners as they never checked him for it. Hunt continued that the paper was anything but an answer to any of the charges…' Hunt was denied a copy of Bridle's document.

A brief introductory note at the beginning of the transcript Hunt, (or Shillibeer?) wrote,

> The whole of the questions put to the chairman by Mr White, were previously written out and arranged by Mr Williams who acted as Bridle's counsel, to select and arrange what evidence should be adduced in his defence; there being assembled in Ilchester a gang perhaps of the greatest scoundrels that ever were collected together, brought from all parts of the county as witnesses for the jailer, in whose custody they had been; they were placed in a public house. A regular guard was kept over them to prevent their speaking to anyone and they were regularly trained every day... However, Mr Williams very prudently packed off the greatest portion of this gang immediately he found out the sort of characters they were; and if he had remained in Ilchester he would not have suffered many of those who were afterwards called to have further disgraced a distressful cause by their prevaricating evidence.

In his book, *The Narrative*, Bridle tells how he received a copy of the *Peep* from one of his officers while he was at Taunton on duty and gave it immediately to the undersheriff together with a letter expressing a desire that investigations would take place to clear his name. When the proceedings began Bridle had no representation, relying on the magistrates to protect him. 'To my astonishment and grief however, I thought I discovered amazing partiality shown to my accuser, and I instantly imagined they feared implication on their own parts, and would try to avoid it, even coalesce with Hunt to procure my ruin'. The case proceeded.

Sir John Palmer Acland a magistrate for over 40 years and chairman from 1805-1820 Acland paid frequent visits to the jail during that period enquiring into every aspect. The jail sessions were held four times a year preceding each court quarter session. A fortnightly report was always made to the magistrates as to the admission or discharge of the prisoners and as a check on the regularity of conduct. 'I always inspected the clothing in wear, and that in store, and if anything were wanting immediately ordered a fresh supply'.

'Before Mr Bridle arrived, there was no prison labour after which a Reformation was set about, we began sinking wells and created personal cleanliness by establishing a laundry'. Bridle found it much more convenient to employ prisoners for various works than to contract out as he has been used to supervising his own men on the prison hulks. He introduced apprenticeships under a shoemaker and the manufacture of cloth, this was taken up enthusiastically with the hope of early remission or a pardon and in a short time they were able to do without contractors at all. Bridle also introduced the occurrence book for recording day to day events bringing the idea from the hulks. Bridle and Acland also instituted the shop system taking orders from the prison to the town and later inviting the shopkeepers to come to the jail with their goods.

During the typhus outbreak in 1817 Bridle fumigated the court and kept the sick prisoners from the others by taking them to a house at Taunton. Acland was not aware of the poor situation of the drains until yesterday when he went out and inspected them for himself.

Debtors, upon coming into the jail, are placed in the upper ward and if they have no means of maintaining themselves are removed to the lower ward to be maintained by labour or by the county allowance. It is illegal to put debtors to work. Women's hair was cut because it was filthy not for any offence, he had even cut it himself when Bridle had not done so. Goods are manufactured in the jail and then sold with the money going to the county. Acland declared that after knowing Bridle for 13 years he believed him to be an exceedingly honest man. He stated that he had resigned due to ill health in July 1820 and could not give an opinion on what has happened since that time.

John Palfryman surgeon confined as a debtor between 1816-18. Found Bridle to be very attentive to the sick and attended upon them himself when the surgeon wasn't there possibly resulting in less visits from the jail surgeon.

Alexander Gane former debtor until 1811 when he was employed as a turnkey at the jail until 1813 now keeper of the house of correction at Wilton. He could not remember any complaint from the magistrates about the jail as everything was kept regular and very clean. Clean stockings were given out by himself every week. He had seen prisoners in irons but had never seen neck irons used in his life. He had never seen Bridle intoxicated.

Dr Woodford

Dr James Woodford a physician residing at Castle Cary who had attended at the typhus outbreak in 1817. Initially about 12 people were infected, one person died then nearly 70 caught the disease of which two died. ... the average number of deaths in typhus fever is one in 15 or 20'. Typhus appeared in the town before the prison and every exertion was made by the governor at great personal risk. The outbreak continued for three or four months and strict attention was paid to ventilation and fumigation. There were 250 prisoners in the jail at the time. The sick prisoners were taken to a House of Recovery at Lymington two miles from here in wards carefully fumigated. Particular attention was paid by Dr Bryer, Bridle, myself and Mr Palfryman who was unremittingly active on the occasion.

John Palfryman re-sworn, supported Dr Woodford by administering to the sick, washing them with vinegar every morning and making tea, coffee etc. Food and drink were abundantly supplied to the sick. The prison was daily fumigated not only with acid of nitre but a quantity of pitch and sulphur in different parts of the prison. He stated that he would have expected about one in 12 to have died of the fever. The prisoners had their stockings and linen changed once a week when he was there and he had never heard any complaints of the debtors not being able to have their wives in private as their wives were brought into the ward the whole of the day.

Martin Webber father in law of Mr Bridle now living at Plaistow in Essex. His family live in Ilchester where he once occupied a large farm making about £1,400 a year. He had known Bridle for between 12 and 13 years, and described him as a man of sober habits. They played cards together with Mr Kinnear who had tried to introduce a higher stakes game but Bridle would not allow it as it was too much money.

Charles Collins ex prisoner employed as a painter, committed for riot and assault. He painted Bridle's gig, and was paid 10/-. Mrs Hobbs got him to paint his house while he was away, he obtained the paint from Yeovil, and made the varnish himself which was not charged to the county. He had never heard Bridle swear or seen him drunk. When he was sick with the 'painters colic', [internal pain caused by lead poisoning] for eight or ten days he was visited regularly every day and given any articles of nourishment that he asked for.

Edward Goodland former debtor, cabinet maker and auctioneer. Undertook all the carpentry work to the cells and arches and acted as foreman. Bridle said that as it was Christmas Day he would pay for a quart of beer for each man out of some charity money. The jail was very clean and the linen was changed regularly. There was a very neat choir of singers in the jail; 'I was the proprietor of them, I taught them; I petitioned Mr Acland for music'. It was all sacred music'. Hillier was a cooper and was asked to make some buckets and tubs out of staves under Goodland's direction but Bridle said not to take any staves that were useful.

Richard Pople Cames one of the county coroners, since 1817 who had attended 14 inquests at the jail. Having received notification, Cames would send back by the messenger, a summons in order that a jury might be assembled before he arrived. The witnesses are then sworn and depositions taken before the jury viewed the body. If they have no questions of Dr Bryar he is released. Sometimes Mr Bridle will be in attendance. The jury consists of six debtors and six of the parish of Ilchester. 'In asking them to reach their verdict the words I generally use are,

> Gentlemen of the jury. You have all seen the body and you have all heard the evidence, there does not appear to be anything very difficult in this business, and I conceive you will find no difficulty in being able to return a verdict.

In the case of Ford the witness said that there was nothing very usual about a man being buried on the same day especially if jail fever was about. Cames was not particularly aware of him being double ironed when he died and found nothing suspicious about his death, the 'outrageous conduct of the man was fully explained by the witnesses'. Dr Bryar's opinion was that death had been occasioned by a rupture on the brain or near the heart. 'Is it not usual to have an operation performed to ascertain which of the two causes, whether from the head or the heart? I did not think it necessary to have an operation performed, I was in my own mind satisfied and the jury perfectly so,'

In the case of Treble were there any of the jury who insinuated that the man had not had sufficient nourishment? There was not. The depositions of the witnesses were unsigned.

[In a clever move, Hunt served Cames with the following notice to undermine his credibility,]

> Mr Cames, if you should be called upon to take an inquest upon my body while I am in this prison, I hereby request you will summon Mr Shorland of Ilchester and Mr Davis of Andover to open my body. H Hunt 19 June 1821

Lucy Smart former prisoner. Sentenced to transportation but has been in the prison for 2½ years working in the laundry. Female prisoners were given fresh linen every Sunday, stockings were washed every week in large quantities as were the mens. She washed things for the Bridles and their visitors and did some sewing. Who got you off from your sentence? 'Mr Bridle and Sir J Acland. Was Sarah Hewitt in the house at the time? Yes. Did you nurse Sarah Lawrence? Yes, How long was she in the house? About a twelvemonth and she was turned away because she was big with child and Sarah Hewitt took her place. Witness had helped out at the Lymington House as a nurse during the epidemic and was paid by the county. Have you been paid anything for your journey here? No sir.'

Edmund Barber ex-felon. claimed that he was treated very well. Did you hear any complaint of Mr Bridle while you are here? Never'. Stockings and linen were changed on Sunday every week which Barber delivered himself enabling him to see that other wards were kept very clean. He had helped to fumigate the jail with pitch and brimstone during the fever, washing every prisoner that came in with warm water and bay salt. The prisoners were allowed by order of the magistrates to smoke tobacco and walk outside. No prisoners were ironed or put in solitary confinement without an order from the magistrates, there were no unlawful irons. The bread was very good and everything was wholesome, we had clean straw and clean bed-tick twice a week.

Edmund Broderip undersheriff. Mr William Mellior of Wells is my partner, Sir Charles Bampfylde appointed him his undersheriff upon taking office on 2nd June 1820 with Joseph Lovell, Edmund Broderip senior and Edmund Broderip junior. Broderip stated that he and his partner had been in the office of undersheriff since 1792, a total of 29 years.

I have known Bridle to be an excellent officer with one exception. Two men named Culliford were confined for some violence in Ilchester. They were removed from the time ward [lodgings for those sentenced to fixed terms] to the upper debtor's ward as a consequence of them also being charged in two civil actions, I was astonished and had them both put back on the time ward.

'There was an order made by the magistrates which states that no females but the wives and daughters of Mr Hunt and Mr Kinnear be admitted to see them, were you present when the order was made? I was. Was the high sheriff Sir Charles Bampfylde present? He was not. Did you consent to the order? I did. Mr Mellior was acting as undersheriff in the court [Wells Assizes] I believe he signed it. Mr Bridle came to me to find out exactly what the order meant and I referred him to the magistrates.

'What is your opinion of the state of the jail and the prisoners? It has always appeared to me that the jail was kept very clean and in good order, and with regard to the prisoners, I never saw or heard anything to the contrary before the magistrates hearing.'

John Poole felon and constable for six months. Gave evidence that Bridle used to ask convicts if they had any complaints sometimes twice a day. He would visit the ward and to give extra coals in the winter or extra blankets, he would come around with the shop wishing every man to buy articles at the best advantage, he would examine the goods to see if they were any good and see that they had good weight; the shop comes between seven and eight in the morning. 'At the assizes and sessions, I have heard the prisoners… wish to return with Mr Bridle, they would sooner come back here then go to any other prison'.

Witness knew Gardiner to be a very bad character and gave him his meals, he was allowed out of his cell every morning between 6 and 7 o'clock for about an hour or more he was always swearing at everyone. Poole put him in the straitjacket and helped with the blister, he was very wicked in a cursing, swearing way. I don't know what the blisters were put on for, he had chamber pots in the cell but he kept breaking them. Poole put the straitjacket on him with help from Mr Pike. Do you think the blister did him any good? I don't know whether it made him afraid, but he was better afterwards than before. I let him out to ease himself, I had a chamber pot very handy in the cell. Hillier was not much better, threatening to set the place on fire.

The men got clean shirts and stockings every Sunday morning. I have heard the men speak in praise of Mr Bridle many times, I told him often that he was too good. I never heard him swear an oath or give the prisoners an angry word, he gave them every indulgence in his power in order to make them comfortable. He attended chapel regularly and I never saw him drunk. Bridle assisted in the execution of Hibbard attending upon him until 2 o'clock in the morning and shook hands with him, he felt very sorry for the man and I did not hear him say 'Damn the man, I am ashamed of him'. Hibbard was aged about 50 with one leg Mr Bridle helped support him with cushions at his execution as he found it difficult to stand.[Church records reveal that Charles *Hibbert* aged 59 of Walcot, Bath was executed for forgery on 8 September 1819 he came from a good family, was the author of a book entitled *A View of Bath*. By a strange coincidence Hibbert had been a follower of Hunt and was involved with him during the meeting at Bath in January 1817].

A little later the following exchange took place,

Poole: I was here before for 12 months before the last time
Hunt; What was that for?
Poole; For knocking down a couple of ducks.
Hunt: Did you do anything else?
Mr Phelps: Mr Hunt, this witness says he knocked down a couple of ducks.
Mr Hunt; What was you sent here for the first time?
Poole For knocking down a couple of ducks.
Hunt: What were you tried for?
Poole: For knocking down a couple of ducks.

Richard Blisset former prisoner. Employed as a labourer carrying stones for the new building. Were you at constant attendance at Lymington? Yes, I was sent there on trust to see that the prisoners did not get off for the place was not safe. The prisoners had everything that was necessary that the doctors ordered described the prison as very clean and says Bridle attended Lymington every day when he was at home. I never knew Bridle give a prisoner an angry word'.

William Hodder a prisoner sentenced for rioting two years ago and employed to wash the prisoners in bay salt and warm water. 'I went to Lymington to look after the sick prisoners and made up anything they wanted according to the doctor's orders'. What was the soup made of? Sometimes leg of mutton sometimes veal and beef, oatmeal to thicken it and skimmed milk'. I never heard any complaints all the time I was there.' Bridle was there most evenings unless he was at the assizes or sessions. What was done with a straw when the beds were emptied? I raked out the long straw and put it into the stable because it did blow all about. Was the straw sufficient for Mr Bridle's use? He never had any other straw because we had plenty of that.

James Morse weaver from Frome. discharged 27 March 1820. Did you carry on your trade in jail and teach others? Yes. 'Bridle spoke like a father to us'. I was sentenced to transportation for seven years and served my time in Portsmouth Harbour. Were you sent for to come here? No, I came here on my own generosity. Then you came all the way from Frome to give Bridle and the jail a character? Yes, I did I would have come if it had been 100 miles.

Sir George Gibbs MD read out his report.

> The jail stands on the northern side of the river in about one acre of ground with a commanding view over adjacent flat country. Epidemics are not common in the immediate neighbourhood, unless, as in typhus fever, they happen to be imported. We have examined the water chemically which shows that there is no noxious ingredient except in the old time ward were, there are ten wells. A deep well sunk below the shale was contaminated but this has been stopped up, other wells lie within the compass and range of several sewers of the jail due to a greater porosity and a gravelly soil. The jail is built of blue lias the principal stone found in this part of the country which at certain times of the year must appear damp. We examined the walls during the prevalence of an easterly wind and they appear to be dry and wholesome. The roof has no gutters and water is driven by the wind against the wall.
>
> There follows a long survey and scientific report on the sizes of the various wards, water quality, analysis of deaths etc. One cell in the refractory ward measuring 10' x 7' 5" is used as a kitchen by Mr Hunt. The female infirmary is also occupied and Mr Hunt as is a yard measuring 29' 2" x 27' 3". At certain times of the day Mr Hunt is allowed to walk in the factory yard. Upon a general view of the state of the prison I was much struck with the cleanliness and wholesome appearance of the several wards, rooms, and cells and of the prisoners confined therein. There seems to be a deficiency by want of a proper infirmary which I am given to understand is about to be erected on the ground purchased for the purpose.
>
> George Gibbs 22 June 1821.

As an aside Hunt tacks on a little report of his own and comments,

In spite of prejudice and in spite of his employers, Sir George Gibbs is much too honourable a man to disguise or conceal this fact, that the back part of the prison where I am placed, is the worst and most unwholesome part of the jail… the convicts and felons are better off. Their health and comfort are promoted while mine are neglected and destroyed by being placed in a dungeon at the back of the prison where the rays of the sun never enter the yard for four months in the year; which yard is surrounded by walls 20 feet high so as nearly to exclude both light and air.

John Westcott debtor. Davis was fellow debtor who died from a stroke. Dr Robertson attended him and said that, 'he must take about a pound of blood from the mad the brain of him'. Davis was given some clysters [enema] Court: 'Had Davis ever been crazy? Yes, he had'.

John Hayes debtor' Did you look into Treble's cupboard when he died? Yes, there was a great fig pudding and bread and cheese and tea and sugar and he had meat in the meat house'. He was an old man and feeble.

Anstice surveyor

Robert Anstice & George Allen Underwood. surveyors. Took their orders from Sir George Gibbs and agreed that they have not measured the fall on the drain and that they had in fact done very little at all. 'Did you not understand that the object of your labours was to ascertain the state of the drains and report it to the Commissioners?' No. Why are you not instructed to open the drains in different parts? I have no recollection of it but I did open the drain in six places. Evidence under cross-examination was largely evasive and of little value.

Rev. Wm Langdon magistrate, and one of the capital burgesses of the borough for more than 30 years. Attended a dinner at Bridle's house with singing and playing cards to celebrate the election (7 March 1820) of Whig candidates, Dr Lushington and Sir Isaac Coffin.

Rev. Mr Valentine. Appointed to the jail since April. 'Did Mr Bridle regularly attend chapel? He did. 'I cannot say anything to the prejudice of Mr Bridle'. Witness had lived in the area for about 20 years and has not heard anything to the disparagement of Mr Bridle's character.

William Hanning high sheriff and magistrate for 25 years. 'I have asked the prisoners if they had any complaint to make and generally speaking no complaint was ever made against Mr Bridle I have looked at his accounts again and again and never detected a fraud or suspected any, I never heard it intimated before this investigation'.

The magistrates journal for 15 December 1820 contains an order by Sir Charles Bampfylde saying that Mr Hunt is to be allowed to see his female friends. 'Since you have been sheriff have you made any order to rescind or counter that order? I have made no order to that effect. The magistrates journal of 13 Feb. 1821 ordered that the previous order of 16 October last be enforced by the governor and signed by Colston, Thring and Thring. I did not know of that order until several days after, I did not alter it because I thought the interior regulations of the jail vested in the magistrates, not in the sheriff. Hunt: 'When I applied to you as sheriff for redress have you not advised me to apply to the court of King's Bench? I have. Perhaps you did not know that my last application cost between £50 and £60? I never heard it till now'. 'Was it in your knowledge that stocks were kept in the jail? I never knew of the boy's stocks until the late investigation, the female stocks I have seen'. ' ...for the past 25 years have the judges ever sanctioned any rules for the government of this jail which have been made and laid before them by the magistrates of Somerset? I don't recollect any rules having being laid before the judges…'

Dr Woodford gave evidence on the state of the jail in general. In the last 13 years there have been 26 deaths in prison. In the last three years the average number of prisoners has been: 1818-408, 1819-519, 1820-478.

'Do you not think it injurious to health to be deprived of the sun three months of the year? I don't think any injury can arise to the health of a man from that'. 'In passing through the jail I was forcibly impressed with the clean and healthy appearance of the prisoners…' The regular and complete washing of the courts and floors once a week and the whitewashing of the whole house four or five times a year is a practice greatly to be commended and very conducive to the health of the prisoners.' There is nothing in the water which could have caused any of the diseases under which the prisoners now labour.'

John Treganzer principal turnkey, left in November 1819 after nearly three years and is now governor of the house of correction at Bedford. Prisoners had clean shirts every Sunday. Bridle was very kind to the prisoners. 'Do you recall the general election, Sir Thomas Lethbridge resigning and Bridle having a large party? I am sure he had not got a large party'.

Ford had been in the jail for three days and was thought to be strange or simple measuring the walls with string. He became violent and Hobbs had him handcuffed to the bed at night he was noisy, continually snapping and biting with his teeth he had dragged his bedstead from its proper place, 'I put additional irons on him. I went to his cell and could not open it… one of the men put in his hand and found it was Ford, when the door was opened, we went in, all three of us and found him dead'. Ford died on 31 October 1817.

At the close of the 1818 election the sheriff donated £10 and there was a large amount of meat and bread leftover at Mr Henry Tucson's house, the mill owner which he donated. Treganzer fetched it three different times in the tail trucks and Bridle said it needed some beer to go with it. The meat lasted 2-3 days there was 1,000lb I suppose. I always found the prison very clean I never heard any magistrate complain of it once. Were the prisoners instructed in reading and writing whilst you were there? Yes. Was it usual to execute prisoners with handcuffs and irons on? It was.'

John Wyatt ex prisoner who served 12 months until the end of May for an assault upon his wife. He was moved to Hunt's ward to wait on him from when he moved in until 6 February. Hunt had a straw mattress with a feather bed placed on top. Bridle used to visit three or four times a day to administer to his comfort when he first came, he repeatedly asked me to point out anything that would render comfort to Mr Hunt. He was accommodated with knives, forks, glasses, wash stands and other useful articles. 'Did you ever hear Hunt speak of Mr Bridle's conduct? Most highly so…till after the order made at Wells in August last, the order excluding Mr Hunt's family. He exclaimed then much against Bridle by saying he was the instigation of that order being put into execution. He declared he would stand at nothing to ruin Mr Bridle and that Mr Hobbs should be governor of this jail'. Hunt used to drink water from Bridle's pump it was clear and good and he never complained of any fault. Did Mr Hunt say anything to you on your release? Yes, he wished me to petition the House of Commons against Mr Bridle'.

Hunt in cross examination; Wyatt agreed that Hunt was charged 4/- per week for the bed and washstand 4/- for dinner 1/6 for breakfast and the same for tea. 'My family were charged 4/- a head when they dined with me'. The sum was later reduced.

I have seen you give presents to Bridle when you once had a brace of hares. You have heard me speak highly of Bridle have you? Yes.' 'You and I were very good friends at first but we quarrelled at last? I did not quarrel with you'. Mr Hunt told me I was a dirty son of a b....h and told me never to enter the place again... I had not access to your room for ten days. I believe Chidley your fellow servant and prisoner waited on me during that time? Yes, he did'. There was further conflict between Wyatt and Hunt after which he was replaced. Wyatt stated that, 'your conduct at times drove me to do that which I have never done before without any provocation, you have so abused me that I have shed hundreds of tears that I never did before'. 'Were you in your right mind when you attempted the life of your wife and children? I have no recollection of what happened.

Wyatt described how he was influenced by the moon and intended to wear green spectacles, given to him by a friend of Hunt's, a large wig and a green coat, mounting himself on a white bull before riding around the country. Wyatt was ordered to leave the room as the Commissioners believed he was in a deranged state of mind despite Bridle wishing to re-examine him. [In another of his asides Hunt claimed that, 'This poor maniac had been kept in Ilchester [town] for three weeks as a sort of superintendent or driller of the witnesses for the defence' and describes him as a spy placed by Bridle.]

During the debate on a petition to secure Hunt's release, brought to the House of Commons by Sir Francis Burdett in April 1822, William Dickinson MP made the following extraordinary statement,

> ... it appeared, that Wyatt had been his servant...for nine months; and the way in which his services were rejected, and the way in which the relation of master and servant was concluded was, by Mr Hunt contriving with Hobbs, a turnkey, to have him placed in solitary confinement for twenty-four hours; and for what?—because he (Hunt) came one day suddenly into his room, and found his ward, Miss Gray, sitting upon his knee. This produced great anger on the part of Mr Hunt, and ended in the punishment stated: the history of this transaction was in the evidence of Wyatt', [Appendix to the Commissioners Report page 335'.]

John Goodford. Visiting magistrate of the county for about 15 years. 'What has been the state, [of the jail] as far as cleanliness? I have never had an occasion to complain of that... I considered his manner to the prisoners sometimes rather too abrupt and sharp to them... When you have visited the jail has Mr Bridle been in the habit of going around with you? Not always. I know nothing of his general conduct which would induce me to speak unfavourably of him'. 'did you sanction the applying of blisters as a punishment? I should have thought myself unworthy to hold the office of magistrate if I had sanctioned it'.

John Newman visiting magistrate about 13 years. 'When you visit the jail has Mr Bridle always accompanied you? Always when he has been at home. Have you ever observed any restraint on the part of the prisoners in consequence of his presence? I never have.'

John Thring (snr) 1753-1830 visiting magistrate. Visiting magistrates are appointed every quarter. 'I always considered Bridle a very correct man; the jail in good order and very clean, and I have heard him spoken of as a very humane man'. Hunt complained about his bell being muffled by order of the governor, and the magistrates had it reinstated.

'Did you make this order (of February 13 1821) relative to the exclusion of female visitors... without the sheriff's knowledge or concurrence?' Yes. Had you seen the order made by Charles Bampfylde? Yes, I had. As visiting magistrate, you did away with the order... without the concurrence of the new sheriff ? The order speaks for itself.' This was on the day that Bampfylde was out of office and Hanning the new sheriff took over.

Thring was asked about James Hillier who he had seen as visiting magistrate and returned to solitary confinement for his insolence despite of the way in which he was ironed. 'Did you then order him to be continued in chains, irons and handcuffs? We thought nothing about chains, fetters or handcuffs at all'. He was ordered to be released from the irons once he showed signs of contrition. Then you would not consider a man chained in the manner I have just described for nine days and nights to be torture? Thring imagined it would be extremely painful but not torture, then, when pressed added that he would not have ordered irons at all but would not interfere with the discipline of the jail.[This was Thring's first visit as a magistrate] 'Perhaps you and your brother magistrates had been so taken up with the amiable project of precluding females from visiting myself and Mr Kinnear that what you witnessed relative to Hillier appeared of a trivial nature? My mind was not taken up with the former or with the other... I returned home feeling I have done my duty and I think so now'.

Rev. Wm Hungerford Colston magistrate for 20 years. Colston was questioned about Hunt's bell being silenced and replied that Bridle had said that there were not enough officers to keep answering it ringing so frequently which is why it was muffled. It was rung at unreasonable hours when the task master and other offices had many other duties but 'as the bell has been ordered by former visiting magistrates I ordered it to be unmuffled.'

Hunt: You resolved that it was improper for matron [Mrs Hobbs]to pick a pheasant or get a pie baked for me? I don't recollect that'.

As regards Hillier being double ironed, 'I have never interfered with it, nor have other magistrates; we have left it to the discretion of the governor'.' I don't understand what you mean by hands and feet chained together, the man came in and stood upright as I do now, he made no complaint or I should have attended to it. 'If then, a prisoner is confined in solitude and in irons for *10 days*, do you consider it is warranted by the regulations of this jail? I should think not'.

Re female visitors. 'you made the order to exclude my female friends with the exception of my family... that was my wife and female children? Yes. Did you know at the time that I had been separated from my wife for 18 years? Knowing that, you made an order for my wife to visit me at the exclusion of all other females... and you don't call that torture? I hope not. Was it not meant as a mockery of a prisoner in your custody?

Those ladies were constantly living in the jail and would perhaps have lived there up to this time if this order has not been put in force'. 'A jail, I think would be no punishment if we were to have all our friends from morning till night and rooms made more of an hotel then a prison, that is my opinion as a magistrate... The magistrates have granted you favours that were never granted to any other man since I was magistrate'.

Rev William Hungerford Colston

John Phelips a visiting magistrate since 1811. With regard to Bridle, Phelips states that he never saw anything that he disapproved of. The jail was the cleanest and best he had ever seen and he was unaware of the jailer having any undue influence over the prisoners when speaking to him with their complaints.

Rev. John Gale Dalton Thring jnr. [1784-1874] magistrate. Prior to the present investigation I never heard any impeachment of Bridle's character or honesty. There is an order saying that, 'William Pitcher is activated by mischievous intentions and he be prohibited from visiting anyone without an officer' dated 12 March 1821. Did you know at the time that he was a person I had employed to write for me, and that he drew up the petition of Charles Hill? I did not. What rule had been violated to cause his exclusion? I cannot give a direct answer.

Thring the Younger

Thomas Poole magistrate. 'I have always considered the jail in excellent order... and the prison is generally in such a state of comfort as men in their situation can be expected to be'.

Prison account books were discussed and it was agreed by Mr Hunt, the Commissioners, and Mr White that the charge respecting the fraud upon the county should be expunged, and all evidence relating to that as it was a question for the consideration of the county, being between Bridle and that authority.

Robert Pinney prisoner and constable. Claimed to be afraid of Hillier who he caught gambling and who threatened to knock his head off. 'I asked Pike to remove me as I was afraid of what he might do to me...' Hillier said that he had taken off his irons every night, he then took out a bit of wire to show me how he took them off and was not more than three or four minutes about it and taking them off and putting them on. He said he took them off every night and put them on again before Pike came. Hunt claimed that this was not possible because, as the magistrates have seen, there was only nine inches of room between his legs and it could not be done in the manner shown. Pinney could not produce anyone else who had seen this done despite claiming that there were others in the room.

'Did you hear Gardiner say anything? I heard him say that locking him up and putting on the blister had not hurt him, he took off his cap and showed me his head, ''this don't hurt I''

Joseph Bayley prisoner seven years transportation. White: did Mr Hunt to give you anything? Yes he gave me half a crown, I told him the men had no bread'.

James Glover prison and cook. Do you know a boy called Wheeler? Yes, a very bad boy I have heard it said one day last week that Mr Bridle ought to be hung and he hoped he will be transported and he would do all in his power towards it.' For these nine or ten weeks I have heard them say 50 times that Mr Bridle has done them no harm.

James Harper. a prisoner sentenced to transportation, he was put in irons for hitting a fellow inmate with the leg of a stool. 'Did you ever know Mr Hunt before you came to this jail? I did not. Hunt;- Did you know Mr White [barrister to William Bridle] before you came to jail? No'. – Mr White, in great passion, 'I wish to know what Mr Hunt means! I have carefully abstained from anything personal although I have ample means if I thought proper!'

> Hunt: 'When you have insinuated that I gave a man 2/6 for some improper motive, when you have brought a madman into the town and placed him to guard over some witnesses at Cotton Garden for three weeks, and now put the book into his hand to swear him as evidence against me; that, knowing him to be mad, you have had the cruelty towards the poor maniac himself and the injustice towards me, to put words into his mouth to traduce me, I cannot acquit you, Mr White, of being personal, particularly when it is considered that the evidence of this unfortunate maniac does not in the slightest degree exculpate your client from any other charges preferred against him, even if the poor fellow had been in a proper state to have been believed upon his oath and now you have had the folly to call a witness to give your client a character… you endeavour to screen your own imprudence by insinuating that such an infamous fellow was acquainted with *me* before he came into this jail. But it is fair to infer, from the rank in life in which you were brought up, that it was more likely he was acquainted with you than with me'.

Peter Auton prisoner. Described Wheeler as very bad. 'Yesterday he was making a false key to undo the door.' [the witness was convicted of housebreaking and found with a bunch of skeleton and false keys.] He would often take off his jacket and try to fight other inmates.

Elizabeth Summers prisoner. What has been Mr Bridle's conduct? He has always treated me of the greatest kindness. Mrs Hobbs did often poison our minds against him saying that he said this thing, that thing, and the other, when at the same time Mr Bridle said no such thing'.

William Phillips. farmer. States that he asked the surgeon Mr Shorland if he got on with his neighbours, Mr and Mrs Stainer. He replied that he did not because of that damned villain Bridle who had caused them to bring an action against him, he said he would drive Bridle out of town.

Edward Sheppard debtor, bookseller and stationer in Wells who used to, 'measure land'. With regard to the 'shop' Bridle told him that the jail door was open at all times of the day for butchers and vegetable sellers when they liked. Four or five come regularly now every week many come with potatoes I suppose the debtors get things cheaper now than when there was only one. Ann Denman should have been discharged on 24 October 1820 but was not released until two or three days afterwards.

Charles Marshall deputy turnkey's servant 'Charles Hill asked if I would be a radical I told him no, that I was a King's man, he said if I'd be a radical I could go down to Mr Hunt's, I could have plenty to eat and drink and something to put in my pocket if I could say anything against Mr Bridle'. I reported this to Mr Pike.

At the election you voted for Dr Lushington ? Yes, he is an honourable gentleman'. He brought or sent down the horseradish I believe? I don't know what do you mean by horseradish...Is it not called horseradish, the money, £30,

Charles Marshall

which is given to each of the voters after an election? I don't know, it is what is dug up in the fields'. I am paid 2/- a day and nothing else.

Richard Pike 'Did you know Bridle complain of Hobbs neglecting his duties? I have heard that he used to go into the town'.

William Bridle. Bridle made brief comments on some of the points raised but seems to have made no attempt to defend himself against any of the specific accusations.

Mrs Pike

It appears that the jail was once reported to be dirty; I entered an order on that in the occurrence book April 16, 1820. With respect to Treble I wish to explain that I know nothing more than that I obeyed the order of the doctor. With respect to boys, the jail is so full that it is impossible to keep boys from the men. With respect to a boy sleeping with men in a very improper matter, I was not aware of it, there was great neglect somewhere. Instead of the fever being brought on by the drains it was brought in from the town of Ilchester. In the early part of the fever there were 77 men in a kitchen that ought to have only had 20 and four men were sleeping in the room of one. When I came here there are five wards and 66 prisoners, and it was three years before the prisoners amounted to 100. We continued to increase until we had 266 prisoners, which was the highest number. With respect to mixing men and boys for misdemeanours together, the same thing applies as the men and boys sleeping together it is impossible to make any classification.

With respect to the drains, I can only say that four men in two days cleaned them out. Prisoners are ironed before trial for felonies and after conviction. I have given my evidence before the House of Commons, that a prison might be built to prevent the necessity of irons but in the present state of my jail it is impossible to do without irons. Orders are made but it is impossible at all times to obey them. I never heard the water complained of till it was complained of by Mr Hunt. I wish to explain that the prisoners have now a greater power to benefit themselves than formally as they can now buy their goods in the jail, and are not obliged to send to the town of Ilchester for them. The charity box was put up at the insistence of myself.

Hunt: a sovereign was traced into the box by Treganzer in 1819. No sovereign is found when the box is next opened in 1821 what has become of the sovereign? Mr Bridle had all the keys in his possession, six keys.

Court, 'You must answer or explain about the sovereign Mr Bridle'. No answer.

With respect to the interlineations in the occurrence book, in my absence the task master used to make so many that I ordered him to keep his memorandums on the separate sheet of paper and enter them after my return.'

With the final witness examined the proceedings drew to a close but not before in a final flourish, Hunt declared his wish to return the cheques which had been given to reimburse him for payments to his witnesses as he wished to pay for it himself. Hunt explains his reasons in a final letter to the Commissioners,

Ilchester Jail June 30 1821

Gentlemen,
In consequence of your refusal to comply with my earnest request to grant your summons to the warden of the Fleet to bring before you a prisoner in his custody John Kinnear Esq late a prisoner in this jail who had resided ten months in the jailers house, and who had thereby become acquainted with all the debaucheries and atrocities committed therein as well as the torture and injustice inflicted it upon the prisoners, and most of the tricks, deceptions and delusions practised on the magistrates by the jailer; also your having refused to grant a summons directed to the sheriff of Middlesex to produce Matthew Hobbs, a prisoner in his custody who had acted as a task master for four years past, I have been totally deprived of the two most material and necessary witnesses to enable me to substantiate the charges that I preferred against Bridle the jailer on behalf of the public, my fellow prisoners and myself, and without whose testimony the honourable Commissioners can have but a faint idea of the transactions that have been carried on in this jail. Under the circumstances and impressed with a feeling of conscious pride that I have never in any occasion in my life, received, either by myself or any of my family, one sixpence of public money. I beg now most respectfully to decline accepting any sum from the Honourable Commissioners towards paying the expenses of those other witnesses, 72 in number, which I have called to substantiate the charges which I preferred.

I am, gentlemen with great respect,
Your most obedient servant
H Hunt

Aftermath

A SPOOF REPORT appeared in the *Morning Post* for 5 July 1821 indicating that the Commissioners had dismissed all charges against Bridle finding his conduct to have proved, 'most laudable'. The article ended with, 'Hunt's mortification is extreme and has produced a visible alteration in his person'. Hunt as usual failed to see the funny side commenting that the editor of the *Morning Post* is 'the most foul mouthed unmanly, and unblushing libeller of women who knew at the time that every charge had been fully substantiated'. He hints but doesn't say that the author was Smith of the *Bath and Cheltenham Gazette* 'a good friend of Bridle, a pot companion and brother gambler'. Hunt estimates that Bridle made between £1,200 to £1,500 a year from the jail and that the whole jail cost around £5,000 to maintain but could be conducted magnificently for around £3,000.

Bemoaning his lot once again, Hunt comments on how unfair it was that his co-defendants, Johnson, Bamford and Healy had been free for the previous three months, 'their imprisonment in Lincoln Castle was rendered a paradise compare it to what I am doomed to suffer in this accursed, pestilential Bastille. They had only 12 months in good airy apartments in better accommodation than they ever were at home with their wives company whenever they chose.'

In the meantime, while the Commissioners were still considering the evidence from their investigation, the conclusions of the magistrate's enquiry into Bridle himself were made public,

> The committee of magistrates appointed to assist the high sheriff in his investigation of the charges adduced against William Bridle the keeper of Ilchester jail have terminated their proceedings by adjudging the keeper unfit to be longer retained in his appointment. The announcement of his dismissal was accordingly communicated to him on Friday last. (3 August 1821) Bridle is to have until tomorrow week to make up his accounts at which time the keeper, to be appointed, will enter on his office. The advertisement for a new jailer will appear in our next publication. The stated salary is to be £400 per annum besides the house, etc and the legal established fees upon the discharge and removal of prisoners.
>
> *Herefordshire Journal* 1821-08-08

Bridle was informed on 27 July 1821 that he had been found guilty of, neglect of duty, playing cards with a prisoner, bad language, not regularly attending divine service, opening the prison doors for election celebrations, withholding part of the salary of the task master, applying a blister to Gardiner, allowing boys and men to associate and share beds, allowing unfortunate women to associate with felons, employing male and female prisoners together under his own roof, and supplying the prisoners with bad water. Most of the matters discussed in the *Peep* in fact. He was given until 3 December to put his affairs in order and move out. He found it unfair that he was expected to stay on until December. He was prepared to do his duty, as he put it, but why were they compelling him to stay in a position for which he was judged unfit? Were the magistrates afraid that their decision would be overturned by the Commission and that they would have to reinstate him?

Bridle was shaken to the core. 'they pass their judgement on me unheard and my years of faithful, honest and arduous services were all forgotten. I had spent the prime of my life and wasted my best energies under their own eye and within their own approbation'. Bridle lists the frequent visits and complimentary comments from the visiting magistrates recorded in their journal. The number of inspections came to 28 in 1809, 25 in 1812, 46 in 1816 and so on, all of them giving reports of good order and cleanliness and signed by many of the magistrates that had given evidence in front of the Commission including, Aaron Moody, William Colston, Thomas Poole and Richard Whalley where they said nothing to contradict their initial favourable reports. On 30 August 1821 Dolby published Hunt's now completed transcript of the Commission's proceedings, *Investigations into the Abuses of Ilchester Gaol* priced at 6/6d for a fully bound set.

In a letter to the *Morning Post*, dated 24 October Bridle claimed that he remained silent before the magistrates because he did not wish to prejudice the report of the Commissioners by following 'in the footsteps of his calumniator by foisting ex parte statements upon the world. The public doubtlessly decided that because I am to be dismissed the charges of Henry Hunt are proved but such is not the fact, and immediately the report of His Majesty's Commissioners shall reach me, I trust to prove to the world that I am the victim of as a malicious a conspiracy as ever disgraced this or any other nation'. Bridle appealed to the sheriff and the magistrates in a letter dated 31 October 1821 pleading his case,

> The committee selected from your own body to sit in judgement on my conduct were biased against me... the subject matter was investigated before a

higher court than that of the committee... acting upon that judgement against me before the verdict of that court was registered I feel to be most harsh and unmerited. It has ever been to me a matter of great astonishment that the motives which governed my accuser should never have been examined by the committee, they must have known that when he was first committed to my charge and for some time after, how profuse he was of his eulogies on me and the state of the jail under my government. Did it never occur to the committee that I incurred his hate by enforcing their own very proper order, directing his concubine to be restrained from keeping up adulterous communication with him within the walls of a jail? I will not anticipate the report of His Majesty's Commissioners, but as soon as that report reaches me my means of defence are complete. I implore you therefore to suspend your judgement until that defence comes forth. I implore you also to give it a fair and impartial perusal. To answer my inveterate accuser personally is beneath me. Truth is the most powerful of all weapons and it alone shall portray how infamously I have been abused and how wickedly I have been treated.

William Bridle.

He makes a fair point about the magistrates acting upon their decision before the Commissioners had finished their report, but it was all too little too late. Bridle finally has his say in his book '*A Narrative of the Rise and Progress of the Improvements...* which wasn't published until January 1822 some months after his dismissal. The first few chapters concern his improvements to the building and workings of the jail already considered in chapter 7. He outlines the effects of the investigations and judgement on the prison population, describing how the jail was in a state of anarchy with disobedience and confusion the order of the day. Despite the findings going against him he was still in nominally in charge as the jail was not to receive its new governor until November.

On 18 August 1821 and the following day, the turnkey, Pike reported the felon's ward to be in great riot and confusion initiated by two prisoners fighting. An escape plot was also discovered, the felon's plan was to demand to be released from their irons, attack the officers in chapel and break out of the jail. The undersheriff visited, immediately and committed some to solitary confinement and applied to the secretary of state for the removal of others to the hulks upon which application 29 of the most desperate were removed. During this time Bridle claims that he had no power of control and that the major part of his officers were paralysed in the execution of their duty by mere fear of Hunt. Bridle finally managed to leave on 10 November as the new man took over.

Shortly before publication, Hunt, having got wind of Bridle's intention to publish, commented, 'Bridle is still here, winding up his accounts, in which it is said, he is assisted by a young man who was an assistant at the village school... those who profess to be in the ex-jailors confidence have given out that he has hired the young man to write the book in which he means to publish his vindication, myself, the sheriff, and those magistrates who dismissed Mr Gaoler are to be attacked and caricatured'.

In September, Matthew Hobbs, Bridle's brother-in-law and former right-hand man, appeared before the Commissioners in bankruptcy applying for relief which Bridle opposed by putting in affidavits attempting to show that he was possessed of sufficient property to discharge his debts. At his final examination Bridle opposed the discharge on the grounds that Hobbs had not accounted for his furniture to which Hobbs replied that his wife had disposed of it to support herself and eight children but he could not say who had been the purchasers as he had been in London. After an adjournment his wife produced a number of affidavits in which she named the purchasers and amongst them was Mr Henry Hunt who also gave Hobbs an excellent character for honesty. The court declared that Hobbs was fully entitled to the benefit of the act and he was discharged.

The most interesting part of the hearing was a letter produced by Hobbs from Bridle wherein Bridle offered to cancel a bond for £120 if he would to go to Ilchester and swear against Hunt's charges before the Commissioners:

To: Mr William Smart, County Store Office, Excise Office, London May 27, 1821

My Dear Smart, the Commission is going on, having been opened three days; things are going so much better than before the committee. I have but one wish concerning the jail, leave it I certainly will, and my only wish is to leave it with credit. I can only do that by the assistance of those who have been concerned in the service with me. I wish you would see Hobbs and tell him there are many things that require explanation from him; things which cannot be well explained but by him, none of which will be to his *discredit* but *otherwise*. I shall get all the rest of my past officers and I very much wish to get him. I am disposed to clear off all differences with him and, as far as myself is concerned, to make him free of the world. I have engaged to spend my last shilling in matters concerning this persecution, if driven to the necessity; and I would rather do it for credit sake, than in retaliation for injuries I may have received. I have a bond against Hobbs on which £120 beside interest is due; I will give him this bond although it is for money borrowed; my anxiety being to beat some of the desperate gang against me and to leave with credit; and this, you may depend, will be to the advantage of many. The post is waiting and I am in great distress yours truly,

William Bridle

Hunt took great delight in re-printing the letter in the introduction to his *Investigations*. Bridle had apparently sent a special messenger with the letter from Ilchester to London, who, by mistake, left it in Hobbs's hands. Bridle attempted to get it back for fear that Hunt should see it, but Hobbs persisted in keeping it.

Hunt writes in his *Address* of 24 December 1821 that 'Within six weeks after the expulsion of the old jailer, who, when he was discarded, published a letter in his friend and associate Smith's *Bath and Cheltenham Gazette* and most of the county newspapers, accusing the magistrates of treachery and desertion and threatening to be revenged in the following words, 'the downtrodden viper will sting my Lords and gentlemen', three days after this on 15 November a serious fire broke out at the northern end of the jail factory most of which was destroyed including the woollen factory and workshops. It was put out by people from the town and many of the prisoners themselves despite raging for about two hours. Hunt claimed that the fire was within ten feet of his bedroom and that his bell was silenced the day before the fire. On 8 December another fire occurred in the wash house destroying some linen and on the 15th yet another in the laundry – three seemingly unexplained fires in the space of 31 days.

The Commission's Report: 4 December 1821

THE COMMISSION'S REPORT into the state of the jail was due by 1 November 1821 but was delayed until 4 December and eventually printed by order of the Commons in February. Its findings were detailed in a 300 page appendix but in summary its conclusions were as below. Please bear in mind once more, that this was written and produced by Hunt and Shillibeer,

> There was a general complaint about the foulness of the water which the Commissioners found to have a disagreeable taste, likewise the bread was found to be well below the standard claimed by the suppliers. Other general complaints amongst the debtors were that the visiting hours were extremely inconvenient and that they were only allowed in the, 'conversation room' and that the most comfortable part of the exercise yard had been converted into a garden to grow vegetables putting it out of use. At the same time, they

are exposed to temptation by the constant sight of the produce of the garden placed completely within reach of the men who, as in the case of the lower or poor debtors have nothing to live on beyond the county allowance of bread and water. These complaints were judged to be well founded.

It appeared that the governor had greatly neglected his duty in inspecting the wards and exercising proper control over his officers. The occurrence book was full of interlineations, interpolations, and additional entries which were, in their judgement, calculated to mislead and deceive. The committee expressed astonishment that two women had been delivered of a child when employed as a servant in the house of the governor, which circumstances appear never to have been brought to the knowledge of the magistrates.

Charges of drunkenness and gambling for large sums were not found to be supported by the evidence. They found that the prisoners letters were opened in disobedience of the Secretary of State's instructions and that insufficient clothing was provided.

With respect to the charges for a proper application of the county stores or goods manufactured in the jail we conceived them to be a matter for the investigation between magistrates and their officer, not falling within the scope of your Majesty's commission.

Complaints of the immoderate severity of certain punishments appeared well founded particularly in the cases of James Hillier, Thomas Gardiner and Mary Cure. Although it has since been discovered that Hillier was enabled by means of a piece of wire which he concealed, to unlock the fetters from his legs at night. There can be only one opinion as to the gross misconduct of the governor in applying a blister to the head of Thomas Gardiner by way of punishment nor can we refrain from expressing our astonishment that any medical man could have lent himself to such a purpose. The case of Mary Cure seems to us to be one of extraordinary cruelty. An iron collar for the neck was produced by Pike for the purpose of chaining a prisoner to the ground or wall but it appears to us from the testimony of the witnesses that this instrument has never been made use of.

It appears to us that there has not been sufficient attention paid to the characters of the persons selected for filling the inferior offices in the jail in many instances persons convicted for the second and third time have been appointed to act as constables of the wards.

It appears that during a considerable period there was a great neglect existing in providing sufficient county clothing for the use of the prisoners in consequence of which they were reduced to a state of extreme filth; this evil however, was removed a few months before our arrival.

Classification does not appear to have been sufficiently attended to and the Commissioners expressed their horror that boys were put to sleep with men convicted of the most disgusting and unnatural crimes. The locking of doors which compelled the offices of nature to be performed in crowded lodging rooms at night could easily have been prevented.

It is to be lamented that the sheriff and magistrates did not, early in the imprisonment of Gardiner and Cure, cooperate with each other and agree in laying down a system of treatment to be observed towards them, instead of separately issuing contradictory and in some instances irritating orders. No evidence of the particular inconveniences alluded to in the order of the 14th of August was adduced before us although repeatedly demanded by Mr Hunt.

It appears that in some instances articles of nourishment ordered by the general surgeon for the sick have not been administered; the only reason assigned being that the market at Ilchester did not supply them. It seems extraordinary at the surgeon should not considered it part of his duty to report the fact to the visiting justices. It is to be observed that these evils seem only to have existed lately, for during the prevalence of typhus fever in 1817 the sick received every possible attention and the activity of the governor and officers as well as of the medical department appears to have been most praiseworthy. To the conduct of the governor on that occasion it is impossible to advert without admiration.

Coroner's enquiries appear to have been conducted in an extremely slovenly manner. In the case of the death of Ford the testimony of Chamberlain that a blow from the turnkey induced his death is in our judgement undeserving of credit.

The lack of accommodation for the sick was felt to a considerable degree. The charge of robbing the charity box was not supported by the evidence. The wards are well suited to the species of discipline here adopted but overcrowded.

In bringing to a conclusion our observations on the internal management and discipline of this jail, we cannot but observe, that a system of irritation, rather than one of steady authority and conciliatory government appears to have existed.

Having in the course of our enquiry found that frequent allusion was made to Mr John Kinnear who had been for the last two years a prisoner in the jail and admitted by the governor to an intimate knowledge of the transactions that had during such time occurred; and likewise, to Mr Hobbs late the task master, we issued our summons directing them to appear before us. Each was prevented from doing so in consequence of their imprisonment for debt, one in the Fleet and the other in the White Cross Street prison. Upon our return to London we deemed it expedient to visit those two prisons that we might examine the above-mentioned persons, but as the information derived from them contained no facts with which we were not previously acquainted we did not consider it necessary to examine them on oath or to reduce their testimony to writing.

4th December 1821

> **INVESTIGATION OF THE HORRID ABUSES OF ILCHESTER GAOL.**
>
> The Seventeenth Number, price 1s. of the
>
> MEMOIRS of HENRY HUNT, Esq. containing, in addition to the continuation of the Author's Memoir, an Address to the Reformers of Great Britain on the termination of the Inquiry in the above Gaol; a Description of the extraordinary and affecting evidence adduced before the Somersetshire Magistrates, and again before his Majesty's Commissioners. Also, just published, the Sixth Edition of the famous PEEP INTO ILCHESTER GAOL. This pamphlet will be now read with peculiar interest, the extraordinary facts contained therein having been established on oath during the late investigation.
>
> Published by T. Dolby, 299, Strand, and may be had of all Booksellers.

Morning Chronicle

During the same month Bridle ceased to pay his subscriptions to his Freemason's Lodge but whether this was because he was leaving the area or lack of funds is uncertain but he did maintain his contacts as we shall see.

10
PASTURES NEW

Visits & Petitions

WITH BRIDLE GONE the new man at the helm was William Erasmus Hardy, formally clerk and principal assistant to Mr Brown, keeper of His Majesty's jail at Newgate. Hardy had known Bridle for 16 years and had always considered him a humane man having kept up a correspondence with him since before his appointment to Ilchester. He took charge from 10 November 1821 and Hunt reported that conditions in the jail had begun to improve a 'vigilant discipline was exercised with humanity and proper treatment, this produced correspondingly good behaviour in the prisoners' and blasphemous swearing formerly, used indiscriminately by the jailer and officers, was nearly abolished and all the chains had been removed'. Soon after, the jail had a new surgeon, a new parson, a new task master and a new matron, but not everything was working out as well as he had hoped.

The previous July, after five months without visitors, Sheriff Hanning had ordered that Hunt should once more have free access to his friends at reasonable times and this situation continued until 22 January 1822, when at the quarter sessions in Wells, Justice William Draper Best, a 'poor hobbling cripple', and Whig turned Tory, endorsed an order by the magistrates which stated that, 'no visitors *male or female* were to be allowed in Hunt's private rooms, all visitors were to be seen at the double grating in the felon's cage.' For the third time, and despite the concerns of the Commons Commission, an order had been issued banning Mrs Vince from the jail. Colston and Newman were still in place as visiting magistrates and thought to be the instigators, while the father and son Thrings had declined to continue their appointments at the jail. This time the exclusion order applied to all visitors including his son and physician, Dr Shorland, (he refused to see Tomkins the jail doctor fearing that he might poison him.) On 25 January Hunt was taken ill with cramp in his chest and spasms in the heart, he asked for Shorland the surgeon who had attended him since the start of his sentence and who lived within 20 yards of the walls but he was denied admittance. Hunt was in pain for eleven days and entreated Colston to admit Shorland but the magistrate claimed that he had no power to alter the order that Justice Best had signed, saying, that the jail doctor, Woodford, who lived five miles distant, and the county medicines were freely available if he needed them.

By now his mental and physical health was deteriorating, the constant cold and damp had brought on rheumatism and the poor light had damaged his eyesight, he was now complaining that he had been in solitary confinement for the same number of days that Jonah was said to have been confined in the belly of a whale … he claimed that, 'one assassin endeavoured to prevail upon the person who supplied me with biscuits to put arsenic in them to poison me, another scoundrel secretly communicated to the same man his wish to assassinate me by shooting me with a pistol.' It is indeed probable that his mental health was deteriorating as well.

Hunt was concerned that Hanning, a man of independent fortune and liberal principles, was not as strong as his predecessor and less able to stand up to pressure from the undersheriffs and magistrates; the new restriction on visitors seemed to prove him right. Naturally politics played a part as it had throughout his sentence. Those most opposed to Hunt and his endeavours were Whigs, including William Dickinson, and Sir Abraham Elton and of course Bridle himself. Sir John Acland was a Tory, 'the Tories sent me to jail but they behaved something like gentlemen… it was left to the Whigs to record their dirty, petty malice upon a prisoner in their custody… tyrannical as the present ministers are they are incapable of lending themselves to such mean dirty grovelling acts as the base Whigs are guilty of'. It was the York Whigs, claimed Hunt, that had selected the jury that convicted him, 'the most determined enemies of reform, it was a Whig jury that found me guilty at York, Sir Abraham Elton another Whig who took the place of Acland, and the present sheriff William Hanning is also a Whig'.

On 8 February Alderman Wood introduced a petition to the Commons by Hunt's son Thomas on his father's behalf. Sir Francis Burdett spoke about the unfairness of the original sentence which had come down to one charge of attending an illegal meeting and argued that Hunt should not be treated as a felon. Dickinson defended the magistrates saying that the rules were in line with other jails and had been signed by Mr Baron Graham and Mr Justice Best. 'A representation had been made that a Mrs Vince had sought to be admitted but from the character of that person it was judged proper not to give her this right'.

Sir Thomas Lethbridge said that all complaints at Ilchester had only arisen since Hunt was confined there. He knew the magistrates were incapable of such conduct as was ascribed to them, they were most worthy men and he was not prepared to believe that Hunt was in solitary confinement which he thought was a state in which a prisoner is forbidden communication with others. This seemed more a case of him not seeing persons of a certain description as and when he chose. He was also of the opinion that the indulgence granted to Mr Hunt had led to the complaints of which the House had already heard too much. If he had been treated like other prisoners from the start all the troubles that had lately arisen would have been avoided. 'There was a time when Mr Hunt thought it a more excellent prison than any other. He was inclined to think that it was not the state of the Gaol, but Mr Hunt's opinions, that had undergone a change.- It appeared almost impossible that a Gaol which Mr Hunt had once described as a perfect paradise, should be so radically bad as some persons would have the House and the country believe'.

It was asked if Hunt should also be shut out from seeing his son who was forced to take a boat down the river until he came under a small aperture in the wall of his father's apartment and communicate through this little hole. The Attorney General pointed out that Hunt was tried by a jury every one of which he had approved, in a county chosen by himself and tried by a judge whom he complimented when the trial was over. Petitions of support flooded in from all parts of the country with thousands of signatures pleading Hunt's case all making the same plea with many copied into editions of the *Address*. In February the Report of the Royal Commissioners was published officially at last much to Hunt's approval, '…it is more complete then we could have expected; the magistrates are of course protected as much as possible. But it is quite enough to condemn the gaoler, the magistrates, and the gaol. I wrote to one of the members, to say that it was wrist-screws, not thumb-screws, that were made use of in this gaol. His answer was, 'I have just read the Report of the Royal Commissioners, and think that had thumb-screws been used they would have added but very little to such a mass of cruelty and horror'. Hunt's delight at the outcome was enhanced by the reaction of his enemies, who,

> …have retreated, eaten their words, and apologised to the worthy Alderman, the Honourable House and the country, for the manner in which they attempted to impose upon them. Amongst this number is Dr Lushington, Sir Isaac Coffin, Mr Fowell Buxton, Mr Bright, of Bristol, Scarlett, and several others. Dickinson and Lethbridge still endeavour to brave it out, as to the Magistrates and the Gaol, in spite of the Report of the Commissioners; and they now lay it on thick and three-fold upon the wretched, abandoned devil of a Gaoler, as if this would take off the odium from themselves and the rest of

the Magistrates of the county, who have so long and so obstinately supported, protected, screened, and upheld the said Gaoler in his atrocious and cruel proceedings'. ....it was mostly the Whigs that endeavoured to stifle the inquiry and to deter Alderman Wood from proceeding to present the petitions of the poor suffering prisoners —you should never forget this. It was they that rose in full cry, and joined the ringleader, Dickinson, to vouch for the character of the magistrates and the Gaoler, who wished the Honourable House to take their words that the above amiables were the most just and humane men in the world, and that all which the prisoners had stated were falsehoods, not to be believed, and which ought not to be attended to. It is the sanction of these mock patriots, the Whigs, that have upheld the system so long, without their sanction it could never have lasted half this time…'

> **MOST IMPORTANT AT THIS TIME.**
> **GAOL TYRANNY,—ILCHESTER.**
> Just published, by T. DOLBY, 299, Strand, price 6s. 6d. in boards, or in Six Numbers, at 1s. each,
> The whole of the EVIDENCE given on Oath before the Commissioners appointed by the Crown, to investigate the ABUSES in ILCHESTER GAOL; containing instances of Cruelty and Oppression not exceeded in any country. This Book will be found of the utmost importance to Judges, Jurymen, Magistrates, Gaolers, Prisoners—and, in short, to all who are interested in upholding the reputation of England for justice and humanity. In the course of the Work are given numerous Engravings of Magistrates and others, connected with that hitherto unexplored Sink of Immorality.
> "My wish is to bring the cruelties practised in this Gaol to light, for the sake of the poor creatures who have intrusted their cases to me, and not on my own account alone; and I know the Court will do me the honour to allow that I have brought forward no frivolous charges, nor have I produced an exceptionable witness."—*Vide Mr. Hunt's Speech to the three Commissioners on the last day of the Investigation.*

Hunt's Advert for his Investigation at Ilchester Gaol

In his *Address* for 25 February Hunt advertised his transcript of the proceedings as available in, 'six closely printed numbers or complete in extra boards for 6 shillings and sixpence'. Also available was part 29 of his *Memoirs* (now to be published on the 1st and 15th of every month),with the addition of letters respecting his solitary confinement and various petitions.'

On Friday, 1 March, three surgeons 'assembled by appointment to perform a painful and delicate operation — that of extracting a tumour from the interior part of my right eye. The operation was performed with great address by skilful surgeons, and it could not have been accomplished with less : while one held the eye-lids wide open, the second had to force the eye nearly out of its socket, while the third seized the tumour with a sharp crooked sort of needle, which he held in one hand, while he cut it out with the other, considerable haemorrhage ensued. Pike, was sent to say that the Surgeons had certified that it was necessary that I should have a nurse to sit up with me, and if I pleased I might have one of the Frome weavers, who had lately been committed for rioting, one of these men might be locked into my room with me all night, if I pleased. I indignantly declined to accept the assistance of a perfect stranger that I never saw, a greasy weaver, from being locked up all night in the same room with me'.

On 13 February Hanning's year as high sheriff was completed and Vincent Stuckey took over. At the beginning of March, it was ordered that visits were once again to be allowed, 'the same as they did immediately preceding the rules signed by Judge Best being put in force'. Hunt was ecstatic, 'my enemies the magistrates of the county of Somerset have sustained another defeat and have been compelled once more to open the doors of my dungeon and admit a free intercourse to my family and friends between the hours of 9 o'clock in the morning and sunset'. At last this battle of wills was over and freedom of visits continued until his release in October. There was further cause for rejoicing when on 18 March Charles Hill was finally released after 16 years and at the age of 76, Hunt expresses his delight in his memoirs,

> I am proud to bear testimony to Rev. Henry Cresswell, the vicar of Creech St Michael whose zealous cooperation to assist me and the worthy Alderman Wood, to procure the liberation of poor old Mr Charles Hill …in spite of his remorseless persecutors, who have repeatedly sworn, ever since I have been here, that he should never leave Ilchester Gaol alive. It will be recollected that it was this poor man's sufferings that I made the ground-work of my charges against the monster of a gaoler and the Magistrates. How much more delightful is the occupation to record the good, than the evil deeds of one's fellow creatures; how much more gratifying is it to me, to write of a Dr Shaw, than of a Dr Colston!

During March and April 1822 various petitions were presented to the House, Sir Robert Wilson took up Hunt's case proposing that he be released arguing that he had suffered far more than was originally intended during sentencing. Thomas Buxton, MP for Weymouth, took part in the debate and apologised for his previous rosy picture of the jail but explained that this was formed in 1818 when Sir John Acland was playing an active part in its running and things might well have altered after his time, he continued,

> The House knew, that the judges in sentencing Mr Hunt, had taken into their consideration the supposed advantages of the prison in which he was at present confined. Those learned authorities believed that prison to be one of the best in England; and they supposed that they were sentencing Mr Hunt to be confined for thirty months in a wholesome and well-regulated gaol. Without meaning to cast any reflection upon those learned persons, he must say they had been misinformed. For twenty months the sentence of Mr Hunt had been aggravated by the treatment he had received, and the unhealthy state of the gaol.

Mr William Peel was of the opinion that,

> Mr Hunt occupied two rooms in the gaol which had a northern aspect; the adjoining ward was appropriated for the reception of two prisoners who waited on him; and he had the privilege of walking at stated times in the yard. That contradictory orders had been issued respecting Mr Hunt, he knew; but he must defend the magistrates from the suspicion of being actuated by unworthy motives in any part of their conduct. He believed that they were much disposed to make the situation of Mr Hunt as comfortable as was consistent with the discharge of their duties. That some of the visiting magistrates had been guilty of negligence, he would candidly admit, but it had obviously arisen from their confidence in the gaoler, who had deserved every praise for his conduct during the time that the typhus fever raged in the prison.

Sir Francis Burdett presented his petition to have Hunt's sentence remitted on 24 April,

> ...the offence of which Mr Hunt had been found guilty was a misdemeanour, for which an imprisonment of from one to six months was deemed sufficient, visiting it with the punishment of imprisonment for two years and a half, was more than sufficient for the purpose of justice. But Mr Hunt's offence, was, of all the charges preferred against him ... the slightest; so that they had the anomaly before them, of a man suffering a heavy punishment for a crime that was as small as possible... at the time of Mr Hunt's committing the offence, he was, in mind at least, as innocent a man as could be. It was an ancient maxim of English law, that 'actus non facit reum, nisi mens sit rea. (An act does not make a person guilty unless there is a guilty mind); but, in Mr Hunt's case, a new practice had been introduced: the

intention of his mind was not considered…When Mr Hunt was sent to Ilchester, it was said that he had been sent there because it was one of the healthiest and best conducted gaols in England. If such were really the motive for sending him there, when that gaol was found to be one of the worst conducted gaols in the kingdom, and to be insalubrious to a degree that could hardly be credited, he had a right to say, that even those who inflicted the sentence on Mr Hunt never intended to submit him to the inconveniences which he had since suffered.

Others were of a contrary opinion, George Dawson MP for Londonderry,

The persons with whom Mr Hunt had been described as not condescending to mix were not felons, but imprisoned for misdemeanours only. For the convenience of Mr Hunt, bells were hung; and the floor of his apartment, which before was of stone, was replaced with one of wood. This was at Mr Hunt's own suggestion. To show that those attentions were felt and acknowledged by Mr Hunt, he would now read a letter from that gentleman, in which he stated—'I believe no man that ever lived was more happy than I am here. In fact, I have every possible care taken of me.' It was dated July, 1820 and published in the *Sherborne Mercury*.

William Dickinson contributed asking that…'as Mr Hunt had unfortunately contracted a complaint in his eyes, that green blinds might be furnished, to give a more commodious shade to the room, and after a very long debate the house divided,

Noes 223
Ayes 84
Majority against the motion 139.

Hunt had pretty much opposed the petition himself. He refused to entertain the idea of any remission in sentence, demanding either a free pardon or to serve the full term. He reprinted the entire 32 page debate from Hansard in his *Address* of 24 April before adding his own hyperbolic comments,

On the 30th of October, in spite of the Borough mongers, I shall leave this place. I want no mercy. I demand justice, and I do not wish one jot of my sentence abated.' Remission of sentence, indeed! I want none of their remission: Mercy, forsooth! mercy from those men who sanctioned the cowardly and cruel murders of unarmed men, women, and children, at Manchester!— Not I, indeed: I scorn their mercy. If the King chooses to kick the rumps of the Judges and his Ministers, by sending me down a pardon, why I cannot help myself; Mr Hardy can, turn me out of this dungeon at once. By Heavens ! I solemnly, declare, that I will accept of nothing short of this! and I would rather cut my tongue out than I would suffer it to pronounce thanks even for that. Not I, indeed…I will accept of no favour: they, know me too well —they dare not offer me any compromise. Mercy, indeed !

Despite his constant complaining in that same month he is quite jubilant,

In consequence of the exertions of my friends, every restriction that I ever complained of is now removed, two new Visiting Magistrates called upon me — Mr Hanning, the late Sheriff (who has not been a Visiting Magistrate these ten years), and General Bathurst, accompanied by Mr Dickinson and Mr Phelips, the two Chairmen of the Quarter Sessions. Every wish that I expressed was complied with, the little trap-door of my yard was ordered to be left open to admit the ingress and egress of my friends, without the intervention of lock or key after they pass the front door; no person of any class is refused admission. Three high walls which surrounded my yard were ordered to be lowered, and they are since, by the activity of Mr Hardy, reduced from twenty to ten feet in height'.

Hunt's Breakfast Powder

Throughout his remaining months Hunt continued to write his *Address* concerning the conduct of the visiting magistrates and the plight of those still imprisoned, he was also demanding that a complete list of the constables on duty at Peterloo should be published and a full enquiry undertaken. Hunt also had problems on other fronts. Some years before, Cobbett had invented a new drink as a substitute for highly taxed coffee, a substitute made from wheat and he devoted pages of his journal to it. At the end of 1819 Hunt made his own from roasted rye which he named *Hunt's Breakfast Powder,* and the two fell out over it arguing bitterly until the end. Politically, it was billed as a protest against paying taxes to the government after Peterloo and for Hunt economically, it was a great success, so much so that the Board of Excise took possession of his factory and his stock worth about £150 and issued a writ for £200 back tax. To make things worse the Court of the Exchequer sought to seize his estates and property in Glastonbury worth many thousands more via the undersheriff, Edmund Broderip, to pay off what was owed. Hunt had no choice but to pay the fine and eventually in June 1822 the government backed down and allowed him to produce his powder without interference on condition that he bought a licence for 2/6. 'Great pains have been taken to bring *Hunt's Breakfast Powder* to great perfection, which have succeeded equal to my most sanguine expectations'.

He may have won a few battles, but Hunt was not going to get things all his own way. He apologises for the lateness of his *Address* for 14 July 1822. The magistrates at least seem to have retained a sense of humour,

> I have to apologise for the delay which has taken place, and the unusual lateness for bringing out this Number. I have been too ill to furnish Dolby with the manuscript before. This illness has arisen from my being prevented, from taking my usual quantity of exercise. I had always been in the habit of walking an hour at least before breakfast, and frequently an hour and a half or two hours, from six to eight o'clock in the morning; and as this exercise was taken in the factory-yard, in a comparatively pure air, before any of the prisoners were employed there, I contrived, to preserve my health much better than my friends expected, or that I could scarcely hope for in such a vile, pestilential, and contaminated pest-house; but when my evil genius, Dr Colston, and his hopeful colleague, Squire Newman, were visiting magistrates, they not only had the door of my yard shut, so as to exclude all possibility of a free circulation of air but, as if for the purpose of destroying me and depriving me of every particle of fresh air, they had two furnaces erected just in the centre of the factory-yard, for making soup for the prisoners, the chimneys of which being within the walls, and so contrived as not to reach above half their height, as if for the purpose of preventing any portion of the smoke or soot escaping.
>
> However, as soon as the fires were lighted in these furnaces, which was every morning a few minutes after the doors were opened, I was not only driven out of the factory, but I was obliged to close the door and window of my dungeon, to prevent myself from being suffocated with smoke, and my clothes, books, and papers being completely covered with soot, which issued in torrents from these bastard, clerical-contrived chimneys, and found its way into every crevice and cranny of my room, and spoiled my milk and covered my food in the pantry with soot to such a degree as rendered it frequently totally unfit for use. It was in vain either to complain, expostulate, or to point out any means of relief while these worthies remained visitors, because any attempt of that sort would certainly have increased the inconvenience, therefore, for that quarter I bore it patiently. When Mr Hanning and General Bathurst, came and ordered the interior walls of my ward to be lowered, and the door which Dr Colston had closed to be thrown open, and evinced a disposition to render my

situation more comfortable and salubrious, I mentioned to them the dreadful inconvenience arising from the soot and smoke which were not above six feet high, and placed as it were just under the nose of my window.

They saw the folly, or rather the wickedness, of the doctor's scheme, and ordered them to be immediately raised, so as to carry the smoke and soot over the walls. There was already what is called a cook-house for the prisoners, where all their soup and meat used to be dressed, at the back of the keeper's house, where there was a large chimney already erected, much higher than the walls, and capable of carrying off any smoke. However, when the prisoners began to raise the chimneys, it was found that, like all the rest of the Doctor's works, there was no good foundation to build upon, and the attempt was abandoned. I was left to endure this another month or two, till the Magistrates came again for they appear to leave Mr Hardy no discretion. In the mean time I found my health evidently declining for want of exercise, which it was useless for me to attempt to take under such a complication of smoke and showers of soot. When the Magistrates arrived, I must do them the justice to say, that they gave orders for having this intolerable nuisance removed by funnels placed on the top of the Doctor's dwarf chimneys, which carry both smoke and soot over the walls, for the benefit of the surrounding country, instead of depositing itself, as it did before, within the walls and in every department of the Gaol.

Towards the end of July Hunt was delighted to hear that, 'Ilchester Bastille is to be razed to the ground as totally unfit and that a sheriff's jail was to be added to the present house of correction at Shepton'.

Hunt obviously welcomed Bridle's conviction but was disappointed by the jury's recommendation for mercy but commented further that, 'bad as he is I think some of the magistrates are worse',

As the clock struck midnight on Tuesday 29 October 1822 Hunt was a free man but could not leave without an audience and so he stayed until 8 o'clock the following morning to be greeted by crowds of people who had assembled for the occasion. The party made straight for the town where a celebratory breakfast was held at the Castle Inn. Festivities and celebrations were held countrywide with bonfires lit on the hilltops and processions through the streets. After the breakfast he made his way to Taunton for a 5 o'clock dinner at the London Inn. There was not a word of his release in Cobbett's *Register*. Hunt claimed a triumphal entry into London on 11 November with half a million people lining the streets, in fact it was far less than that and nothing like the events during 1819. He and Mrs Vince moved to Stamford Street in London close to his breakfast powder factory, while the enigmatic

Miss Gray had apparently chosen a career on the stage and disappears from the record. The breakfast powder, which along with other inventions like his matchless blacking for waterproofing boots, now formed his main business interest and day to day activity. Public subscriptions had only covered part of his legal costs and he threw himself into his work with increasing success despite a failed attempt to expand into France with a patent ink and a new type of fuel. As ever politics was foremost in his mind and his activities continued, he stopped writing his *Memoirs* when he reached his sentencing making about 48 numbers in total. The *Address* also ceased publication, the date of the last issue being 8 July 1823. He continued with letters, pamphlets, petitions and public meetings and announced his intention to publish a monthly periodical called *Hunt's Union or the Radical Recorder*.

In an issue of the *Address* the previous February he had summed up his place in history,

'… the benefits which I have accomplished in this jail and in this county, will hang upon the lips of the babe as yet unborn. The name Hunt will last longer than the walls of this Bastille and centuries hence, when not one stone shall stand upon another in this jail, tradition will hand it down to after ages and he that passeth by will say, 'There once stood the Bastille in which Hunt was imprisoned for two years and six months for advocating those rights which the people of England now enjoy…''

Despite his faults, and there were many, he wasn't far wrong on this occasion…

Dr John Robertson

At the Taunton Sessions during May 1821 John Robertson submitted a bill for £10/16/-to cover his medical services at Ilchester jail. The magistrates found this extravagant and refused to pay it allowing him only £6/6/-which was agreed and Robertson's original bill was altered to reflect that amount. However, before it reached the treasurer for payment it had been altered back to the original sum which was paid and although knowing it to be the incorrect amount Robertson made no attempt to correct the error and appeared at the Epiphany sessions in 1823 charged with fraud. Even though witnesses had claimed that Robertson had told them how he had 'done the magistrates' the jury were swayed by considering the risk involved to the defendant for such a small amount which was bound to be discovered and he was found not guilty. Despite this victory things did not go well and by May

John Robertson surgeon and apothecary, late of Northover and now of Wilton was declared bankrupt and a London publication, *The Beacon,* revealed that Robertson was the nephew of John Kinnear the convicted swindler and Hunt's roommate at Ilchester jail.

Business As Usual?

LEST IT BE thought that all was sweetness and light at Ilchester after the eviction of Bridle, in August of 1824 a 22-year-old gentlemen debtor named C Smith was said to have been handcuffed, pinioned, and chained to an iron bedstead in a damp cell 7' x 6" and imprisoned for 11 days after his discharge had arrived. The allegations were published in the journal *John Bull.* Hardy sued for libel on the grounds that the report was totally false and won an apology from the proprietors of the paper plus 40/- in damages. That would have been an end of the matter were it not for Thomas Swymmer Champneys, baronet of Orchardleigh near Frome and a magistrate of 30 years' experience who, 'made the most minute and particular enquiries into the allegations and found them all confirmed except for the number of hours which the petitioner remained in irons and chained down to the bedstead'. Champneys obtained 'clear and decided confirmation upon every point upon which Smith has charged the jailer, such testimony extending to no less than nine different witnesses'.

Thomas Champneys, a flamboyant character and heir to massive debts had been in Ilchester jail for debt himself from 1822 to 1824. During his time there, he wrote to Vincent Stuckey one of the visiting magistrates at the jail, complaining that he was being deprived of any proper exercise and that Governor Hardy was guilty of many infringements of the prison rules including cruel and inhumane treatment of prisoners and misuse of prison property for his own purposes. The matter was complicated by Champneys main witness, a turnkey named Davis who had given evidence at the Commons Commission into Bridle having some trouble on his own account. He had agreed to act as a witness in support of Champney's claims, and brought a civil case of his own against Hardy claiming damages for malicious prosecution which included having him lodged with felons in his own jail and other cruel treatment. Hardy had charged Davis with having pocketed a sum of money that was to pay for transporting a debtor to court in Taunton but when the matter came to court no witnesses could be produced and the case was dropped, leading to the malicious prosecution charge. The whole case, claimed Davis, was untrue and brought maliciously to discredit the forthcoming Champneys case. In the meantime, Davis had been sacked by the magistrates for other misdemeanours and his character blackened meaning that any evidence brought in Champneys favour would not have carried much weight. Neither case went any further.

Cobbett Returns November 1819

DELIGHTFUL AND RELAXING though America may have been it was not England and Cobbett returned to Liverpool on 21 November 1819 carrying with him the bones of Tom Paine. He was reunited with Nancy and although Cobbett never spoke about her without great affection, it is perhaps significant that he never taught her to read and write despite writing books on the English language and perhaps she was content in her role as housewife and mother – for now.

Large crowds followed him everywhere, he tried to enter Manchester where he had been invited to attend a dinner in his honour but found himself banned by the magistrates from entering the city. The authorities, fearing another Peterloo had posted sentries on the road to give warning of his approach but he turned around and headed back to London. A lot had happened in the two years since he had been away. Several abortive attempts at armed insurrection had ended in disaster and his great friend Hunt was now in custody following the tragic events at Peterloo a few months before. He found the atmosphere more oppressive than when he left particularly the six acts, the last of which imposed heavy taxes on political publications spelling the end of the *Twopenny Register* and causing its sales to fall by 80%. Cobbett still fearful of arrest, published articles on the evils of tea and coffee and a defence of Tom Paine's religious opinions. As for the bones which he had brought back with him, his plans for a memorial and burial service were met with indifference and he kept them until his death, what happened to them after that is not known.

Cobbett's Evening Post published a full report on Hunt's trial but was very guarded in its comments being conscious of the new laws, nonetheless he managed to support the demand for a new trial on the grounds that the jury had been prejudiced without actually spelling it out. When they first met again after Hunt's release and under what circumstances is not known but we do know that after three years apart they met in London in December at a dinner organised in Cobbett's honour. Nothing was drunk but water in line with Hunt's pledge not to pay tax until the government set up a public enquiry into the events in Manchester. The *Political Register* had made few references to Hunt and many more to Cobbett's own achievements. Relations between the two men had cooled and Cobbett declared that he was to go his own way cutting himself off from the main stream of reformism and his former colleagues. The main elements in their estrangement arose from Cobbett's personal jealousy of Hunt's achievements and popularity, his desertion to America without informing his best friend was still incomprehensible to Hunt, and nagging in the background there must have been some uncertainty over the 'whore' letter and then of course Cobbett's wife Nancy's personal hatred of Hunt.

In the general election campaign of March – April 1820 and despite being on bail, Hunt stood as a candidate for Preston pledged to secure an immediate parliamentary enquiry into Peterloo together with his full radical programme. Cobbett's *Register* did not mention the campaign which was cut short when his trial began but nonetheless he gained well over 1,000 votes. Cobbett was also running a campaign in what proved to be a violent election in Coventry in March 1820 in which he polled 517 votes against the successful candidate Edward Ellice with 1,474.

Cobbett's increasing feud with Hunt even went to the extent of interfering with the distribution of his publications and Hunt published the following in his *Address* of 22 June 1822,

TO COUNTRY BOOKSELLERS AND READERS OF THE MEMOIRS.
Having had numerous complaints lately made to me by letter, that the Memoirs have not reached their destination at various places, I wrote to Mr Dolby, to whom I leave the whole management of printing and publishing, to urge him to be more particular and attentive in future and from whom I received the following answer :—

'I understand the *Memoirs* are not regularly conveyed to Hull, Greenock, and some other places. I am very sorry to hear it, the more so, because I do not send parcels to those places, and, therefore, have no remedy. Hull, Greenock, Glasgow, and several other important places, are now supplied direct from Mr Cobbett and wherever his influence extends, not a single number of the *Memoirs* can go.' This, certainly, is one way of accounting for the delay. I had observed, with pain, the publisher's notification, two or three weeks following. Does Mr Cobbett think to put me down by such, or by any means ? If he does —But we shall see ! ! !

I am, my friends,
Yours steadily and faithfully,
H. Hunt

The situation between them had been made worse the previous May when Hunt wrote in his memoirs that Nancy was a bad mistress to her servants and unable to keep them for very long. Cobbett had carried reports of Hunt's trial when it began in March 1820 publishing a full account at the end but did little more than mention Hunt's name along with the other defendants. Hunt resented the lack of support from Cobbett who never once visited him throughout his time in Ilchester. It is sad indeed that the two should become so estranged when they needed each other the most. Hunt was now barely mentioned by Cobbett, his jealousy overwhelming his political judgement. Hunt the all-conquering hero, now martyred, and Cobbett the coward who had fled to America and was struggling to regain his position.

Cobbett was now having serious problems of his own, having been taken to court several times for debt he was forced to declare bankruptcy and take refuge just across the Sussex border in Kent where writs for his arrest were invalid. He surrendered himself at the end of April 1820 and spent five months in the King's Bench until he could clear his debts. During October 1821 Cobbett took a major break. He saddled up his horse and set off across the British countryside gathering material for what was to grant him everlasting fame, his *Rural Rides,* which he detailed irregularly in his *Register* over the next ten years.

In February 1826 things between the two deteriorated further when Hunt sued Cobbett for libel over some trifling matter. The jury found for Cobbett and Hunt was ordered to pay costs of £25. That same month they both appeared independently at the Freemason's Tavern in London to launch a subscription to fund Cobbett as MP for Preston at the election set for June. Cobbett came last but was overjoyed at the enthusiasm of his many supporters. Despite all that had gone on between them the two were reconciled to some degree and met again in May 1827 at an election dinner at the Crown and Anchor. The high sheriff had tried to ban the meeting and the police were tearing down the hustings platform as they arrived, it was just like old times. The event turned into an all out riot which was nonetheless considered a great success and the two old comrades left arm in arm.

Nancy Cobbett was devastated that her husband had rekindled his friendship with Hunt. She had even threatened suicide if such a reconciliation was to go ahead and true to her word she cut her throat with a knife which left her dangerously ill. Whether there was more behind this act than Hunt we do not know. She was 53, had survived 14 pregnancies and lived through Cobbett's bankruptcies, imprisonment, exile in France and America, changes of address and the strain of being married to a man of unbending principles and boundless energy. Hunt stood as candidate for Somerset in the general election of 1826 opposing Dickinson and Lethbridge but he was no match for the sitting MPs, polling only 309 votes against Dickinson with 1,812 and Lethbridge with 1,719.

In following years they joined together to fight for Catholic emancipation and in July they published a joint declaration, *Radical Reform in the Commons House of Parliament* their main points were soaring taxation, social injustice, poverty, with those in prison better fed than the average labourer, their demands were that no man be taxed without his consent and of course annual parliaments universal suffrage and vote by ballot. It led to the inevitable meeting in London on 13 July 1829 which both Hunt and Cobbett attended. Hunt was on form, asking the rhetorical question, 'Was there any man in the world who would you bold enough to look another in the face and say, 'I am entitled to a certain right which you are not entitled to?' Despite the show of unity cracks began to appear. Cobbett was worried that including such radical atheist republicans as Richard Carlile in their newly formed Radical Reform Society would frighten off many from taking part but in general the pair were working together harmoniously as before.

The fatal wedge between them was to come from a totally different direction. Cobbett had engaged a secretary since 1826, Charles Riley whose wife was having an affair and reconciliation having failed he sent her off to her family. Nancy Cobbett had decided that he had disposed of his wife so that he could have a gay sex with her husband; as might be imagined their domestic affairs had been poor for some time. Cobbett had moved into a separate part of the house seeing no one but Riley who panicked fearing a major scandal. One of Mrs Riley's lovers was David French a reformer and friend to both Cobbett and Hunt and Cobbett believed that the rumours had started with him. On 12 August 1829 Cobbett's sons beat him up bringing the matter into the public domain. Hunt had every sympathy with Riley and French and they joined forces against their common enemy, Nancy, convinced that all the slurs began with her. Cobbett would not believe it and during September there was a tense exchange of letters between he and Hunt after which they resumed attacking each other in print. It had been a long, hard road but Nancy Cobbett had finally achieved her aim and this time the two were never to be reconciled.

In December 1830 Hunt was elected member of Parliament for Preston under the Whig prime minister Earl Grey with 3,730 votes. Cobbett was green with envy. After a hectic round of celebratory processions, speeches, dinners and theatre visits, Hunt made his way through the radical heartland to Manchester where he visited the site of Peterloo. At the Commons he was dismayed to find his desk piled high with mundane constituency work taking up all the time which he should have spent reforming the institution itself, added to which

House of Commons

were 657 colleagues who opposed him. The chamber was preposterously small with members having to clamber over each other for seats and the noise was intolerable. For Hunt it was a depressing and disappointing experience, he had achieved nothing, the suffocating atmosphere of the parliamentary chamber, the constantly braying, 'yells groans and hootings' of the opposition rendered even his powerful voice and determination ineffectual. To add to his woes, Cobbett's pen was constantly at work criticising and belittling his activities in the House turning at times to undisguised hatred attacking him politically, personally and in business. The established press loved it of course, pitting one against the other and enjoying the fray. A self-professed independent, Hunt made over 1,000 parliamentary speeches between February 1831 and August 1832 claiming to be the only parliamentary spokesman for the unrepresented poor and the working classes and, from March 1832, 'the only self-avowed radical in the House'.

After initial enthusiasm both were disappointed by the terms of the Great Reform Bill of 1832. It abolished the rotten boroughs and enfranchised all the large towns, which was very welcome, it gave the vote to small landowners, tenant farmers, shopkeepers, and householders who paid a yearly rental of £10 or more increasing the electorate from about 400,000 to 650,000, making about one in five adult males eligible to vote. But it was a far cry from universal suffrage, the act did not enfranchise the working class since voters had to possess property worth £10, a substantial sum at the time, possibly around £1,600 today. Hunt paid the price for maintaining his ideological purity. Cobbett, who ended up in support of the bill, accused him of working for the Tories and he was ostracised by most prominent radicals.

On the final day of the old Parliament, 18 August, Hunt presented a petition calling for the whole bill to be repealed except for the abolition of the rotten boroughs after which he left the Commons never to return. Ironically, the great reformer lost his seat in the first election to the reformed Parliament as the Whigs and Tories hired gangs of thugs to discourage his supporters and bribed those entitled to vote to swing their allegiance back to the old guard.

William Cobbett c 1831

ON 13 DECEMBER 1832, Cobbett was elected MP for Oldham just as Hunt was evicted from Preston. The newly elected member was now able to experience first hand all the trials and tribulations of his former friend. He took his seat on 29 January 1833 but was to fare no better than Hunt. His 70th birthday was only days away and the volume of work coupled with the extremely long hours took its toll, he was by now extremely fat with swollen ankles and shortness of breath along with a cough which had troubled him for some time. If things were bad in the Commons, they were worse at home. At the end of 1833 he returned one night to find no fire and no food. Nancy then spent the entire night criticising the exhausted MP and as the next day dawned he moved out to his office in Bolt Court off Fleet Street and never went back, dividing his time between there and his farm in Normandy, Surrey. Nonetheless he continued to write and publish, desperately short of money; when not asleep he was at work.

In the House he condemned the Poor Law Amendment Act which was greatly influenced by the theories of Malthus who Cobbett, a man renowned for his hatred of a great many people held in special detestation. The act established prison-like workhouses into which the poor were herded like cattle, families broken up and conditions kept at a basic and uncomfortable level to exclude the workshy and the feckless. He questioned why the crime of bastardy was confined to the poor when there are so many bastards in high places. During an adjournment of the house in September 1834 he felt well enough to take a trip to Ireland and was overwhelmed by the poverty that he found there.

Hunt continued the attack on his old friend writing in the *Poor Man's Guardian* while in failing health with very bad rheumatism and in financial difficulties himself with his blacking business struggling to make money. In

November 1834 his 61st birthday was widely celebrated all over northern England. Shortly afterwards while travelling to Winchester he suffered a stroke which paralysed his left arm and left him unable to speak. His speech recovered but he had another stroke two weeks later and died at Alresford in Hampshire on Friday 13 February 1835 surrounded by family and friends. His opposition to the reform bill had cost him a lot of the popularity that he had enjoyed during the Peterloo days but he never stopped campaigning or moderated his views. He was buried in the churchyard of St Peter's church in Storrington West Sussex on 21 February.

William Cobbett

Cobbett made no mention of his friend's death in his writings but his own was not far behind. He gave his last speech in the Commons on 25 May 1835 and feeling increasingly ill retired to his farm. After being carried around his land to see how his crops were growing he slipped peacefully away on 18 June at the age of 72 and was buried at St Andrews Church, Farnham. His son William who had supported him throughout was the sole beneficiary of his will. The *Gentleman's Magazine* wrote: 'like other noisy demagogues, he soon found his level (in the Commons), and became harmless and insignificant, except in his votes'. The *Poor Man's Guardian* acknowledged his intense egotism and added: 'to sham reformers he was particularly obnoxious; while to turncoats and trading patriots he was a perfect raw head and bloody louse' Brougham's private secretary recalled him as a small landed proprietor in Somerset of broken fortune and profligate habits, ill informed, but clever and resolute, with a fine person, and (when he pleased), rather prepossessing manners so that altogether he was able to gain an ascendancy in the disaffected districts greater than any man of the day'.

He and Hunt were of course terrific egoists; Hunt had behaved with insufferable vanity and self pity during his imprisonment, and Cobbett's irascible nature and jealousy did him no favours, but they may be forgiven in many ways as it takes a particular type of personality to achieve as much as they did and it is very sad that they were apart at the end. They had always had differences of opinion in their political views but managed came to terms in the early days, it was their personal lives that drove the wedge between them, two cantankerous old men who refused speak to each other at a time when unity could have achieved so much.

Hunt's estranged wife Ann (Nancy) died at the age of 85 at 1 Green Park, Walcot in Bath and was buried on 27 April 1860. His daughter, Anne was educated at Mrs Crouch's of Andover, one of the top schools of the time; she married an English gentleman, James McGhie IV in 1818 before moving to Paris. Eldest son Henry Hunt went to America after the election of 1818 and remarkably, married Mrs Vince's daughter, Catherine Maria Ann Vince (born 23 August 1800) on 4 December 1834 at St Martin in the Fields, London. Mrs Vince snr. died a widow at the age of 74 in Islington, her effects were less than £100.

11
TRIAL & SENTENCE

THE ANNOUNCEMENT OF Bridle's dismissal in July of 1821 meant that he was to lose his home, his occupation, a large income, and presumably the respect of many who had supported him. He had run his jail in his own way and by his own rules but now he was awaiting criminal proceedings, after what must have been a year of uncertainty he was faced with the possibility that he could lose his liberty as well. Shortly before his departure in November he sent an open letter from the jail to the *Morning Post* dated 31 October 1821 and addressed to the 'High Sheriff and Magistrates of the County of Somerset'. He begins by thanking magistrates for their support over the years enabling him to 'bring the jail at Ilchester to a state of superiority above all others', before expressing regret,

> ...that such kindness and protection should ever have suffered diminution is to me a source of great and unavailing regret. It is an old and a true axiom that the trodden worm will turn – the trodden viper, my Lords and Gentlemen, will sting too. My weapon of defence is *truth* a weapon with which my enemies are unacquainted'.
>
> It is fortunate for me that none are better acquainted than yourselves with the mode in which for 14 years I discharged my duty to you and the public – a mode which must have been meritorious since it called from the magistrates of other counties, as well as from your own body, unqualified, and I may add, unlimited praise. A strict and straightforward performance, of my duty became my bane.
>
> The demagogue who disturbed the national quiet was committed to my charge and from the moment of his disapprobation nothing has been spared to overwhelm me. No charge, however vile, no accusation however false and malignant was wanting, and amongst the dark spirits of his own nature, he found the hearts to strengthen, and the tongues to swear to whatever the blackness of his own mind chose and delighted to concoct.

The Committee, selected from your own body to sit in judgement on my conduct, were, by such means biased against me and although that right to dismiss me whenever you pleased, cannot be doubted, yet, seeing that the subject matter was investigated before a higher court than that of the Committee, their judgement and their acting upon that judgement against me, before the verdict of that court was registered, I feel to be most harsh and most unmerited.

Bridle then quotes from what he calls 'remarks made during the investigation, by my accuser's chief organ',
'We have begun at the wrong end. The eyes of the whole world are on this case, someone must be sacrificed and the weakest will go to the wall. We do not want to hurt Bridle, we had better impeach the magistrates and let everyone carry his own load.' And again, when he found my defence growing rather too mighty for him, 'We are all wrong, we should have brought this against the justices, Bridle is only their agent'.

What he did during this period is not known but presumably he had prepared the ground should the worst happen and secured whatever assets, he may have had for the future. How he must have wished that he had possessed the power to have given Mrs Vince unlimited access…

In April 1822 Bridle wrote two letters to the press, firstly to the *Bath and Cheltenham Gazette* in the following terms,

> It has been stated that thumbscrews, gags, neck irons, body irons, &c with which the limbs and bodies of the prisoners in Ilchester Gaol were heretofore manacled are now all abolished. To this Sir, I briefly reply, thumbscrews, and gags are unknown to me, never in my life having seen either. Neck irons I have seen used out of the county of Somerset but never in it. One such iron was in my jail and as such in my power to use but I never used it there or elsewhere. Body irons are sometimes used in refractory cases and sometimes for safe conveyance. Of such irons I believe there are two in Ilchester Gaol, where, I believe one prisoner only was subject to the use of them for the last three years of my governance and that was to prevent suicide, the same prisoner having once before attempted his life by hanging himself and had then a very narrow escape. In such irons I have never removed a prisoner. I have known Mr Hardy the present governor for the last 15 years and I believe him to be a very humane man but he has already been compelled to use them in the same gaol. They have also been used in Newgate, and in removing convicts from the county gaol to the hulks.

In his second letter he refutes various allegations about his character,

That I am a drunkard was denied even by Shorland, the Sheriff's Committee and the Commissioners also deny it.

That I am a gambler, the commissioners also deny observing when speaking to me that, 'although in one instance a game had been introduced for a considerable amount *in his absence* by the prisoner Kinnear, who was then living in his house, as soon as it came to his knowledge he put a stop thereto'. In fact, I know no game but whist and cribbage, and even these but very indifferently. I did occasionally play a rubber in the winters evening for sixpences or a shilling; and this is the amount of my gambling!! But as play for higher sums did take place in my house I conceive it to be my duty to make a few observations thereon. Kinnear took his meals at my table and his evenings in my parlour becoming acquainted with, amongst others, the late Rector of Ilchester who unfortunately was fond of play. He lent himself *in my absence* to a very high stakes game and lost considerable sums of money. This, for a long time was concealed from me, as those who had the care of the establishment in my absence were not only themselves implicated but bound by other ties to conceal it. It came to my attention that having become a considerable loser he attended whenever invited in the hope of recovering the money he had lost. As soon as these matters were made known to me I did what I conceived to be my duty. I removed some from my house and complained to the magistrates of others who assembled at the jail and enquired very minutely into the charges. [The Commission] having very kindly excused my attendance thereby sparing me from much distress they examined every servant of the jail and in my own house and also the Rev. Gentlemen before alluded to, the result was that four servants of the jail were dismissed, one of whom on leaving the committee room was heard to declare that she would be revenged, she was called again before the Committee and admitted to such a declaration. [Mrs Hobbs].

How far I have deserved the appellation of, debauchee or pander, the sheriff and magistrates have made a sort of lapse in their report touching on the birth of two children in the jail, I feel myself bound to call attention thereto as it will materially show what reliance ought to be placed on that report formed on such ex parte evidence and also how much I am abused and misrepresented. The report states that 'these women could not be examined on oath as to the fathers of such children insomuch as the mothers at the time were convicted felons'. One of the women was in jail at the time and her examination before the Commissioners had no reference whatever to me! The other woman alluded to is Sarah Lawrence, she is living in Frome; after her discharge from prison she applied to the magistrates at Frome and affiliated the child to Thomas Palme of Ilchester who had been in jail for debt and was occasionally employed in the house. On being asked if her master had ever taken any liberties with her, she declared most positively, 'Mr Bridle never touched me in his life; nor did I ever see him take liberty with any woman, or speak an improper word, in my life, although I was in jail three years, and was nine months of that time in his house, and I always thought Mr Bridle as much above a prisoner as the king is above a beggar.'

To establish these charges against me, no attempt was made further than the subject of these women; and I would ask, what would be the report of men generally if they were tried as I have been?

The Trial of William Bridle 15 August 1822

THE PROSECUTION OF Bridle was ordered by Home Secretary Peel in May and despite the large number of charges that Hunt had brought against him previously he was brought to trial on only two and was convicted of one, the facts of which he did not dispute. The bulk of the evidence produced has already been rehearsed in chapter nine on the Commons Commission and so I have kept the witness evidence short unless it is greatly different and concentrated more on the court and its characters.

Proceedings opened at the Wells Assizes on Thursday 15 August 1822. The town was described as 'quite alive at five in the morning, with the influx of persons to hear the trial. By half-past seven the doors were surrounded with expectants of all ranks; but no one except those who had immediate business in the courts were admitted until after the arrival of Mr Justice Richardson at 8.00am when the doors were thrown open to the public'. Most of the county magistrates were in court. Mr Sargeant Pell, Mr Gaselee, Mr Adam and Mr Selwyn acted for the prosecution, Mr CF Williams, Mr Erskine and Mr Manning for the defence.

William Bridle faced two charges.

> Firstly, that between the 18th and 25th November 1818 on divers dates he, being a person of malicious mind and disposition intended to hurt, injure, aggrieve, and oppress Mary Cure a prisoner in his charge, confine said Mary Cure, she having an infant of six months at her breast, in a cold and unwholesome cell neglecting to supply her during that appointment with necessary firing or with the bread and water necessary for her sustenance.

Secondly that on 20th of November 1820 the defendant intended to injure one Thomas Gardiner, put a blister upon his head for the space of 20 hours and a straight waistcoat on his body confining him at the same time in a solitary cell, did beat and ill-treat the said Thomas Gardiner.

Mary Cure, to whose case the first part of the information referred, entered Ilchester Gaol in the year 1818. She had been sent there for committing some trifling offence, sufficient of course to justify her detention, but not of a gross or aggravated character. This unfortunate woman, who had a child at her breast, when she went to prison, was so unfortunate, somehow or other, as to excite Mr Bridle's displeasure.

Cure was called to give evidence (a plain looking country girl of about 30 years). She had quarrelled with a woman named Smith who was her fellow prisoner — a thing not unlikely to occur in such a place as a Gaol; but admitting that she had conducted herself in a refractory manner, there was nothing to, justify that brutal and wanton cruelty which the defendant, had caused to be inflicted upon her. In consequence of this woman's supposed misconduct, Mr Bridle thought fit, on the 19th of November, 1818, (being a Thursday) to confine her in a dark and solitary cell. 'I had no fire until Saturday morning it was a stone floor, I was allowed bread and cold water which I was obliged to drink out of the bucket. I had nothing for the child, my milk had failed me. The weather was extremely cold, snow had fallen and was upon the ground and Ilchester Gaol was at all times subject to severe damps, but not withstanding all those circumstances, she was shut up with a sucking infant at her breast, without fire in a solitary cell, and kept in that situation from Thursday the 19th, to Sunday the 22nd of November. She was taken very ill on the Sunday and Mrs Hobbs gave her something to relieve her. The child and herself were very well when they first went into solitary confinement but both very ill on being released.

Mr Williams in cross-examination: Cure is unmarried with three children, two surviving. Mrs Jane Hobbs supplied her with some crockery, her original crime was stealing some turnips. Bridle had got a subscription to get her released from a fine. Another witness claimed that, Mary Cure was not kept on bread and water; she had bacon and butter on Thursday evening, I saw it carried to her. She used to sell gooseberries and fruit to Mr Hunt and he had spoken to her as recently as last Thursday. 'I often went down to Squire Hunt. He was very good to me. I can't swear that Mr Hunt never talked to me about this in his cell – I spoke to him last Thursday about this [her treatment and solitary confinement]. I don't know how many times before. It was not five or six times, He mentioned it to me once or twice, when I went down with things, but I never went on purpose'. Cure was released early following a promise of good behaviour. Jane Morgan, under sentence of transportation, remembers Cure taking a basin with her and going into the pantry to get cheese and bacon she also saw her suckle her child whilst in the cell.

According to another witness, Ann David, [Bridle] 'was universally looked on by the prisoners as their friend and these deponents never knew a single complaint of him until the order of the high sheriff that all prisoners should have access to Hunt's room to make complaints. Witness spoke of the shameful manner in which Hunt abused the power so foolishly granted to him, and asserts that Mary Cure after giving her evidence to the previous court, confessed to her that what she had said against Mr Bridle was dictated to her contrary to the truth'.

As to the second charge, Thomas Gardiner had been very idle and refractory having refused work altogether after being accused of stealing a purse from another prisoner he denied it but his wages were stopped after which he claimed to be ill which was not believed. He was put into solitary confinement for three days his head shaved and a blister applied with a straight waistcoat to prevent him removing it. This was done at Bridle's request the surgeon not having visited him. Gardiner was called to give evidence, a 'decent looking well dressed young man of around 20 years of age' now living in Bristol. He denied having picked the pocket and said that he was genuinely ill at the time. The blister was tied to his head from which he suffered a great pain and rubbed it off against the wall, it was then replaced. 'I asked Bridle to forgive me but he said he didn't think I was quite well enough yet'. Gardiner denied stabbing a fellow prisoner in the knee and 'damning all justices to hell'. Under cross examination he denied having told a fellow prisoner that the blister did not pain him so much as he had said but that he would get well paid for it as he had been put up to it.

Those were the basic facts of the case against Bridle, further details of which have been recorded in previous chapters.

Mr Williams now rose to address the jury for the defendant, but was for a moment so overpowered by his feelings, that he was unable to proceed beyond the first sentence. He begged leave to retire into the open air for a while. One local paper commented that, 'an absurdity was Little Williams weeping when he began to speak, if he had been crier to the court, it might have been in place,-as a barrister it was sheer tomfoolery'. Upon his return, he said, that never, in the whole course of his professional life, had he risen under such feelings as those which at that moment almost overpowered him. He was not ashamed to avow those feelings. He re-commenced his address which was exceedingly able, eloquent, and impressive. He proceeded to speak in high terms of his client whom he was proud to call his friend he declared that he could fill the hall with men of rank, magistrates and gentlemen of the county, all of whom would speak of him in terms of the highest commendation, as the most honest and intelligent man; but he would do more, he would examine the poor prisoners themselves who at their own expense will come forward and say that when they had been placed in his hands his heart had always been open to their afflictions. Williams speech was at great length and even caused the audience to applaud on one or two occasions.

Williams dismissed the evidence of Cure as inconsistent and moved onto the case of Gardiner a 'thief from his cradle' who had been sentenced to death but reprieved. Punishment by the application of a blister was done in the army constantly and in the Bluecoat school when an idle lad shammed sick. Mr Bridle had been at Ilchester for over 12 years during which time he had received more than 4,500 prisoners and all that could be found against him were two, 'got up' cases. Evidence was taken from ex-prisoners some of whom declared Mary Cure and her baby to be in excellent health when they came out, others to the good character of the defendant; and some to the bad character and fained illness of Gardiner.

Jane Long was awaiting transportation in 1817 and Bridle was instrumental in obtaining her pardon and making sure she got proper medical attention when she was ill in the prison. Upon hearing that he was to be tried at Wells she came forward to give evidence on his behalf. She was one of a party of about 40 at an inn in the town willing to be witnesses in his favour, newspaper reports of her evidence include the sentence, 'This deponent states several circumstances relative to the means adopted by Hunt to induce the prisoners to complain against Mr Bridle of which we do not think it proper to state'. Bridle claimed that he had nearly 500 persons who had been in his custody prepared to come from all parts of the kingdom to testify to his character and conduct and that it was his inability alone to pay their expenses that prevented their appearance.

Witnesses as to character were Sir John Acland who has known Bridle since 1808 and described him as kind and humane of an excellent disposition. Magistrate F Poole described him as the best man for the job. Sir John Cox Hippisley the county magistrate found him to be kind and humane as did Mr Cole the Clerk of the Peace along with the high sheriff Vincent Stuckey and undersheriffs Edmund Broderip and William Melliar. William Hardy, successor to Bridle, stated that he had been a deputy keeper of Newgate before his appointment to Ilchester, and had kept up correspondence with him for 16 years, he had always considered him a humane man. Charles Allen had known Bridle for 24 years since he was in the fencibles and described him as a kind and worthy man. Captain Smith, in charge of the hulks at Woolwich stated that he had behaved with great humanity and firmness while there and that great numbers of those who had been under his care sought to testify in his favour. His commanding officer in the fencibles, Charles Anderdon, now a Somerset magistrate deposed to his outstanding conduct in several situations in the regiment. Several other magistrates, the coroner and gentlemen of the county followed giving similar testimony in his favour, as did Mr John Browne described as 'the police officer at Bath'. Mr Williams stated that the case was the result of unparalleled malignity; the author was a man who produced discord whenever he came, like the champion of whom it was said, 'where his horse placed its foot grass never grew.'

There were no petitions or statements from the prosecution, Sergeant Pell outlined their case once more and Mr Justice Richardson summed up after which the jury deliberated for a few minutes before finding Bridle guilty on the charge that referred to James Gardiner only and strongly recommended him to mercy on account of his former excellent character. The trial had lasted from nine in the morning until eight in the evening and sentence was deferred until his appearance at the King's Bench on November 21 in front of Justice Bayley.

The court officer was about to pay the special jury their fees when they asked if they, or any proportion of them were payable by Bridle himself and in that event, they would decline receiving any part of it. Immediately following this highly unusual gesture, counsel for the defence, Williams, Erskine, and Manning followed suit and returned their fees amounting to 75 guineas. According to one newspaper this was the second time that they had returned their fees to Bridle.

Hunt records in his *Address* for 12 December 1821 that after Bridle left Ilchester he, 'has taken up his residence in Bath with one Smith the editor of the *Bath and Cheltenham Gazette*' and he continues his sour remarks after the verdict.

> What such men as Smith, the editor of Bridle's Bath Gazette, may say, is of little consequence he was, and has been for many years, one of Bridle's pot-companions, not only in the Gaol, but at the Sessions and Assizes, where they were equally notorious for their gambling and profligate conduct. To this Smith I am willing to give credit at least, for sticking to his friend to the very last. It was expected by Bridle's cronies at Wells, that so favourable a Jury,

with Mr Rodberd as their foreman, would have acquitted him through thick and thin, and they had actually got a car decorated with ribands, etc with the intention of having him carried to his lodgings in triumph, as soon as the words not guilty had been pronounced; and while this feeling lasted, Bridle was surrounded by a number of the said cronies; but, as soon as the Jury had, although reluctantly, found him guilty, all his friends deserted him but Smith, the editor of the *Bath and Cheltenham Gazette,* and he was the only person who would accompany him out of court.

I am willing to give Smith his full share of credit for this conduct towards his fallen, deserted friend. Smith, it is said, has received some substantial marks of Bridle's friendship, which possibly he is not prepared to repay in any other way than by his personal exertions in his favour during his trial; and, under such circumstances, it is very excusable in Smith to endeavour, by all that lays in his power, to save him, if possible, from punishment. But 'we shall see' since he has been found guilty, acts of greater atrocity and more fatal in their results have come to my knowledge; and if we ever get a committee of the House of Commons to inquire into the conduct of the Magistrates, (which, if there be any justice remaining in the country, we certainly shall) these things will come out. The eyes of all England will be fixed steadily upon these Judges when Bridle is brought up for judgment; then we shall see whether the Government is disposed to lay the blame upon Bridle or the Magistrates; for a light sentence upon Bridle would be a severe and heavy denunciation upon the heads of said Magistrates.

The Sentence 22 November 1822

BRIDLE HIMSELF PUT in an affidavit in mitigation of sentence outlining his own history both before and during his time at the jail as reported before. He admitted that the treatment of Gardiner was unlawful as it was contrary to prison regulations but he was not influenced by any personal motive of malice or hostility and said that he had exceeded his duty in his individual instance and trusted that this solitary act of indiscretion would be amply counterbalanced by his previous conduct and a life devoted to public service. He had been subject to great mental agony from libels upon this character and conduct previous to his trial. He added that nearly one half of what he had saved had, at various periods, been expended in subsisting his aged parents now nearly 80 years old and some dear but indigent relatives. He claimed further that inability to bear the expense had alone prevented his accepting the voluntary offers of nearly 500 persons who had been in his custody to come forward from all parts of the United Kingdom and testify to his conduct and character. The defendant having taken his station on the floor of the court, Mr Justice Bayley [the judge in the case of Hunt it will be remembered] proceeded to pronounce the judgment of the court in the following terms:

> William Bridle, you have been found guilty by a Jury of your country, and now stand to receive the judgment of the Court, for unlawfully punishing a young man, named Gardiner, who was about 18 or 19 years of age, and who had been sentenced to death, but had his sentence commuted to imprisonment in the House of Correction, and to be kept to hard labour for a period of 18 months in the Gaol of Ilchester. It appears, that whilst he was in your custody he was punished for offences committed within the Gaol. In the month of November, 1820, he complained he was ill; but on the surgeon's examining him, the surgeon declared he was not. He was confined in a solitary cell, between which and the punishment an unfortunate interview look place between you and a surgeon of the name of Bryar, and, according to the affidavits, he suggested to you to apply a blister to this man. Whether the suggestion came from one or the other, it made no difference; both were in the wrong to suffer an application of that kind. It is of importance for a gaoler to know he should keep within the limits of his duty, that subordination may be preserved; and if he goes beyond those limits' subordination will cease.
>
> It is of importance to prisoners to know, that when gaolers exceed those limits they will be punished. It is stated, that this was a blister calculated to produce pain, but not to have dangerous consequences; and it further appears, that for many days he (Gardiner) was kept in a strait waistcoat. It is the duty of the gaoler to report anything uncommon that may happen in the course of the discharge of his duty, in an Occurrence-book; but no mention is made by you in the Occurrence-book of the punishment of Gardiner. You must have been conscious to yourself, at the time, that you were not acting correctly, or you would have mentioned it, that it might have met the eye of the visiting magistrate, who would have given his opinion whether it was proper to be continued or not. While the man was in solitary confinement there was no reason why the strait-waistcoat should have been applied. It was not a punishment attended with danger to the prisoner, but it was a deviation from the course of your duty.
>
> From the evidence it appears that he misconducted himself, but that does not justify you. A good character has been given you by many respectable persons. It appears that you were under the eye of Captain Smith for many years, and had his highest approbation. In the general tenor of your duty you have conducted yourself with great propriety, which has been taken into

consideration by the court. It appears that you even went beyond your duty as a gaoler in attending to the comfort of the persons under your charge, and that you even exposed your person to danger in visiting persons who had contagious disorders, to see if they had every comfort their situation required.

I sincerely believe this offence is a solitary instance of a deviation from your duty. The court look at whether it has not produced any inconvenience to yourself. It has contributed to your removal from the situation you filled at Ilchester, and you have suffered great uneasiness of mind. You are conscious that a man must be brought to punishment by deviating from his duty, and that you have, in this instance, sacrificed your character; great bitterness, regret, and anxiety of mind, must have been produced by this thought.

You are conscious that you are looked upon with a different eye – now from what you were before this transaction. It is the bounden duty of the court to take care that offences of this sort do not occur, and they are to punish, in order to deter individuals from repeating similar offences; and what you have already suffered will, in all human probability, prevent any other man from being guilty of the like. The line of your duty was plain. The keeper of a gaol is to keep in safe custody all committed to his charge, but not to annoy them in any manner. If any are refractory there are rules by which you should be regulated, and from which you should not have deviated. The court does not consider it necessary to visit your offence with imprisonment; the purposes of justice will be fully answered by imposing on you a fine; and, taking all the circumstances of the case into consideration, the court doth order and adjudge, that, for this offence, you do pay a fine of £50 to the King, and be imprisoned in the custody of the Marshal of the Marshalsea until such fine be paid.

The defendant who appeared much affected during this address burst into tears at its conclusion, bowed respectfully to the court and after paying the fine, withdrew.

Before the end of the year an appeal for financial donations, was launched, in order to 'afford Mr Bridle's friends and the public an opportunity of expressing their approbation of his general conduct and to reimburse him for his ruined fortunes, he having expended his last shilling in enormous costs attending this threefold persecution, it has been thought by his friends that an appeal might be made to a right-judging and liberal-minded public, affording an opportunity to their generous feelings to secure this deserving but unfortunate man from that ruin which must otherwise prevent him from raising its head again in life and which can only be done by opening a subscription in his behalf'.

The advertisement on the front page of the *Sherborne Mercury* for 9 December 1822 showed that subscriptions so far had reached over £176 including £100 from Sir John Acland and £20 from the Earl of Cork with 26 different towns or cities listing addresses willing to accept contributions and the appeal was repeated the following week. Help was also at hand from a different direction. Bridle had been an active freemason since 1806 and although his subscriptions seem to have stopped in December 1821 he wrote to them in January 1823 saying he was 'reduced to the greatest penury and distress'. On 23 January 1823 the Lodge passed a resolution in the following terms :

> A very interesting correspondence re worshipful brother Wm. Bridle, a Past Master of the Lodge and his prosecution for cruelty and ill treatment of prisoners whilst governor of Ilchester Jail.
>
> The minute referring to this matter is a bright illustration of the truly Masonic spirit evinced by the Brethren of the Lodge. As the minutes are couched in polished and a beautiful phraseology, the following extract may prove very interesting.
>
> It was unanimously resolved that it is the opinion of the Brethren present that Bro. William Bridle, Past Master of this Lodge, is reduced to the greatest penury and distress by the late proceedings relative to the investigation of his conduct in Ilchester Gaol. They have always considered, and do still consider him to be a man of the strictest integrity and eminently distinguished by the virtues of humanity and kind-heartedness, that they cannot but believe him to be harassed, a persecuted and a much injured man, and as such, entitled to the liberality and assistance of every good Mason. That, as a subscription has been most generously set on foot by his friends, Lord Cork and Sir John Acland, (the former contributing £20 and the latter £100), the Treasurer of this Lodge be desired to pay to the receivers of such subscriptions the sum of £16 from the funds of the Lodge, as a mark of the regard and esteem of the brethren, and as an earnest of their good wishes for his future prosperity and welfare.
>
> It was resolved to transmit a copy of these resolutions to the PG Secretary and to Bro. Bridle and a congratulatory letter to Bro. Bridle on the favourable termination of the, 'most cruel and vindictive proceedings with which he has been persecuted'. In this letter the secretary goes on to say,' Although anxious to avoid everything foreign to the Masonic character, I cannot forebear from stating the position of the Lodge, that you are the victim of a cruel and most merciless persecution and to assure you that nothing which has transpired during the whole of these proceedings has in the least degree shaken the high

opinion which we have long entertained, both of your public and private character.'

Bridle wrote to the Lodge with his thanks both for the donation and their support and 'the kindness towards me in this particular, will never be obliterated from my memory.'

In March of 1823 Bridle wrote to Edward Coles from 2, Thanet Place, The Strand, London. He appealed to Coles for a letter of recommendation as, 'Some valued friends have done me the honour to interest themselves deeply on my behalf', and he is 'about to apply to some persons in power to procure me an appointment at home or abroad as may enable me by fidelity or industry to obtain a reputable subsistence.' He continued that he has written to several magistrates individually and asks if Coles could possibly obtain some more favourable recommendations for him. His reasons for being in London are not explained but the address is of course near the river and maybe he was hoping for something from the hulk establishment presumably based nearby and he may also have been visiting the Freemason's Charity.

Coles replies from Taunton suggesting that he is giving himself, 'unnecessary trouble upon the subject as his character is already recorded and enough to entitle him to the appointment of any situation which you may be confident to undertake without the necessity of you addressing the magistrates individually or anyone else.' He also implies that no matter how highly he is regarded by individuals they are unlikely to say so in writing other than affidavits already existence… presumably this included himself.

Bridle writes back immediately explaining that the testimonials he is hoping for are to be annexed to his, 'memorial to the crown praying for service', ' if the government cannot find me immediate service I must direct my attention to another quarter and another source'. He finishes with, 'I shall be at the Assizes to receive anything which may be awarded me'.

12
SYDNEY GARDENS, BATH 1824

LETTER WRITING ASIDE, how he occupied the two and a half years between his leaving Ilchester in November 1822 and taking on the tenancy of Sydney Gardens in Bath at the end of June 1824 is not known but like a butterfly emerging from its chrysalis the 'hulk educated monster'; the, 'heartless, cold-blooded, inhuman, remorseless ruffian [that] ever disgraced the face of the earth', turned to running a pleasure garden in what was becoming the most beautiful and fashionable city in the country. Sydney Gardens opened in May 1795 as a place of amusement and recreation with dining rooms, underground passages, a sham castle ruin, walks, swings and grottos plus many other attractions of a similar nature. It also featured a large hotel and tavern. Initially the attraction was owned by the Pulteney family with 40 shareholders paying £100 each. A lease was created with the tenant to take charge of the day-to-day running including the organising and advertising of the functions and entertainments, the catering, keeping the grounds in good order as well as any necessary refurbishments. The financial arrangements are uncertain as to whether the tenant kept all the takings and had to pay for all the improvements himself, but it does seem as though they provided all their own provisions and equipment including stocks of wines and spirits. Bridle took over the lease of the gardens on 24 June 1824 having advertised the fact in the newspapers from the 15 June. How he was able to finance this is not known, did he have backers or was there capital set aside from his time at Ilchester? The latter is unlikely given his prostrations of poverty after his trial. The previous resident George Farnham was surrendering the lease after seven years unable to make it work to his advantage. Bridle announced his arrival in the *Bath Chronicle;*

> Sydney Gardens Vauxhall, Bath
> William Bridle respectfully announces to his friends and the public that he has taken the above establishment which he will enter upon on the 24th of June instant.

WB is determined to render the gardens deserving of public patronage by adopting every improvement which can increase their attraction. The future GALAS will be conducted by artists of the first eminence, and upon the same liberal style as the Royal Gardens, Vauxhall. THE TAVERN DEPARTMENT will be conducted upon the superior principles.-wines, spirits, and every other article, will be of the best quality and flavour, and the prices will be uniformly moderate.

A Grand Gala
Unprecedented for magnificence, diversity and interest
Will take place at these gardens during the ensuing
Race Week

Full particulars of which will be given as soon as the necessary arrangements are completed.

The next week further details were announced, the Grand Gala was to take place on 15 July,

... accompanied by many thousand lamps and flags, a grand vocal and instrumental concert which will consist of the pleasing variety of the most popular airs and modern comic songs. The celebrated and inimitable Il Diavolo Antonio will display his wonderful feats on the Rope Volante in which he will introduce various new astonishing and unequalled performances, never before attempted. Other performances and amusements will be introduced which will be particularised in the descriptive bills. The fireworks will be on a superior scale of magnificence, and will consist of the most brilliant, rare, astonishing specimens of the pyrotechnic art – conducted by the celebrated De Mortam. Military and Pandean bands will perform during the evening. The celebrated French Hercules, Monsieur Clyne, Balance Master from Paris will go through his wonderful and astonishing feats of agility, balancing and strength wherein he will balance a ladder 13 feet high on his chin with a boy on the top; also a pyramid of 13 glasses filled with wine all illuminated and 10 feet high, with which he will lie down and rise again, beat a drum to the tune then playing etc etc. A private carriage entrance will be provided. Additional police and other officers will be stationed in various parts to reserve strictest order. Refreshments will be furnished the price of which with those of wine spirits etc will be fixed up in each box to prevent imposition. Any box or room maybe set apart for a private company by timely application. To prevent a delay at the entrance doors it is advisable that the parties should previously provide themselves with tickets which maybe had, price 2/6d each.

One of Il Diavolo's specialities was, 'leaping through a balloon twenty feet from the stage and twenty feet from the rope, blowing a trumpet the whole time with the rope in full swing.' A pandean band consisted largely of panpipes and drums, for a time they were all the rage at fashionable places of entertainment in which every band member played the pipes and a percussion instrument with trumpets, drums, cymbals, and triangles, they were thought of primarily as a dance band, playing marches, quick steps, minuets, waltzes, and airs.

Pandean Minstrels

A late addition, although he had appeared in the gardens before, was Mr George Graham, balloonist extraordinaire performing in his new silk balloon to raise money for the Bath General Hospital. He ascended from Sydney Gardens at 6.30 on the evening of 16 July, accompanied by one of his assistants, and lifted off faultlessly at the start of a flight which took them to within five miles of Ramsbury in Wiltshire, having flown about 50 miles in an hour and a half. George was soon to be overshadowed by his wife Margaret who

George & Margaret Graham in their Balloon

became a celebrated balloonist in her own right, probably the first woman to do so. Reports stated that the three day event had been a huge success with about to 3,000 people attending under the excellent arrangements of the new proprietor and that the gardens were now to be called the 'Bath Vauxhall', after the original pleasure ground in London. During the closed season Bridle would carry out alterations and improvements replanting, installing paths, and in the early days a cascade and theatre. He employed John Kerr a London theatrical figure to write a small handbook or syllabus in which he described all the attractions in grand and enthusiastic terms including a plan of the labyrinth, 'nearly as big as Hampton Court', and drawings of the various features including the sham castle and hermit's cottage.

A man of 60 years arrived one day and applied to Bridle for work as he had 'been under his protection' before having been in Ilchester for debt. He had been paymaster in an English regiment for 25 years but had fallen on desperate times. Bridle gave him a job sweeping the walks but he became ill and unable to work before cutting his throat at his lodgings in Avon Street. In another act of kindness, he took in a fox from the huntsman and added it to the menagerie. On 29 June 1825 he organised a Grand Military Gala re-enacting the tenth anniversary of the glorious victory of Waterloo which included a military band of 34 performers. This was in addition to the annual race day gala in July when attendance was put at 5,000 over the three days. In September the 'unfeeling fiend in human form' put his name to a declaration or 'Anti-Peggery Proclamation,' in a, 'notice to fisherman and fishmongers respecting the practice of pegging the claws of crabs and lobsters'. Apparently, it was the done thing to put wooden pegs through their claws rather than tying them with string which not only caused great suffering but rendered the meat unpalatable and disgusting. The petition was signed by over 100 residents in Bath along with 11 fishmongers who in turn blamed fisherman for the practice.

January 1826 saw the addition of the Diorama, a scenic painting, viewed through a peephole, in which changes in colour and direction of illumination illustrate changes in the weather, time of day, etc. This one featured moonlight views of the ruins of Hollyrood Chapel and Canterbury Cathedral to great effect. In March of the following year he organised a collection at the gardens for the Crocker family, respected agriculturalists, who had fallen upon the hard times and been burnt out of their home. The gardens opened for the season in April having undergone, 'complete renovation' with the walks enlarged, the trees 'judiciously thinned with the different ornaments and amusements beautified to which has been added a complete aviary'. Other attractions included the Labyrinth, Merlin's Swing and Grotto, the Miller's House and Water Mill, Hermit's Cot, Cosmorama, etc'. The victory at Waterloo was celebrated once more in June this time under the patronage of Colonel Horner of the North Somerset Yeomanry Cavalry; there was a triumphal arch to welcome home survivors of the battle with Congreve rockets, shrapnel shells, bombs and the explosion of mines. The entertainment included Sylvia Zeppora an infant prodigy whose performance on the tight rope exhibited, 'a wonderful combination of juvenile talent and self-command'.

The Height of Fashion Cruikshank 1826

In July at the Somerset sessions in Bridgwater a man named Richards was sentenced to five months for stealing glass, the property of William Bridle of Sydney Gardens. The presiding judges were William Dickinson and J Phelips names which were more than familiar to him. During the same period, as the

21st Regiment of Foot were about to leave the city they asked Bridle if he had anywhere where they could have breakfast. He not only provided a sumptuous meal but refused to take any payment for it.

The following August there was a fete to celebrate the king's birthday on the 12th which was again well attended by thousands of people and a great success but at the same time the gardens were advertised for rent, presumably something to do with the terms of the lease, but there seems to have been no takers as by mid November, 'W Bridle respectfully announces to the nobility, gentry and general public that he has re-taken the premises for a term of years'. In the same month he announced that the roadway is in a complete state of dilapidation and that he is going to have it thoroughly restored and improved; he issued a scale of charges for its use. When the gardens opened for the new season in April of 1827 he declared that he had engaged a bigger band along with a saloon of considerable dimensions with a sprung floor, 'should young ladies feel disposed for a dance'. He also organised another benefit concert for the United Hospital which raised £139 and introduced archery as an additional attraction.

And so it went on. Bridle seems to have put his heart and soul into the enterprise, celebrations, amusements, balloons, breakfasts, dinners, galas, all presided over by 'the most liberal and generous of hosts', 'Mr Bridle's Gardens attained a degree of fashion which they had never previously enjoyed, various improvements which have been recently affected, render it at all times a delightful promenade and on gala nights nothing in the way of attraction is left to be desired'.

But it all came at a price. At the end of his trial he had claimed that his resources were depleted and as we have seen collections were raised in his honour to get him back on his feet, possibly he borrowed heavily or found some enthusiastic backers, but not everyone was happy. An anonymous letter in the *Bath Chronicle* during July of 1827 complained about an excess charge payable by subscribers wishing to walk in the gardens of a summer's evening.

By now the new aviary had grown to 140 canaries plus several other songsters of the feathered fraternity. In a most bizarre raid, between 80 and 100 birds plus eggs were stolen during April 1828. The thief was apprehended and his fascinating story along with that of his confederates is detailed by way of a diversion, in Appendix 1. In December 1830 Bridle was presented with a cuckoo for his aviary taken from a sparrow's nest the previous June and so presumably the attraction had been reassembled after the thefts. Crime was not his only problem during this time. Under the terms of his lease he paid £160 a year, 'inhabited house duty' and in 1829 the Commissioners increased this by £90 making a total of £250 to cover the Sydney Tap, a pub which formed part of the Sydney Hotel and which he sublet to a Mr Answorth. He appealed against this amount but initially refused to provide details of the amount of rent he received causing his appeal to be disallowed. He kept trying and eventually a couple of years later received judgement in his favour.

The air balloon attraction was now handled by a Mr Green who in May 1830 in front of an 'immense crowd' attempted to soar into the sky, unperturbed by the fact that his balloon was leaking he jettisoned his companion and some ballast before managing to reach the height of about 400 yards after which it descended rapidly into a garden at Kingsmead Terrace. Once returned to the gardens the gas continued to escape – so rapidly that a young boy was almost suffocated but recovered. Among his most remarkable engagements during this period was an appearance, in May and 'for four days only' of the, 'Extraordinary Double Boys', the 'original' Siamese twins Chang and Eng then embarking on a world tour, 'with nothing of a nature offensive to the feelings.' Just as remarkable in July was a walk through an avenue of blazing fire 24 feet in length more than 20 times by a man in an asbestos suit invented by Italian scientist Giovanni Aldini. Pigot's trade directory of 1830 has Bridle listed as a Wine and Spirit merchant of Great Poultney Street

Sydney House

In October 1830 his father George, retired tallow chandler, died at the age of 81 and was buried at Evercreech on 3 November. Also in that month Bridle installed a large star seven feet in diameter lit by gas and placed over the doorway of the Sydney Hotel and following its success he installed 127 more lights throughout the gardens. Not content with this in March he rearranged the aviary, installed an eagle chained to an ivy tower, a bear, (quite secure), which climbed a pole, some monkeys, 'to amuse juvenile visitors' and a pheasantry with some rare gold and silver specimens.

In early July 1831 an advertisement appeared in the *Bath Chronicle* putting the lease on the gardens up for sale by private treaty. This was organised by Mr George Robins a highly successful auctioneer of Covent Garden in London and seems to have been prompted by the death of the freeholder Richard Godman Temple of The Circus, Bath. Presumably the lease had to be renegotiated but whatever the reason Bridle continued in occupation.

Bridle organised a Grand Coronation Gala to take place on 8 September 1831 in celebration of the coronation of William IV. His Highness, it was said, disliked ceremonies and it is perhaps for this reason that no illuminations were planned for Bath on that date. Seizing, as he thought, a golden opportunity, Bridle organised his gala anticipating a great success as the 'only show in town' and tripled his normal expense in organising attractions, illuminations and events including a Mr Ryan who had erected an equestrian amphitheatre specially for the occasion and probably at great cost. Unfortunately for Bridle, Bath had a change of heart and organised celebrations after all, 'it is therefore expected a general illumination will follow, and that it will operate against my gala, such loss I must put up with but as I took upon myself the risk of providing this great fete to amuse the citizens of Bath when they had no other amusements for the evening, I cannot listen to the advice of my friends and give up my gala, but to render mutual accommodations I have ordered that the performance shall not commence until 9 o'clock so that the citizens of Bath and also the visitors may be able to view the illuminations …' Nonetheless, the newspapers gave a glowing report of Bridle's effort claiming an attendance of 2,000 persons and then gave a detailed list of all the other illuminations in the town.

The following October, 1831, Bridle was treated to a 'Bath Reform Dinner' for the, 'staunch friends of reform, served up in the style of comfort and abundance of variety which gave the highest satisfaction to the guests' and held at his Sydney Hotel. The event was chiefly intended as 'a compliment to the liberal landlord who on many public occasions has so promptly and gratuitously offered the use of his premises to his fellow citizens'. All was gaiety fun and enjoyment, few could have predicted how short a time this, 'style of comfort and abundance' was going to last.

13
DESTITUTION & DESPAIR

During March, 1832, after eight years, Bridle announced that he was not going to renew his lease which was due to end on 24 June. Advertisements were placed in the local papers offering the 14 acre 'Sydney Gardens with a labyrinth, bowling green trees and shrubs to a high perfection with a commodious hotel and an adjoining a public house known as the Sydney Tap', the tenure was for 7, 10 or 14 years but it was still being advertised in January. His final, 'Grand Reform Gala' was held on Monday 18 June with a concert, fireworks and the inevitable Diavolo Antonio and his flying rope [otherwise Antonio Migasi who shortly after moved to America and started his own circus]. On 27 June all his furniture and effects were put up for auction on the premises including a cellar containing '500 Dozen of Choice wines selected by Mr Bridle from the London bonded cellars with French and Rhenish wines imported by him direct'. Also included were fruit trees, forest trees, evergreens and shrubs. The main sale took place from the 27th to the 29th of June with the wines held back until 30 June and the 2nd and 3rd of July. The latter sale could not have been a complete success as 100 dozen bottles were reoffered for sale on 5 July 'at about one half the usual retail price'. By the following March there were still quite a few bottles left now removed to 14 The Market Place and these were finally auctioned off on the 27th.

Throughout his time at Sydney Gardens he was never accused of anything underhand or in poor taste, possibly he limited his audience by trying to attract the 'better class of customer' rather than including cheaper more popular attractions or possibly the whole thing was just not a viable proposition from the start. Nobody else could make it work, his successor a Mr Norriston survived only a few months as did William Chatterton the one after him, both perhaps frightened off by Brunel's plans for a new railway which was to run right through the middle. In the eight years of his occupation Bridle tried harder than anyone else to make a go of it but the income was just not there and it wiped him out. In June of 1833 his mother, Betty died at the age of 84, she had been an annuitant on the Rev. William Hetherington's Charity for the Blind at Christ's Hospital in London for many years but was still resident in Evercreech and buried in the local church. One enduring mystery is what became of his wife Maria? She is not mentioned after the Commons Commission of 1821 and has not been found in the death records nor is there any indication that they had children.

In November 1834 it was reported in some local papers that Bridle was committed to Ilchester jail as a debtor but nothing has been found to substantiate this. The newspaper accounts began on the 6th stating that while he was there he addressed a long letter to Francis Popham the then high sheriff of Somerset in which he '…recapitulates the services he had rendered to the county during his governorship and solicits pecuniary aid from the magistrates'. Whether in Ilchester or elsewhere, it seems to have been for a very short period and he was certainly free by January 1835 as he laments his situation in a letter to the *Bath Chronicle* mentioning both his arrest and release,

> … on my quitting the premises I believed I had enough to pay every person in full the amount of their claims with still a little to spare; I therefore never thought of making a compromise with my creditors but as fast as my property sold, and I got the position of money I continued to pay them. The produce of my sales amounted to £1,796/19/3d and I paid to 61 of my creditors, £1,721/10/3d and then discovered that it was impossible to pay all in full… I had made no reserve whatever for myself and there was yet £138/8/2d unpaid. For the principal part of this sum I had been arrested – the magistrates of the county commenced a subscription, the debt was satisfied and I got released. By documents accompanying this you will see that I brought £4,100 to the Sydney Hotel and Gardens the whole of which, besides the sum unpaid, I lost upon the premises; I am heavily affected and my ways and means are exhausted…
>
> W. Bridle, White Lion Inn, Bath 19 January 1835.

The United Grand Lodge of England, Board of Benevolence Minute Book for 30 April 1835 responds to his appeal for funds and records that he had been a mason since 6 December 1806 and paid his contributions until December 1821. Since that time he had been, 'unfortunate in business having lost more than £4,000 and is now afflicted with paralysis and in great distress. He was awarded a donation of £10.

In December of the following year he published an open letter to, *The Very Noble and Most Mighty, The Aristocracy of England,* and dated London December 26 1836. In this he once again outlined his early life on the hulks and the improvements that he made upon his appointment to Ilchester jail. His letter is not always easy to interpret, consisting in parts of hints and unnamed persons but he seems to be referring back to the general election of June 1818 at which Sir John Palmer Acland, chairman of the Somerset sessions, proposed the renegade Tory Sir Thomas Buckler Lethbridge as a parliamentary candidate. Acland made some remarks at a dinner in support of Lethbridge for which he was called to account in the public court, exactly what this was is not reported but it caused a 'schism' amongst the magistrates and Sir John retired from the chair soon after. The new magistrates on the standing jail committee directed that Bridle could not correspond with Sir John on the affairs of the jail 'hinting that they strongly suspected I had been an agent in the Lethbridge interest'. It was shortly after this that Henry Hunt began his campaign against Bridle. In an interesting footnote he states,

[When] Mr Hunt… was publishing the memoirs of his life; the sheriff was a gay widower and it was said that he had been induced to meet Mr Hunt's wishes to stop the publication of certain anecdotes which were otherwise to appear in the said memoirs'. [the unnamed sheriff was Sir Charles Bampfylde, and their relationship is mentioned in an earlier chapter. Bampfylde certainly had a most rakish reputation and was an associate and drinking companion of the Prince Regent at Carlton House. He was well liked and later curbed his youthful vices which did not save him from being shot dead by jealous husband on the streets of London in 1832.]

Bridle goes on to outline the conflict between Hunt and himself claiming that various witnesses had been bribed while given access to Hunt in his rooms, 'for the long period of 109 days under the orders of the sheriff, it was the rendezvous of the outcasts of society who were daily fed and bribed to insure the threats of revenge declared by Hunt against me'. Also, 'the sheriff and certain magistrates who suspected that I had interfered with a certain election became the friends of Henry Hunt'. Bridle quotes at length from an affidavit by Esau Whitcombe a former prisoner made after he was discharged from jail and shown to him by Sir J Cox Hippisley, Whitcombe was of Hunt's servants who swore,

…that he was 14 weeks servant to Mr Hunt, that he frequently seen money passed from the hands of his said master to the hands of several prisoners, for the purpose of inducing them to give evidence against the governor and that he heard Mr Hunt say, "When I ask you a question speak out sharp and never mind a lie or two to prosecute such a rascal as Bridle; never mind what you say to get him out of this place, as that is what I want"; 50 prisoners at least were so admitted to interviews in the presence of the deponent, some of them repeating their visits 12 times at the least; one of them told the deponent £40 were to be given them by Mr Hunt if they gained the day against Mr Bridle; that he had frequently heard his fellow prisoners express themselves satisfied with Mr Bridle's conduct towards them, and drink his good health in water, and after many of them expressed their regret when he was dismissed from the jail.'

Bridle claims that there were four magistrates who worked against him along with Sheriff Hanning but does not name them other than to say that they were the same four who challenged Sir John Acland over his election dinner remarks. When the Commissioners assembled for their enquiry at the jail, he claims that Hanning claimed to, 'know nothing of the Commission and expect you to attend our court, [the magistrates] or we will make a report against you upon the evidence we have taken'. Basically, telling Bridle to ignore the newly arrived Commons Commission and give his defence to the magistrate's enquiry. As we have seen Bridle took legal advice and chose instead to attend the Commission which had, of course, a much higher authority. This is a slightly different version to that given by Hunt who claimed that the magistrates called an end to their enquiries as Bridle chose not submit a defence. His dismissal by the sheriff, and the magistrates, claims Bridle, arose from political divisions amongst them, 'for party revenge', but does not elaborate. He was destroyed, he claims, 'first by Hunt because he suspected that I had prevented him from enjoying the private society of another man's wife in the jail and secondly by the anger of certain magistrates who suspected that I had put them to expense by opposing their interest at an election, but I neither did one or the other'.

He then gives more examples of prisoners being paid or given food to give evidence in favour of Hunt naming four petitioners, Chidley, Hill, Wheeler and Hillier, all of whom had since retracted their statements. Hillier claimed that he had put his X on the paper because Hunt told him that he should perhaps get his liberty, gave him something to eat and drink and something worth four shillings adding that, 'if that is what the gentleman read to me, then was not true'. Another witness, Charles Hill, when asked why his evidence differed from the magistrates to that given before the Commission replied that, 'I was not on my oath in the Sherriff's court and therefore did not think it any harm to stretch my conscience in a good cause'. Apparently, the Sherriff's court did not have the power to administer an oath. Bridle continues that Hunt caused the town of Taunton to be posted with caricatures representing the cruelties which were stated to be practised on the prisoners in Ilchester jail during the time of the Assizes.

Bridle states that he had 'incurred heavy and extraordinary expenses to the amount of the earnings of my whole life to protect that character which I had so nobly earned from my boyhood'. He concludes his 32 page letter by giving examples of support and recommendation during his years as prison governor and states that, 'I have so long suffered these runs to lie dormant because I depended on provision being made me; to wait longer is impossible, for I am now without the means of subsistence.' It does seem likely that the egotistical and childlike Hunt was used by the magistrates as a pawn to get at Bridle for their own political ends. Hunt's incarceration must have been a godsend to them, the more they could wind him up the greater the case against Bridle.

London & The End of the Road

IN THAT SAME year, 1836, Bridle wrote another long address, *To the Honourable Members of the British Parliament* which he sent from 76 Myddleton Street, Clerkenwell, London. It goes over much of the old ground and reveals that the person who wrote out the petitions for Hunt, presumably, William Pitcher, was desperate for Bridle to pardon him describing himself as one of the, 'devils in the conspiracy' confirming that the petitions were made up and the contents unknown to those who had their names affixed to them, he claimed further that the petitioners had since been traced and agreed that this was indeed the case. 'Those in the plot have since sworn that they were liberally treated at his table that repeated supplies of money were given them on the visits to be trained for witnesses… pardons promised… and as a general reward £40 – the price fixed upon as blood money for my ruin was to be presented to them by Mr Hunt and he permitted them the use of a private room for their amours!'

Once more he dates the source of his undoing to the General Election of 1818 and Sir Thomas Lethbridge's stand as a candidate for Somerset, a move which split the sheriff and magistrates into competing factions and the belief that Bridle was heavily involved on the Lethbridge side. Hunt became the means to get at Bridle and through him to Acland. As before no names are mentioned making it hard to work out who plotted what or why. Lethbridge, he claims assured him that he would go to the Home Office and insist that Bridle be looked after but nothing came of it. 'I have no income, am much afflicted by the effect of hard circumstances, and am destitute of a solitary day's subsistence'. Bridle claims that he had intended to publish his account of the whole affair but Acland said it would give him pain and so nothing appeared in print. Bridle reveals that he spent some of his income buying a house for his aged parents, and another for his brother either John, a grocer in Shepton Mallet who died in 1837, or George who had worked for him at the jail but moved to New York with his family in 1831. He ends his pamphlet by appealing for an enquiry into the whole affair. It is perhaps strange that he doesn't seem to have tried to achieve redress or justice, as he might term it, during his time at Sydney Gardens when he would have had friends and contacts who could have supported his plea for an enquiry. Instead he chose to leave attempts to re-establish his reputation until he was penniless and friendless. Bridle's great friend and supporter, Sir John Palmer Acland, died in 1831 and perhaps it was a deference to him and his wish that nothing be published about the affair to save his embarrassment that Bridle had kept quiet for so long, plus he was having the time of his life in Bath.

Bridle established contact with his son Sir Peregrine Palmer-Acland and in January he wrote saying that he has no home, is rendered incapable of earning the means for his future, and that he is being kept alive and from becoming a beggar in the streets by strangers ending, 'that unless aid is forthwith provided I am doomed to perish'. He writes to him once more at the end of March again from Myddleton Street describing his 'wretched misery' during the last two years. He continues, 'this poverty was described to the grand jury of Somerset at the last Spring Assizes by Sir TB Lethbridge who on his return to town writes that the gentleman, 'all agreed that they have no power to aid me and that many objected to taking the matter into consideration on the grounds of my dismissal from the service of the county.'

By the summer of 1838 Hardy was suffering from 'extreme debility' and ill health and in July the magistrates advertised the position of Keeper for the Common Gaol the with a salary of £250 per year, along with a free house, taxes and legal fees paid. Despite his claim of paralysis dating back to at least 1835 and to what must have been the amazement of everyone, Bridle put his name forward in an attempt to get his old job back. He sent a 'packet' presumably containing testimonials, to the long-suffering clerk of the peace Edward Coles from, 13 Yardley Street, Wilmington Square, Clerkenwell along with a letter highly recommending himself and appealing once more for Coles help and requesting further details of the appointment. He addressed a similar letter to the High Sheriff and magistrates of the county and heard with some dismay that Hardy's son might be offered the position; he remarked in a helpful but hastily scribbled note that, 'I feel myself bound to represent that this young man sometime since took a hasty flight from England for America to avoid the dangers of being tried at the Old Bailey for forgery, not one case in fact, but as his father told me, 'enough for a dozen necks if he had as many'.

When Coles replied, the news was not encouraging, 'you stand no chance whatever of being re-appointed' which Bridle in his reply stated, 'surprised me very much'. He then alludes to the, 'secrets' that both of them know relating to his dismissal but cannot talk about, and how he has 'forborne publication' of the whole story hinting that his silence should be enough to insure his reinstatement. Bridle continues that he has been wholly without income or property for the past four years and is alive due to the generosity of some good friends. Various subscriptions which he said came from well-wishers, 'from a duke to a guard on a mail coach', totalled £847/16/6d. 'Sir A Hood told me the other day that he had subscribed to this fund three times, yet when I had paid the postage on my last letter to you I was left with only 3d in the world'.

Not everyone saw his cause as lost, an article in the *Taunton Courier* gave Bridle its wholehearted support claiming that the then sheriff, Hanning, 'gave Mr Hunt every facility to examine the prisoners on account of an election pique, Mr Bridle having favoured the side of Lethbridge as the third candidate for Somerset. If Mr Bridle was ever fitted for this office he is now and if innocent his restoration to such situation would be a triumph due to integrity, and a reward for the heavy sufferings he must have endured' the *Salisbury and Winchester Gazette* continued in a similar vein, 'we have always considered Mr Bridle as a cruelly persecuted and deeply injured man, his conduct distinguished by great ability and a remarkable sense of judgement, effective discipline and a singular kindness of heart'. His application was probably as much to do with an attempt to publicise his cause and regain his reputation as it was to gain employment.

Letters to Coles become more formal and on 15 October Bridle wrote again on this occasion from the Winchester Arms, Taunton presumably he was lodging there awaiting the outcome of the election. Complaining that although he had been told that all relevant papers must be in by 15 October, Coles had neglected to tell him that the names of sureties in the sum of £10,000 were also required by that date. He included ten testimonials attached to his note presumably with minutes to spare. Unfortunately, only the list has survived which included,

Robert Smith late commander of the *Justitia* hulk
Vincent Stuckey

Colonel P Anderton
Mayor & magistrates at Bridgwater
Portreave Corporation and magistrates
Edward Alan Esquire
Colonel Danberry

Bridle didn't get the job and a scribbled note, this time addressed simply to 'The Clerk of the Peace' stated that he wished to leave Taunton immediately and would like his papers returned, he was waiting at door of the court the note continued, and was later, signed at the bottom, 'Received the above M Bridle'

In October 1838 Hardy retired from Ilchester with a pension of £150 a year. It had already been decided to 'break up the establishment' in the near future and despite the proposals to turn it into a county lunatic asylum the old jail was demolished shortly after 1843.

By February of 1839 it seems that Bridle had moved back to Bath and was in desperate straits. It was reported in one of the provincial papers that he 'is now a patient in Bath hospital, on leaving which it was said, he has not, "[any]where to lay his head".

On 2 November he wrote a long letter which was published in the *Bath Chronicle* on the 7th, and addressed to 'the Worshipful Mayor of Bath'. The letter was posted from 3, Hot Bath Street, although not stated this was probably part of the Bath Infirmary.

At some point between 1839 and 1843 he moved back to London. He has not been found on the census for 1841 and next appears in 1843 when he tried to petition Parliament asking to get his case reheard and in this he was fully supported by the *Cheltenham Journal*. He repeated his claims that his dismissal was due to political rivalry, with Hunt being used as a pawn. It states that 'Mr Bridle is in a state of great destitution and scarcely one remove from death's door… he is endeavouring to get some member of Parliament to lay his case before the House of Commons'. Worse was to come. In August of 1843 an elderly man on crutches and in a state of destitution appeared before magistrate Twyford at Bow Street in London. The man had entered the Home Office and asked to see the Home Secretary, Sir James Graham but was asked to write down the nature of his business which he was then allowed to deliver in person. He returned after a short period, raised his crutch and smashed three panes in the fanlight saying to the porter, 'You may take me to prison if you think proper.'

William Bridle, described as 'of good address', was arrested and asked to account for his actions to which he replied that he had committed the offence for the purpose of getting protection or relief as he was reduced to the upmost distress and privation'. He had no intention of doing anybody any injury but broke the windows in order to be taken into custody. Bridle then proceeded to outline the events at Ilchester many years before including details of his being supported at the time by Sir John Acland, and Sir Abraham Elton amongst others but the majority of the magistrates, he claimed, were influenced by party motives. This led to his total ruin and he had spent everything he had seeking redress. Understandably, the magistrate would not have been particularly interested in a long sob story and Bridle was just asked to pay for the cost of the damage at 6/- but as he was penniless he was committed to the house of correction for six days. His paralysis was first mentioned in 1835 when he applied to the Masons for relief and he was on crutches by the time of the above account, a situation which was to become increasingly severe; obviously a degenerative disease affecting possibly the last 20 years of his life. Although he does not record any particular accident or injury it is worth noting that when telling of his adventures on the *Retribution* he said that, 'In this excursion I had to pass through stagnant water and mud up to my middle the effect of which, and similar services prevents me now from the power of walking without support. [letter of 1836]. He probably had some disease of the spine which would certainly have prevented him from pursuing any active occupation as the symptoms became worse. It is possible that the disease had other symptoms affecting the brain which may account for his obsessive letter writing, of which we only have a tiny sample, and his determination to re-establish his reputation after many years in Bath where he does not seem to have pursued the matter.

Once more he was forced to depend upon the charity of his fellow masons and on 25 January 1844 he applied for relief which was approved on 17 May 1844 having been voted for by the governors and subscribers of the fund at the annual general meeting of the Royal Masonic Benevolent Annuity Fund on 19 June at Freemasons Hall in London. He was one of 12 applicants selected to receive an annuity as a, 'poor, aged and infirm Freemason', the brief entry gives few details except to record his address as 5, Duke Street, Westminster, his occupation as, 'late a hotel keeper in Bath, [presumably Sydney Tap in the Gardens], and his situation as married with no children. 'Having lost upwards of £9,000 from speculation he is now penniless and afflicted with 'paralytic affection' deprived of all power in the lower extremities and unable to stand.' He was granted an annual amount of £10.

He disappears from sight until 22 June 1846 when increasingly desperate, he began to write letters to Francis Henry Dickinson the son of

William Dickinson the Somerset MP and his long time supporter who had died in 1837. On this occasion he says that he has sent his dying affidavit to the Premier and Home Secretary and is being forced into a premature death by injustice. He continues that he had advanced sums amounting to £9,000 in keeping others from the poorhouse and the jail and is now destitute of everything. In a rather strange claim he says that, he had been advised at one point that if he would join Hunt in an impeachment of the whole bench but five, he would 'lay open the plot which they had worked for my ruin'. He concludes that 'on the honour of his country he could not stoop to such terms', but gives no further explanation. He adds further that, 'Mr Thring as a visiting magistrate sent £30 to my subscription fund, saying, 'before I could have acted the part performed by the sheriff I would have chopped my hand off'.

Yet another appeal for help appeared in the *Salisbury and Winchester Gazette* during February 1847 asking for funds 'for the poor old man who is now starving and in a miserable condition, the Bath papers will, we understand, receive subscriptions…' During the same month a slightly longer appeal appeared in the *Dorset Chronicle* described him as still at White Lion Street. The article describes his excellent record at Ilchester and Sydney Gardens, saying that with regard to the latter his expenses exceeded his precarious income which was dependent so much on the weather and other unforeseeable circumstances. 'he was obliged to leave for some other means of support, but this also failing, he is reduced in his old age 'when nearly dying for want, to solicit charitable aid'. What the 'other means of support' consisted of we do not know nor do we know why he moved to London. It is tempting to assume some family connection but from the little we know of his family this seems unlikely. His brother John died in 1837, George and family moved to New York in 1831 Mary has not been traced, Elisabeth was a widow living in Bath aged 75, Sarah died in 1848, and Amelia and Ann are not traced after the 1820s.

A long article in *Lloyds Weekly* for February 1848 outlines the gross injustice done to him again citing the election of 1818 and continues that he was threatened with dismissal and that, 'for two years every petty persecution that could be invented was put in operation for the purpose of involving Bridle in disgrace but without success for at the end of that time he came out of that ordeal with cleaner hands that at the commencement of the period'. 'The attorney general', continues the article, said that, 'the case against Bridle was produced by a party split on the bench and that Lord Wynford said to his brother judges at his trial in 1822 that, 'if any sentence more than nominal was pronounced he would enter his protest against it, the cause whereof he would publish to the world'. We have room for further testimony', concludes the article, 'but we venture to assert that the affidavits of the prisoners contain sufficient matter to induce the secretary of the Home Department to instantly institute an enquiry, the result of which must be to rescue an innocent man from the degradation of imputed crime and the sharp and stinging curse of poverty'. He may have been living in London for a while but he certainly retained his contacts in the west country. There is no indication of who was behind the publishing of all these desperate cries for help, possibly some were fellow masons, nor do we know if it had any good effect but it is curious that the Bath newspapers should have carried his story for so long after he left Ilchester and Hunt's death in 1835.

He writes again to Dickinson from 5 Winchester Terrace, Pentonville in a letter dated 31 December 1850 and mentions that he had turned down an appointment of £300 per annum in order to take the job at Ilchester. Presumably this was the offer of his own prison hulk on the Thames allegedly proposed by Arron Graham. He continues that he is unable to stand and has to be carried about like a child and that further information about his condition can be obtained from Mr Newman of Berwick House, Yeovil.

Bridle is next found in the census for 30 March 1851 a widower aged 71 and still living at 5 Winchester Terrace, where he is head of the household and described as an annuitant, presumably still receiving money from the Freemasons charity. Living in the same house as a lodger is Mary Steeple a milliner and widow aged 32 and her daughter Ida Josephine aged three. Intriguingly, Mary was born in Bath in about 1819 possibly a relative looking after him but no connection has yet been found. It is curious that in his oft repeated list of woes he never once mentions being a widower or the that he lacks a wife to look after him.

He writes to Dickinson once more on 5 April 1851 thanking him for his letter of 7 January he rambles on making the same old points. He does give one interesting quote from the magistrates enquiry of all those years ago, 'Thomas Poole',[one of the visiting magistrates], claims Bridle, 'addressed me in the following words, 'this will be an extraordinary event in the history of your life Mr Bridle you are to be put upon your trial when no person can be found to accuse you; what the result of this enquiry is to be it is impossible for me to say, but I pronounce it to be intended for your removal from office, which as measures are now laid, it is impossible that you can escape; to call for professional aid will be useless but it may be advisable that you call in some person to watch the proceedings and take notes.'

He finishes by declaring that he had been the inmate of a hospital, 'in the hope of obtaining relief from my bodily sufferings but in vain by my being dismissed as incurable. To be confined for life to a seat and suffering every want. For all my expenditure I now have 10d only per week, you may therefore soon hear of my worldly account being closed. This is followed up by another letter in May within which he wishes he was back in Bath where 'he could have medical advice and a warm bath free of expense plus a wheelchair for a trifle – and also a room on the ground floor, a person to attend me and a trifle for subsistence'. Whether any of these pleas were met with financial help is not recorded as we only have one side of the conversation but the litany of misery continues,

17 June 1851, 5 Winchester Terrace.
You once sent a person, on the subject of my being taken care of, and I now send you the copy of a letter I have written, 'By a paralysis I have lost the use of my lower extremities and for five years [1846] I have not been able to stand, or to breathe in the fresh air, but when at the age of 73 I am carried out as a child. As the muscles of the leg are connected with the muscles of the bladder, the orders of nature are in my person interrupted and my water leaves me by a perpetual dripping so that by day and by night I am obliged to be provided with any means I can contrive to receive this water, distressing as this may be I have symptoms that induce me to believe my stools will pass away in a similar manner unless means can be adopted to prevent it. Look sir, I implore you, at the state I must be in under these afflictions and see if the second part may not be prevented, or should it really be so it would be a charity, an act of mercy to shoot me. I have been carried into the open but three times for the past two years. I'm deprived of the power of obtaining medical aid being unable to call for it or to pay for a visit; I have been to one hospital but the water complaint is declared to be incurable. If I could be removed to any of my old friends in the country, where I could have an attendant and the daily use of a wheelchair I should be relieved of that distress which is now driving me mad, recover strength which is the surest way of saving me from this new dreadful affliction. My complaint throws me from my seat, and when down I am unable to get up again. I have fallen on the fire grate, cut my head open then forced to lie scorching with the fire until by my cries I obtained relief. I ask you sir in the name of the county which you represent if I can be conveyed to the county and provided it for as aforesaid'.

By the 1 October he is living at 18 Upper Winchester Street, Caledonian Road and writes that he has spent the past three winters without a bed and that his bones are now so prominent that he has to wear padding between his knees. 'I have desired to wear a steel bandage around my loins but as the bones of my back are covered only with skin I am unable to wear such bandage… the clothing I wear is nothing but rags…' and in what his possibly his last letter on 22 October,

> My afflictions and wants hath forced me to make an appeal to the parish for relief, in consequence I have received notice to quit my apartments the reason assigned being my afflictions are offensive, in my present distress it is wholly impossible for me to go into other apartments, unless I can find some friend who will afford me aid for that purpose… I appeal to you for relief that I may be enabled to obtain shelter and not to be forced to die in the street.
> I am sir your suffering and dying humble servant William Bridle.

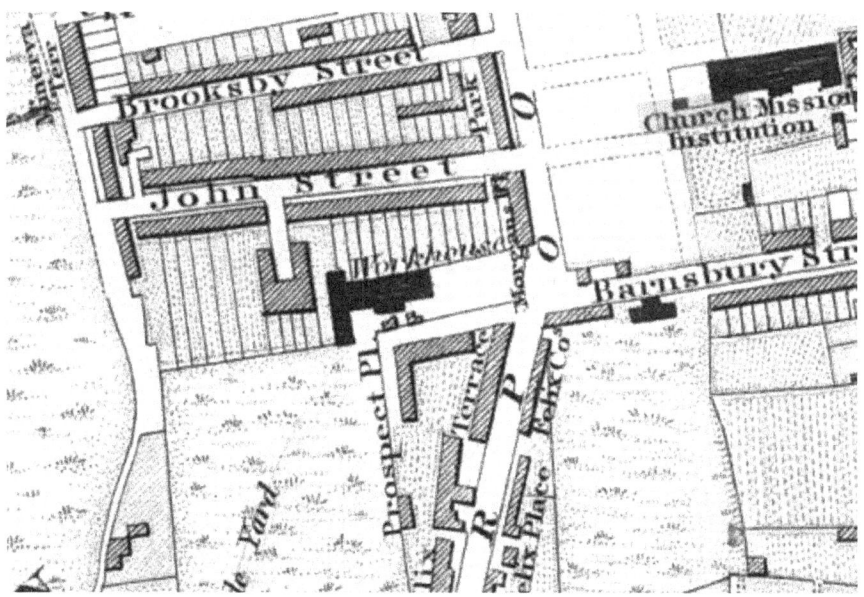

Workhouse, Islington

Within three weeks on the 16 November 1851 he was dead. He died at the workhouse in Liverpool Road, Islington. His cause of death was given as 'paraplegia' or a paralysis of the lower limbs, and 'typhus' caused by the bite of fleas or lice infected with *rickettsia orientia* a bacteria once known as jail fever and almost certainly picked up by insanitary conditions at the workhouse. The supreme irony is that after having survived that very disease for years at Ilchester it should cause his death all those years later. He was buried in St Mary's, Islington, London on 24 November aged 72.

There is almost ten years between him leaving Sydney Gardens in Bath and dying in Clerkenwell, London and there were numerous appeals for funds on his behalf but how he occupied his time or why he moved to London in the first place remains to be discovered. If he had written his memoirs like Hunt what a tale he could have told.

APPENDIX I
SHELLEY, THE MASK OF ANARCHY

Modern Propaganda' website

Percy Shelley's *The Mask of Anarchy* is a powerful and influential poem that has had a lasting impact on political and artistic movements and is often seen as one of the most important political poems of the 19th century. Written in response to the Peterloo Massacre the poem is a call to arms for the working classes to rise up against their oppressors and demand their rights. The poem is structured as a series of visions, each one building on the last to create a powerful indictment of the ruling class and the state of British society at the time. The first vision depicts a figure named Hope who is stricken with grief at the state of the world. She is then visited by a group of figures representing different aspects of the ruling class, including Murder, Fraud, and Hypocrisy. These figures taunt Hope and declare that they will continue to rule over the people with impunity.

In the second vision, the poem turns to the Peterloo Massacre itself, depicting the soldiers and police as brutal and merciless oppressors who trample on the rights of the working classes. The poem describes the violence and chaos of the scene in vivid detail, highlighting the injustice of the authorities' actions.

The third vision is perhaps the most famous and powerful in the poem. Here, Shelley describes a group of people rising up against their oppressors, clad in the titular mask of anarchy. These figures are described as 'the multitude,' and they are presented as being heroic and noble in their struggle for freedom. Shelley's use of the mask of anarchy as a symbol of resistance has been hugely influential, inspiring many other political movements and works of art.

The final vision of the poem is a call to action, urging the working classes to rise up and overthrow their oppressors. Shelley's language here is passionate and persuasive, urging the reader to join in the fight for freedom and justice perhaps the most famous in the poem, and it encapsulates the message of the entire work. Shelley is urging the working classes to recognize their own power and to use it to overthrow their oppressors. He is calling for a revolution, not just in the political sense, but in the sense of a complete transformation of society.

Shelley's use of vivid imagery and passionate language makes the poem a stirring and persuasive work that continues to resonate with readers today. The guilty soldiers, he says, will return shamefully to society, where 'blood thus shed will speak / In hot blushes on their cheek'. Women will point out the murderers on the streets, their former friends will shun them, and honourable soldiers will turn away from those responsible for the massacre, 'ashamed of such base company'.

The poem mentions several members of Lord Liverpool's government by name: The Foreign Secretary, Castlereagh, who appears as a mask worn by Murder, the Home Secretary, Lord Sidmouth, whose guise is taken by

Hypocrisy, and the Lord Chancellor, Lord Eldon, whose ermine gown is worn by Fraud. Led by Anarchy, a skeleton with a crown, they try to take over England, but are slain by a mysterious armoured figure who arises from a mist.

I

As I lay asleep in Italy
There came a voice from over the Sea
And with great power it forth led me
To walk in the visions of Poesy.

II

I met Murder on the way -
He had a mask like Castlereagh -
Very smooth he looked, yet grim;
Seven blood-hounds followed him:

III

All were fat; and well they might
Be in admirable plight,
For one by one, and two by two,
He tossed them human hearts to chew
Which from his wide cloak he drew.

IV

Next came Fraud, and he had on,
Like Eldon, an ermined gown;
His big tears, for he wept well,
Turned to mill-stones as they fell.

V

And the little children, who
Round his feet played to and fro,
Thinking every tear a gem,
Had their brains knocked out by them.

VI

Clothed with the Bible, as with light,
And the shadows of the night,
Like Sidmouth, next, Hypocrisy
On a crocodile rode by.

VII

And many more Destructions played
In this ghastly masquerade,
All disguised, even to the eyes,
Like Bishops, lawyers, peers, or spies.

VIII

Last came Anarchy: he rode
On a white horse, splashed with blood;
He was pale even to the lips,
Like Death in the Apocalypse.

IX

And he wore a kingly crown;
And in his grasp a sceptre shone;
On his brow this mark I saw -
'I AM GOD, AND KING, AND LAW!'

X

With a pace stately and fast,
Over English land he passed,
Trampling to a mire of blood
The adoring multitude,

XI

And a mighty troop around,

With their trampling shook the ground,
Waving each a bloody sword,
For the service of their Lord.

XII

And with glorious triumph, they
Rode through England proud and gay,
Drunk as with intoxication
Of the wine of desolation.

XIII

O'er fields and towns, from sea to sea,
Passed the Pageant swift and free,
Tearing up, and trampling down;
Till they came to London town.

XIV

And each dweller, panic-stricken,
Felt his heart with terror sicken
Hearing the tempestuous cry
Of the triumph of Anarchy.

XV

For with pomp to meet him came,
Clothed in arms like blood and flame,
The hired murderers, who did sing
'Thou art God, and Law, and King.

XVI

'We have waited, weak and lone
For thy coming, Mighty One!
Our purses are empty, our swords are cold,
Give us glory, and blood, and gold.'

XVII

Lawyers and priests, a motley crowd,
To the earth their pale brows bowed;
Like a bad prayer not over loud
Whispering – 'Thou art Law and God.' -

XVIII

Then all cried with one accord,
'Thou art King, and God and Lord;
Anarchy, to thee we bow,
Be thy name made holy now!'

XIX

And Anarchy, the Skeleton,
Bowed and grinned to every one,
As well as if his education
Had cost ten millions to the nation.

XX

For he knew the Palaces
Of our Kings were rightly his;
His the sceptre, crown and globe,
And the gold-inwoven robe.

XXI

So he sent his slaves before
To seize upon the Bank and Tower,
And was proceeding with intent
To meet his pensioned Parliament

XXII

When one fled past, a maniac maid,
And her name was Hope, she said:

But she looked more like Despair,
And she cried out in the air:

XXIII

'My father Time is weak and gray
With waiting for a better day;
See how idiot-like he stands,
Fumbling with his palsied hands!

XXIV

'He has had child after child,
And the dust of death is piled
Over every one but me -
Misery, oh, Misery!'

XXV

Then she lay down in the street,
Right before the horses' feet,
Expecting, with a patient eye,
Murder, Fraud, and Anarchy.

XXVI

When between her and her foes
A mist, a light, an image rose,
Small at first, and weak and frail
Like the vapour of a vale:

XXVII

Till as clouds grow on the blast,
Like tower-crowned giants striding fast,
And glare with lightnings as they fly,
And speak in thunder to the sky

XXVIII

It grew – a Shape arrayed in mail
Brighter than the viper's scale,
And upborne on wings whose grain
Was as the light of sunny rain.

XXIX

On its helm, seen far away,
A planet, like the Morning's, lay;
And those plumes its light rained through
Like a shower of crimson dew.

XXX

With step as soft as wind it passed,
O'er the heads of men – so fast
That they knew the presence there,
And looked, – but all was empty air.

XXXI

As flowers beneath May's footstep waken,
As stars from Night's loose hair are shaken,
As waves arise when loud winds call,
Thoughts sprung where'er that step did fall.

XXXII

And the prostrate multitude
Looked – and ankle-deep in blood,
Hope, that maiden most serene,
Was walking with a quiet mien:

XXXIII

And Anarchy, the ghastly birth,
Lay dead earth upon the earth;

The Horse of Death tameless as wind
Fled, and with his hoofs did grind
To dust the murderers thronged behind.

XXXIV

A rushing light of clouds and splendour,
A sense awakening and yet tender
Was heard and felt – and at its close
These words of joy and fear arose

XXXV

As if their own indignant Earth
Which gave the sons of England birth
Had felt their blood upon her brow,
And shuddering with a mother's throe

XXXVI

Had turnèd every drop of blood
By which her face had been bedewed
To an accent unwithstood, -
As if her heart had cried aloud:

XXXVII

'Men of England, heirs of Glory,
Heroes of unwritten story,
Nurslings of one mighty Mother,
Hopes of her, and one another;

XXXVIII

'Rise like Lions after slumber
In unvanquishable number,
Shake your chains to earth like dew
Which in sleep had fallen on you -
Ye are many – they are few.'

APPENDIX II
CLARKE & MADDEN

THE *BATH CHRONICLE* of 24 April 1828 carried a strange report,

> In the night of Thursday last some thieves broke into Sydney Gardens and plundered the Aviary of canary birds, cages, &c. A reward is offered for their apprehension. The Aviary is rather a new feature in the Gardens: its stock had increased to about 140 birds, in fine plumage and full song. From 80 to 100 of the feathered songsters, and a greater number of eggs, are lost, together with property connected with the fitting up of their colony! These birds were of considerable value, and had been carefully kept, with stoves to warm their habitation in the winter.

The reward offered was ten guineas, a very tempting sum and on 14 July 1828 at the Somerset quarter sessions at Bridgwater a 26-year-old plasterer named Joseph Madden of Bath was convicted of simple larceny, and committed to Wilton jail. The description book describes him as a married man five feet seven inches tall, of sallow complexion with hazel eyes, dark brown hair, three cuts to his forehead and a mole on his left arm; he was unable to read or write. Madden was sentenced to eight months imprisonment including two weeks solitary confinement for stealing 50 canary birds, two stone pitchers and other items. How he was caught and what happened to the birds is not recorded but the aviary was re-established so presumably they found their way home. Stealing birds was quite different from his usual occupation. Despite professing to be a plasterer Madden was a full time grave robber or resurrection man who worked with a gang in Bath the leader of which was a William Clarke otherwise claiming to be an industrious weaver. Born in around 1800 Madden first came to the attention of the authorities in July 1821 when he was detained at Shepton jail until he could pay the maintenance owing for his bastard child. He was discharged in October.

At the Lent Assizes in Taunton on 18 February 1826 Madden was charged, along with William Clarke, with attempting to steal a corpse from Walcot Churchyard in Bath. Clarke had been found with four bodies in his house and confessed that he had assisted in the procuring of 2,000 more for anatomical purposes having been introduced to the trade since he was six years old by his father, a London gravedigger. In his confession he claimed that when subjects were scarce, he had been paid as high as ten guineas a piece and had been tried 28 times for this offence but from various flaws in the indictments he had managed to escape from all but two on which he was convicted and punished. Clarke had, with an assistant, hired a small house at Hat and Feather Yard with a view of Walcot burial ground so that as soon as people were buried he was fully aware of the time, place and subject.

He and Madden had set about their task so industriously that between October and February of 1826 they had plundered the burial-ground of at least forty-five bodies which they packed up in hampers and sent off to London by coach. When his house was searched three bodies were found packed in hampers ready for conveyance by coach and a fourth in a closet covered with straw. In the cellar, there was an immense quantity of human bones which he was preparing to assemble into complete skeletons.

Clarke did not deny the charge but complained, rather foolishly, that the medical gentleman who had promised to come forward in his support had not done so. A Bath anatomical lecturer named Norman along with a surgeon named Knight advised him to plead guilty before the magistrates after which he would be bailed from Shepton Mallet jail and the matter would be hushed up. He acted upon that advice but was imprisoned to await trial before the assize court where he was convicted. He pleaded for mercy maintaining that *subjects* as he referred to them, must be obtained for the purposes of medical science and that the obtaining and acting upon them was very advantageous to the living, drawing a connection between his profession and loyalty to the king. Clarke claimed that he had procured four subjects for Sir Astley Cooper so that he might practice on them before operating on George IV himself. In mitigation he claims that he had lost a good situation in life and with it his character from which he was unable to recover claiming a wife and five children dependent upon him.

Mr Justice Burrough was less than impressed and expressed his disgust at the boastful conduct of the prisoner saying that he considered the case to be very serious and sentenced Clarke to twelve months in the 'common jail' plus a fine of £100. The sentence may seem light in view of the huge number of *subjects* that he claimed to have excavated, its unsavoury and shocking nature, and the insolence of his boasts, but legally the dead did not belong to anyone and were something of a grey area and the offence was classified as a misdemeanour rather than the more serious felony. Had the robbers taken a shroud or any other item from the grave the charge would have been much more serious. Although the public were horrified by the practice, many professionals saw the need for bodies to facilitate research. On this occasion Joseph Madden was discharged with accomplice William Broderip due to lack of evidence.

Confined in Ilchester jail, that August Clarke sent a petition to the secretary of state claiming as before that, 'the practice of dissecting is necessary to the study and practice of medicine and surgery and that as no legal mode exists of procuring bodies for that purpose your petitioner has been guilty of a crime against the law but has, at his own peril, assisted in the useful object of a profession whose occupation is the preservation of life and the alleviation of human misery. Your petitioner has a wife and three children, (reduced from five at his trial) now in the greatest distress and not having the most distant hope of ever being able to pay the fine. Therefore, having no prospect of ever being released from prison but by death unless he receives the Royal mercy and having always born the character of an honest and industrious man he confidently hopes you will be pleased to take into your consideration the severity of the sentence'. Remarkably, the petition was signed by 17 doctors and members of the Royal College of Surgeons as 'a fit object for the Royal Clemency'. By the end of September having received no reply he wrote again to Robert Peel and once more in November this time with the added claim that his wife had gone blind during the last five months and that he has had an offer of employment as a coach builder in London.

By the middle of December with still no response Clarke moved things up a gear. He was instrumental in organising a conspiracy to break out of Ilchester, he suggested to his fellow prisoners that they place a large stone or similar in their prison stockings ready to attack the turnkeys and make their escape from the prison. It seems that the inmates were agreeable to this but shortly before the plan could be put into effect Clarke exposed the whole scheme to the prison officers. Whether the plot was real or contrived prison governor William Hardy was convinced and it provoked a letter from him not only chasing up the petition but saying how useful Clarke, 'a constable of the ward' had been in a plot carried out by some desperate offenders in which murder was contemplated'.

The following January he uncovered yet another escape plot at the jail and at last somebody listened. He was visited by local magistrates Stuckey and Hanning in January who interviewed him at some length probably about his connection to those worthy gentlemen of Bath, Mr Norman and Mr Knight who he claimed had renegaded on their promise to get him out of the scrape, and their connection to the resurrection business. Encouraged to give an account of his life he freely admitted that he had moved to Bath in October specifically to obtain bodies for the London market but the interview revealed far more than that. It was reported in the local newspapers during February that he claimed to be the masked man in the blue jacket that had decapitated Arthur Thistlewood and his fellow conspirators on 1 May 1820 after they had been hanged by executioner Botting. James Botting was described as repellent and illiterate, his number of kills probably totals around 175. He prepared his charges in the normal way on the front section of the gallows in which he was assisted by James Foxen and attended by the Rev. Cotton, the Ordinary of Newgate. At 8 o'clock, the drop fell and the traitors were suspended. It took about five minutes for all visible signs of life to be extinguished, but they were left on the ropes for half an hour just to make sure.

An axe had been placed on the platform for the final indignities and their bodies were laid in wooden coffins with their heads hanging over the edge and then a remarkable thing occurred. Contemporary accounts describe the event,

When the rope had been removed, and the coat and waistcoat forced down, so as to leave the neck exposed, a person wearing a black mask, which extended to his mouth, over which a coloured handkerchief was tied, and his hat slouched down, so as to conceal part of the mask, attired in dark-grey trowsers, dressed like a discharged seaman in an old blue jacket, buttoned close to him and worn out at the elbows, mounted the scaffold with a small knife in his hand, similar to what is used by surgeons in amputation. He hastened with repeat steps to the head of the coffin performing the operation in such a manner as immediately to convince everyone who saw him that his dress was a disguise; and his skill as surgeon and his dexterity as an anatomical and surgical operator were of no ordinary character he advanced to the coffin containing Thistlewood and in a little more than a minute he severed the head from the body. This man knew the best way to decapitate men, and begun with a deep cut across the front of the neck, angling the knife under the jaw to the foramen magnum, where the skull opens to allow the spinal cord to interact with the brain. The man would continue this angle of cut all around the neck of the deceased. When this was done, this man took hold of the head and violently twisted it in both directions, separating the head from the neck without needing to saw through fibrous ligaments that remained uncut by his blade. When Brunt's turn came, the man dropped the head, spurring cries from the gathered audience of, *Yah! Butterfingers!*

The Decapitation of Arthur Thistlewood

Some of the crowd were greatly distressed at the scene issuing groans and expressions of horror and detestation at that part of the ceremony. Some were heard to cry out, 'Damn the butcher! Shoot him! As soon as the severance was complete he handed the head to the executioner, who held it up to the surrounding multitude and cried out in a loud voice, but evidently not much relishing the task, 'This is the head of Arthur Thistlewood – a traitor! This was repeated three distinct times, turning the head to the people on every side. The expressions of the crowd seemed to have an effect on the operator and he retired from the scaffold to the lodge below until another subject was prepared for him. The five Cato Street conspirators became the last to suffer this fate in England.

A fascinating tale but was it true? Clark himself protested in a letter to Robert Peel, Secretary of State at the end of March that it was a story, 'inserted by some enemy to injure me' and that he 'hopes it will not injure his case'.

If it wasn't true it was certainly a very odd thing to make up. Unfortunately, a letter from John Wontner the governor of Newgate prison sent from the Old Bailey and dated 7 February 1827 states that, 'the whole statement in the paper of his being the man who decapitated Thistlewood and others is a falsehood and that he never was brought up to the profession of a surgeon and that from the accounts obtained from the hospital he is a very bad character and unworthy of leniency being shown to him.' One theory is that he made it up to show how useful he had been in discharging such an odious duty but then changed his mind thinking it might be counter-productive. 'The man who really decapitated the conspirators', reported the press, 'is well known at the hospitals and is now in London'. Taking all the evidence together it seems that Clarke was a fantasist and it is difficult to believe anything he said. He was obviously educated as his petitions are well written and in a good hand. Compulsive liar or not his case was at last recommended for, 'consideration by his majesty's government' the magistrates report finishing with the words, 'We understand that the case of Mr Clarke is to be forthwith represented to the secretary of state with a strong recommendation of the county magistrates. Probably before they realised that the whole escape plan was ploy to gain a reduction of sentence. Clarke was still in Ilchester in the middle of April 1827 having served five weeks over the 12 months sentence because he was unable to pay the fine. He wrote once more this time enclosing a letter from his wife Mary in which she described her children as almost starving as she is unable to find their bread and they are almost without clothes, she declares that she has lost all hope. The correspondence ends there but in the jail register there is a note saying that he was discharged on 6 May 1827 the fine having been remitted and he then disappears from the public record.

Madden continued in his chosen profession being acquitted of stealing three bodies in 1830 after being accused of association with, 'the notorious Clarke who was some two or three years ago in Bath' but eventually his luck run out and in July 1833 he was sentenced to be transported for seven years for stealing a gown and other articles – from a Mr Norrison's premises – at Sydney Gardens!

BIBLIOGRAPHY

Bamford, S. *Passages in the Life of a Radical* Simkin, Marshall & Co. 1844
Belchem, J. *'Orator' Hunt* Breviary Stuff Publications 2012
Branch-Johnson, W. *The English Prison Hulks* Johnson 1937
Bridle, W. *A Narrative of the Rise & Progress of the Improvements Effected in His Majesty's Gaol at Ilchester.* 1822
Bush, M. *Casualties of Peterloo* Carnegie Publishing 2005
Clarke, J. ed *Naval Chronicle Vol 7* Bunney & Gold 1802
Cox, J. *A History of Ilchester.* Ilchester 1958
Davis, M. *A Surfeit of Magnificence.* (Thomas Champneys) Hobnob Press 2021
Davis, M. *The English Convict Hulks 1600-1868*, Pen & Sword, 2024
Elliot, K. *No Swinging on Sundays* Akeman Press 2019
Gee, A. *The British Volunteer Movement 1794-1814* Oxford 2003
Graham, H *The Annals of the Yeomanry Cavalry of Wiltshire* Marples 1886
Hannon, K. *Designing and Dangerous Men* Inspiring Publishers 2021
Huish, R. *The History of Henry Hunt MP for Preston* Saunders 1835
Hunt, H. *A Peep into a Prison or The Inside of Ilchester Bastille* Dolby London 1821
Hunt, H. *Investigation at Ilchester Gaol into the Conduct of William Bridle* Dolby 1821
Hunt, H. *Jail Journal* Manchester Libraries 1821
Hylton, Lord *Somerset Fencible Cavalry* Privately Printed 1932
Ingrams, R. *The Life & Adventures of William Cobbett* Harper Collins 2005
Lennox, S. *Bodysnatchers* Pen & Sword 2016
Masonic Material *An Epitome of 100 years of Lodge of Brotherly Love* Yeovil, 1910
Perkins, D. *The History of The Lodge of Brotherly Love* 2010
Poole, R. *Peterloo* Oxford 2019
Reid, R. *The Peterloo Massacre* Windmill 2018
Rogers, W. *West-Country Sketches, Biographical and Historical* Commin 1895
Snaddon, B. *The Last Promenade Sydney Gardens,* Bath Millstream 2000
Thomis/Holt *Threats of Revolution in Britain 1789-1848* Macmillan 1977
Trow, M *Enemies of the State* Pen & Sword 2010
Vaux, J H. *Memoirs of James Hardy Vaux* Hunt & Clarke 1827
Wilkes, S. *Regency Spies* Pen & Sword 2015
Young, P *Two Cocks on the Dunghill* Twopenny Press 2009
Wilkinson, G. *An Authentic History of the Cato Street Conspiracy.* Kelly 1821

RESEARCH
Somerset Archives
Brunel Way
Norton Fitzwarren
Taunton
TA2 6SF
01823 278805
somersetarchives@swheritage.org.uk

Museum of Freemasonry
Freemason's Hall
60 Great Queen Street
London
WC2B 5AZ
020 7395 9257
museumfreemasonry.org.uk

The National Archives
Ruskin Avenue
Kew
Richmond
Surrey
TW9 4DU
020 3897 1575
nationalarchives.gov.uk

Find My Past
For newspaper archive
findmypast.co.uk

Ancestry
General historical research
ancestry.co.uk

INDEX OF PERSONS AND PLACES

Abbott, Lord Chief Justice 37, 98
Acland, Sir John Palmer 123, 124, 126, 131, 132, 134, 137, 140, 144, 175, 177, 183, 184, 186, 187, 211, 215, 236, 241, 253–56, 259
Adam, Mr 233
Adlam, Mrs 130, 131
Alan, Edward 258
Aldini, Giovanni 249
Allen, Charles 237
Allen, George 191
Alresford, Hants 228
'Amelia' 101, 260
Amesbury, Wilts 44
Amiens, Peace and Treaty of 43, 61, 103
Anderdon, Charles Procter 103, 237
Anderton, Col P 258
Andover, Hants 39, 69, 187, 229
Andrews, Jonathan 82, 87
Anstice, Robert 126, 191
Answorth, Mr 249
Antonio, Il Diavolo 244, 251
Arkwright, Richard 18, 19
Ashworth, Mr 10, 11
Astley, Francis Dugdale 43–45, 65
Austen, Jane 119
Australia 105, 109, 119
Auton, Peter 199
Axbridge 118

Badcocks, Mrs 173
Bagguley, John 32, 33
Baillie, Mackay Hugh 103
Baines, Edward 91
Bamford, Samuel 9, 70, 75, 78, 90, 96, 97, 152, 202, 280
Bampfylde, Sir Charles 150, 151, 187, 188, 192, 195, 253
Bantry Bay, Ireland 108
Barber, Edmund 187
Barber, John 101
Barnard, William 180
Bath 54, 71, 101, 114, 119, 124–26, 139, 169, 179, 189, 202, 206, 229, 231, 237, 238, 243, 245, 246, 248, 250, 252, 256, 258–62, 264, 274–77, 279, 280
Bathpool 135
Bathurst, Gen Bragge 67, 217, 218
Bayley, Justice 75, 78–80, 84, 87, 89, 92, 94–98, 147, 198, 237, 239
Beckhampton, Wilts 43
Bedford 193
Bellingham, John 86
Birmingham 70
Bisshopp, Col Harry 52
Blackburn, Lancs 70
Bley, John 109
Blisset, Richard 189
Botley, Hants 61, 66, 72
Botting, James 277
Bradford on Avon, Wilts 42
Brandreth, Jeremiah 33, 34
Brest, France 108
Bridgwater 70, 101, 119, 126, 159, 247, 258, 274
Bridle, William 100-261 *passim*, 263, 280
Brighton, Sussex 52
Bristol 54, 63, 64, 67–69, 71, 160, 212, 235
Broderip, Edmund (sen and jun) 144, 145, 149, 168, 179, 187, 217, 236, 276
Brougham, Henry 228
Brown, Mr 210
Browne, John 237
Bruce, Charles Brudenell, Lord 43, 45–47, 51
Brunel, Isambard K 251
Brunswick, New, Canada 57–59
Brunswick, Caroline of 142, 153
Bryan, - 114
Bryar (Bryer), Dr James 135, 175, 176, 185-6, 239
Burrough, Mr Justice 275
Burton's Mill, Lancs 26
Bush, Michael 11, 12
Bussell, John 179
Buxton, Thomas Fowell 135, 161, 212, 214
Buxton, Mr 3, 6, 9

Calne, Wilts 42
Cambridgeshire 65
Campbell, Duncan 105
Campden Clubs 26
Canada 14
Canning, George 86
Canterbury Cathedral, Kent 247
Caribbean 13, 14
Carlile, Richard 3, 11, 225
Carlton House, London 31, 253
Caroline of Brunswick 142, 153
Carrington, Rev 40
Carter, - 175
Cartwright, John 26, 27, 29, 66
Castle, John 28, 29
Castle Cary 185
Castlereagh, Robert, Viscount 72, 86, 266, 267
Cato Street Conspiracy 28, 36, 37, 278, 280
Chadwick, John 77, 88
Chamberlain, John 176, 177, 208
Champneys, Thomas Swymmer 221, 222, 280
Chapman, John 174
Chapman, Mr 88
Chatham, Kent 57, 108
Chatterton, William 251
Cheshire 10, 11, 77, 83
Chester 82
Chidley, William 153, 154, 194, 254
Child, Henry 176
China, Honor 180
Chippenham, Wilts 42
Chisenbury, Wilts 44, 45, 50, 54
Chorley Mill, Lancs 19
Christ's Hospital, London 100, 252
Clarendon, Assize of 116
Clarke, William 274–76, 278-9, 280
Clerkenwell, London 27, 61, 255, 256, 264
Clevedon Court 144
Clifford, Henry 49
Clifton, Bristol 54, 63
Clydeside, Scotland 37
Clyne, Monsieur 244
Cobbett, William 21, 24, 27–29, 32, 49, 57–74 *passim*, 107, 144, 217-228, 280
Cochrane, Thomas, Lord 29, 30, 62, 71, 72
Coles, Edward 176, 236, 242, 256, 257
Collard, Nicholas 178
Collins, Charles 186
Colson (Colston), Dr 143, 150, 160, 171, 179, 214, 218
Colston, William Hungerford 132, 144, 146, 192, 196, 203, 210, 211
Combe, Mr 151

Commins, John 107–10
Congreve, William, rockets 247
Cork, Ireland 108, 241
Couldwell, Abel 33
Coutts Bank 55
Covent Garden, London 250
Coventry, Warwicks 223
Cox, Elisabeth 173
Cox, Francis 101
Cox, Sir John 236
Creech St Michael 214
Cresswell, Rev Henry 214
Crocker family 247
Crouch, Mrs (of Andover) 229
Cruikshank, George 141, 182, 247
Cuer (Cure), Mary 174
Culliford, Jane 101, 129, 130, 132, 149, 173
Culliford 'Big Jim', 148
Culliford, - (two) 149, 150, 188
Cumberland 43

Danberry, Col 258
Darlington, Earl of 136, 148
David, Ann 235
Davidson, William 38, 137
Davis, Richard Hart 67–69
Davis, Thomas 147, 170
Davis, Mr 187
Davis, - 191, 221
Davison, Alexander 136
Dawson, George 216
Denman, Ann 199
Despard, Edward, plot 23, 24, 29
Devizes, Wilts 42–45, 47, 55, 72, 126
Devon 29, 103, 107
Dickinson, Francis Henry 259–61
Dickinson, William 125, 144, 159, 173, 194, 211–13, 216, 217, 224, 225, 247
Dodington, Glos 100
Dolby, Thomas 141, 142, 156, 165, 203, 218, 223, 280
Dorset 44, 101, 260
Doulting 100
Drake, Francis 145, 178, 180
Dundas, Henry (Lord Melville) 55
Dyke, William 43, 44

East Indies 17, 49
Edwards, George 28, 29, 37
Eldon, John Scott, Lord 267
Ellenborough, Justice 49
Ellice, Edward 223
Elson, William 90
Elton, Sir Abraham 119, 144, 211, 259
Ely, Cambs 65

Enford, Wilts 39, 44, 45, 51, 52, 65
Entwistle, Roger 78, 79, 88
Erskine, Mr 233, 237
Essex 106, 185
Estcourt, Thomas Grimstone 165
Everleigh (Everly), Wilts 42-4, 65
Evercreech 100, 101, 249, 252
Evill, Mr 179
Exeter, Devon 130, 131, 134

Farnham, George 243
Farnham, Surrey 57, 228
Fawkes, Guy 37
Fildes, Mary 3
Fildes, William 5
Fitzgerald, Lord Edward 57
Ford, - 176, 177, 186, 193, 208
Foxen, James 277
France, French 3, 13, 14, 16, 20, 27, 32, 40–42, 44, 59, 61, 68, 101, 108, 220, 224, 225, 244, 251
Frome 114, 126, 180, 190, 214, 221, 233
Fry, Elizabeth 135
Fryer, Mr 142

Gane, Alexander 184
Gardiner, Thomass 158, 169, 170, 182, 188, 198, 203, 207, 208, 234–39
Gaselee, Mr 233
Gatton Park, Surrey 62
Gaunt, Elizabeth 9
Gibbs, Sir George 190, 191
Gibbs, Robert 180
Gillingham, Dorset 101
Gillray, James 58, 71
Glasgow 223
Glastonbury 145, 217
Glover, James 198
Goodford, John 195
Goodland, Edward 186
Gordon Riots 48
Gosport, Hants 107
Gould, Mr 120
Graham, Aaron 61, 106, 107, 111, 261
Graham, Baron 65, 166, 211
Graham, George and Margaret 245, 246
Graham, Sir James 258
Gray, Miss 142, 143, 145, 154, 194, 220
Green, Mr 249
Greenock, Scotland 223
Grey, Earl 141, 225
Griffin, - 120
Grundy, Mr 88
Guildford, Surrey 57

Halcomb, Nancy 44
Halifax, Yorks 86
Hampshire 39, 44, 69, 228
Hampton Court 246
Hanning, William 150, 151, 156, 162, 163, 192, 195, 210, 211, 214, 217, 218, 254, 257, 276
Hansard, Thomas 61, 66, 216
Hardy, Thomas 20, 49
Hardy, William Erasmus 210, 217, 219, 221, 231, 236, 256, 258, 276
Hargreaves, James 18
Harper, James 198
Harrowby, Earl of 36, 37
Hayes, John 191
Healy, Joseph 75, 96, 97, 202
Henlade 103
Hetherington, Rev William 100, 252
Hewitt, Sarah 157, 168, 172, 173, 182, 187
Hewitt, William 168
Hibbard, - 189
Hibbert, Charles 189
Hickwood, - 126
Hill, Charles 158–60, 174, 175, 197, 199, 214, 254
Hillier, Elizabeth 130
Hillier, James 158, 160, 161, 169, 171, 186, 188, 195–97, 207, 254
Hindon, Wilts 42
Hippisley, Sir John Cox 144, 236, 253
Hobbs, Jane and Matthew 114, 126, 142, 154, 155, 181, 186, 193, 194, 196, 199–201, 205, 206, 208, 232, 234
Hobbs, Samuel and William 171–73
Hodder, William 189
Hodges, Jeremiah 173
Holborn, High, London 22
Holbrook, - 170
Hollyrood Chapel 247
Holroyd, - 98
Honiton, Devon 29
Hood, Sir A 257
Hooper, John 28
Horner, Col 247
Horsham, Sussex 37
Horton, Hernry 80, 81, 88
Howard, John 119
Howe, George, Lord 41
Huddersfield, Yorks 86
Hull, Yorks 223
Hulton, William 4, 7, 82, 89
Hunt, Henry *passim*
Hursley, Hants 39

Ilchester *passim*

India 13, 32
Ings, James 38
Ireland, Irish 52, 57, 103, 104, 108, 145, 158, 179, 227
Islington, London 229, 263
Italy, Italian 249, 267

Jacobins 20, 40, 42, 69, 71
Jacob's Well, Bristol 54
James, Mr (surgeon) 114
Jeffreys, George, Judge 117
Jerusalem 153
Johnson, Joseph 1, 3, 9, 10, 75, 81, 85, 86, 96, 97
Johnson, James 178, 202
Jones, Joseph Robert 75, 96

Kent 108, 224
Kerr, John 246
Kinglake, Dr 177
Kinnear, John 141–44, 147, 149, 154, 171, 175, 181, 185, 188, 195, 201, 208, 221, 232
Kirkheaton, Yorks 138
Knight, John 3, 75, 96, 275, 276

Lake, Daniel 127–32, 134
Lancashire 5, 19, 21, 26, 32, 74
Lancaster 74, 77, 82, 88, 98, 99
Langdon, Rev William 191
Langston Harbour, Dorset 107
Langton, William Gore 137
Laurel (convict ship) 107
Lawrence, Sarah 157, 172, 187, 233
Leeds, Yorks 86, 91
Lees, James 11
L'Estrange, Col Guy 3, 7, 9, 82–85
Lethbridge, Sir Thomas Buckler 137, 144, 193, 211, 212, 224, 225, 253, 255–57
Lettsom, Dr John 121
Lincoln 98, 102, 152, 202
Lincolnshire 26, 27
Lindo, Charles 178
Littlecot Farm, Wilts 39
Littledale, Mr 97
Liverpool 21, 90, 100, 141, 222
Liverpool, Lord 31, 36, 69, 266
Lomas, Henry 77
London *passim*
Londonderry, Ireland 216
Long, Jane 236
Lovell, Joseph 126, 187
Lowe, James 111
Ludd, Ned (King) 24, 25
Luddites 19, 24, 26

Lushington, Dr Stephen 147, 148, 191, 199, 212
Lymington, Hants 126, 134, 154, 173, 185, 187, 189

Macclesfield, Cheshire 9, 33, 70
McGhie, James IV, 229
Maggs, - 119, 120
Maidstone, Kent 113
Malmesbury, Wilts 42
Malthus, Thomas Robert 227
Manchester 1, 3–7, 9, 11, 12, 18, 20, 32, 68, 74–83, 85, 86, 88, 90–92, 98, 99, 142, 165, 166, 216, 222, 225, 280
Marlborough, Wilts 42, 45, 52
Marmion, - 47
Marsh, James 176
Marshall, Charles 148, 199
Marsh, William 11
Marshman, William 181
Martock 115, 126, 137
Mather, Ralph 19
Mathews, Parmenas 174
Maxwell, - 73
Medway, Kent 107
Meliar, Sarah 101
Melliar, Elizabeth 100
Melliar (Mellior), William 144, 150, 180, 187, 188, 236
Melville, Henry Dundas, Lord 55, 56, 62
Mere, Wilts 157
Mersey, River 33
Middlesex 55, 109, 201
Middleton, Lancs 26
Middleton Cottage, Hants 69, 147
Migasi, Antonio 251
Minories, London 28
Modbury, Devon 103
Monmouth rebellion 117
Moorhouse, James 75, 96
Moorlinch 100
Morgan, Jane 235
Morgan, Mr 122
Morris, William 78
Morse, James 190
Morton, Samuel 77
Moscow, Russia 80
Murray, John 77

Nadin, Joseph 4, 5, 9, 81, 82
Napoleon Bonaparte 14, 47
Nelson, Horatio, Lord 24
Newfoundland, Canada 106
Newgate Gaol, London 22, 28, 37, 65, 66, 68, 210, 231, 236, 277, 279

Newman, John 179, 195, 210, 218, 261
Norman, Mr 275, 276
Normandy, France 59
Normandy Farm, Surrey 227
Norrison, Mr 279
Norriston, Mr 251
Northover, Ilchester 116, 221
Norwood, Mary 118
Nottingham 33, 34, 68, 70
Nottinghamshire 24, 26

Oldfield, Thomas 136
Oldham, Lancs 9, 11, 227
Oliver, William 34
Orchardleigh 221
Oxford 39, 280

Paine, Tom 13, 16, 20, 222
Palfryman, John 184, 185
Palme, Thomas 233
Palmer-Acland, Sir John 172, 256
Parham, Sussex 52
Paris 59, 143, 229, 244
Peel, Sir Robert 38, 215, 233, 276, 278
Pell, Sergeant 233, 237
Pembroke, Lord 51, 52
Penselwood 101
Pentonville, London 261
Pentrich Rising 33
Perceval, Spencer 86
Pergami, Bartolomeo 153
Perrot, Jane Leigh 119
Peterloo Massacre 11, 12, 21, 31, 33–36, 68, 74, 99, 142, 155, 165, 217, 222, 223, 225, 228, 266, 280
Phelips, John 196, 217, 247
Phelps, John Delafield 165, 189
Phillips, Francis 79
Phillips, William 199
Piccadilly, London 111
Pike, Richard 143, 146, 161, 168–70, 188, 197, 199, 200, 204, 207, 214
Pinney, Robert 197, 198
Pitminster 117
Pitt, William (the younger) 16, 17, 20, 22, 31, 51, 55, 56, 60
Plaistow, Essex 185
Platt, James 81, 82
Poole, F 236
Poole, James 188, 189
Poole, Robert 12
Poole, Thomas 197, 203, 261
Poore, Lieut 44
Popham, Francis 252
Portland, Dorset 107

Portsmouth, Hants 41, 57, 72, 107, 108, 134, 190
Poulett, John 101
Powell, Elizabeth 39
Preston, Thomas 28
Preston, Lancs, 223–25, 227
Pulteney family 243

Raine, Mr 87
Raines, Thomas 101
Ramsbury, Wilts 245
Reed, Capt George 110
Rees, Maria 114
Reid, Ann 59
Richards, - 247
Richardson, Mr Justice 233, 237
Riley, Charles 225
Robertson, Dr John 177, 181, 191, 220, 221
Robins, George 250
Rochdale, Lancs 86
Rodberd, Mr 238
Romilly, Sir Samuel 67, 68, 73
Rothwell, Mr (London Sheriff) 38
Rousseau, Jean-Jacques 13
Rowfant, Sussex 66, 69
Ryan, Mr 250

Saddleworth, Lancs 78
St Peter's Field, Manchester 1–3, 11, 74, 84
Salford, Lancs 4, 7, 82
Salisbury 42–44, 65, 110, 122
Salisbury Plain 39
Sarum, Old 62
Savernake, Wilts 45
Saxton, John 3, 9, 75, 96
Scadding, Joseph and Edward 117-19, 120, 122
Scarlett, Mr (lawyer) 76, 89, 92, 94, 212
Scotland 104, 179
Selwyn, Mr (lawyer) 233
Shaw, Dr 214
Sheerness, Kent 107
Sheffield, Yorks 20, 68
Shelley, Percy Bysse 265, 266
Sheppard (Shepherd), Edward 175, 179, 199
Shepton Mallet 100, 101, 119, 122, 123, 219, 256, 274, 275
Sherlock, - 120
Sherry, John Hutfield 177, 178
Shillibeer, Henry Blatchford 154, 165, 166, 182, 183, 206
Shockerwick 147
Shorland, Dr William 148, 149, 177, 180, 187, 199, 210, 211, 232
Sidmouth, Viscount 31, 32, 34, 35, 37, 72,

167, 179, 266, 268
Slade, George 130
Slater, Joseph 85, 86
Smith, C 221
Smith, John 90
Smith, Joseph 178
Smith, Capt Robert 237, 239, 257
Smith, Miss 158, 234
Smith, - 202, 206, 238
Smithers, Richard 37
Smithfield Show 113
Somerset *passim*
Somerton 116, 174
South Wingfield, Derbs 33
Southampton, Hants 61, 74
Southwark, London 48
Spain, 68, 109
Spence, Thomas (and Spenceans) 22, 23, 27, 28
Spithead, Hants 107, 108
Staffordshire 68
Stainer, Mr and Mrs 149, 199
Standring, William 78, 88
Stillman, James 170, 178
Stockport, Cheshire 9, 33, 70, 77, 78
Stokes Croft, Bristol 63
Stoneaston 144
Storrington, Sussex 52, 228
Stuckey, Vincent 214, 221, 236, 257, 276
Summers, Elizabeth 199
Surrey 57, 62, 227, 281
Sussex 52, 66, 145, 224, 228
Sutton, James 42
Swindon, Wilts 42
Sydney Gardens and Tap, Bath 243, 245, 247, 249–52, 256, 259, 260, 264, 274, 279, 280

Tambora, Mt, Dutch East Indies 17
Taunton 101, 103, 117, 119, 120, 122, 125, 132, 134, 135, 149, 151, 153, 160, 161, 165, 178, 183, 184, 219–21, 242, 255, 257, 258, 274, 281
Taylor, - 126
Temeraire, mutiny 108, 109
Thames, River 105, 261
Thanet, Kent 142
Thistlewood, Arthur 27, 28, 29, 37, 38, 277–79
Thring, Rev John (sen), and Rev John Gale Dalton (jun) 150, 152, 171, 179, 192, 195, 197, 210, 260
Tidd, Richard 38
Tilshead, Wilts 39
Tite, Robert 101

Tomkins, Dr 210
Tooke, Horne 49
Travis, Joseph 78
Trayt, John 181
Treganzer, John 136, 174, 176, 177, 193, 201
Tresur, John 172
Tucson (Tuson), Henry 122, 136, 193
Tuileries Palace, Paris 59
Turkey 3
Turle, James 126
Tuson (Tucson), Henry 122, 136, 193
Twyford, Magistrate 258
Tyas, John 3, 7, 9, 91

Underwood, George Allen 191
Upavon, Wilts 39
Utrecht, Netherlands 107

Valentine, Rev 192
Vaux, James Hardy 111
Vince, Catherine 52, 62, 64, 69, 73, 142–45, 152, 210, 211, 219, 229, 231
Vince, Catherine Maria Ann Vince 229
Vince, Henry Chivers III 52
Virgil 93
Voltaire 13

Waddington, Samuel 49, 50
Walcot, Bath 101, 189, 229, 275
Wales 41, 106, 141
Walker, John 85
Ward, - 119, 120
Warminster, Wilts 42
Warren, Henry 180, 181
Watson, James 28
Watt, James 19
Webber, Jane 172
Webber, Maria 113
Webber, Martin 113, 114, 174, 185
Webber, William 114
Wellington, Duke of 14
Wells 144, 145, 147, 151, 175, 177, 180, 187, 188, 193, 199, 210, 233, 236, 237
Westcott, John 191
Westhoughton Mill, Lancs 26
Westminster 29, 30, 46, 47, 61, 62, 64, 71–73, 259
Weymouth, Dorset 42, 102, 113, 161, 214
Whalley, Rev Richard 129, 179, 203
Wheeler, John 170, 171, 198, 199, 254
Whitcombe, Esau 172, 253
White, Mr (lawyer) 168, 170, 182, 183, 197, 198
White Moss, Lancs 77
Widdington, Wilts 39, 44

Wilcombe, John 179
Wilde, Robert 75, 85, 96
Wilkins, Elizabeth 181
Williams, Charles 168, 182, 183, 233–37
Wilson, Sir Robert 214
Wilton Gaol, Taunton 122, 123, 126, 127, 184, 221, 274
Wiltshire 39, 42, 43-7, 51, 62, 66, 126, 147, 245, 280
Winchester, Hants 65, 110, 228, 257, 260–62
Wingfield, South, Derbs 33
Winsham 101
Wontner, John 279
Wood, Alderman 159, 160, 163, 211, 213, 214
Woodford, Dr James 135, 185, 192, 211
Woolwich, Kent 105–9, 111, 115, 237
Wright, John 64
Wyatt, John 139, 149, 154, 193, 194
Wynford, Lord 260

Yeovil 114, 124, 137, 142, 168, 186, 261, 280
York 59, 72, 74–76, 86, 87, 211, 256, 260
Yorkshire 24, 138

Zeppora, Sylvia 247

www.ingramcontent.com/pod-product-compliance
Lightning Source LLC
Chambersburg PA
CBHW061251230426
43664CB00025B/2924